198

John Williamson
NEVIN

AMERICAN REFORMED BIOGRAPHIES

D. G. HART AND SEAN MICHAEL LUCAS
Series Editors

John Williamson
NEVIN

High-Church Calvinist

D. G. HART

PUBLISHING
P.O. BOX 817 • PHILLIPSBURG • NEW JERSEY 08865-0817

Page design and typesetting by Lakeside Design Plus

Printed in the United States of America

Library of Congress Cataloging-in-Publication Data

Hart, D. G. (Darryl G.)
    John Williamson Nevin : high church Calvinist / D. G. Hart.
      p. cm. — (American Reformed biographies ; 2)
    Includes bibliographical references and index.
    ISBN 0-87552-662-4 (cloth)
    1. Nevin, John Williamson, 1803–1886. 2. Theologians—United States—Biography. 3. Reformed Church—United States—Doctrines—History—19th century. 4. Mercersburg theology. I. Title. II. Series.

BX9593.N4H37 2005
230'.57'092—dc22
[B]
                                                 2005047676

To Bruce Kuklick

Contents

Series Preface

"All history is biography," Ralph Waldo Emerson once remarked. Although the wayward Unitarian may not be the best source to justify a series of biographies on the most influential proponents of Reformed Christianity in the United States, Emerson's aphorism still contains a good deal of truth. History is the memory and record of past human lives, thus making biography the most basic form of historical knowledge. To understand any event, period, or text from the past, some acquaintance with specific persons is crucial. The popularity of biography among contemporary book buyers in America supports this insight. Recent biographies of John Adams and Ben Franklin have encouraged many, who fear for America's historical amnesia, to believe that a keen and formidable interest in history still exists among the nation's reading public. To be sure, the source of this interest could be the stature and influence of the subjects themselves—the founding fathers of the United States. Still, the accessibility of biography—its concrete subject matter, intimate scope, and obvious relevance—suggests that the reason for the recent success of these biographies is in the genre of writing itself.

American Reformed Biographies, coedited by D. G. Hart and Sean Michael Lucas, seeks to nurture this general interest in biography as a way of learning about and from the past. The titles in this series will feature American Reformed leaders who were important representatives or interpreters of Reformed Christianity in the United States and who continue to be influential through writings and arguments still pertinent to the self-understanding of Presbyterian and Reformed theologians, pastors, and church members. The aim is to provide learned treatments of men and women that will be accessible to readers from a wide variety of backgrounds—biography that is both sufficiently scholarly to be of service to academics and those with proficiency in American church history and adequately accessible to engage the nonspecialist. Consequently, these books will be more introductory than definitive, with the aim of giving an overview of a figure's thought and contribution, along with suggestions for further study. The editors have sought authors who are sympathetic to Reformed Christianity and to their subjects, who regard biography as not merely a celebration of past accomplishments but as a chance to ask difficult questions of both the past and the present in order to gain greater insight into Christian faith and practice. As such, American Reformed Biographies is designed to make available the best kind of historical writing—one that yields both knowledge and wisdom.

John Williamson Nevin, the subject of this volume, may seem like an odd pick for this series because he is not well known to many Reformed Christians. A son of American Presbyterianism, Nevin during the middle of his career switched denominations to teach theology for the German Reformed Church. He served in German Reformed circles throughout the rest of his life, chiefly at its educational institutions, teaching theology and history and performing administrative duties at Mercersburg Theological Seminary and Franklin and Marshall College. Although Nevin is better known to church historians and theologians because of his introduction of German theology and philosophy to intellectual life in the United States, D. G. Hart argues that this theologian's significance may be greater for the nonacademics who are unaware of this man, for while carrying out his many responsibilities as a theological educator, first for the Presbyterian Church and then for the German Reformed, Nevin discerned fundamental changes in American religious life that were undermining the vitality of Reformed Christianity in the United States. His articulation of a "high-church" Calvinism was a unique response to the dilemmas posed by religious enthusiasm on the one side and the growing presence of Roman Catholicism on the other. Hart argues that, even though Nevin's theological and liturgical proposals were not fully embraced within the German Reformed Church or by other Reformed or Presbyterian denominations, his critique of the trends of popular Protestantism in the nineteenth century was prophetic for both Nevin's day and all Protestants since then. This book, the first biography of Nevin in over a century, remedies the neglect of arguably the nineteenth century's most creative theologian and provides a persuasive case for renewed attention to his high-church Calvinism.

Acknowledgments

The year 2003 was the bicentennial of John Williamson Nevin's birth. Most American Protestants failed to mark the anniversary with appropriate fanfare. It is likely just as well, because celebrations of Nevin's birth would have had to compete with the tercentenary of Jonathan Edwards. And that would have been a match for which no theologian would have wished. Just as Nevin thought, wrote, and taught during the middle decades of the nineteenth century in the shadow of New England Calvinism and the reputation of its most famous proponent, so even in death on the half-century and century anniversaries of his birth he will always be eclipsed by the theological prodigy that was Jonathan Edwards.

This book is not intended to correct this historical imbalance. For good reasons, Edwards and Nevin each deserve their relative rankings in the annals of American church and intellectual history. But an important contention of this biography is that Nevin understood better than Edwards the nature of Reformed Christianity and the obstacles it faced in the modern world. Unlike Edwards, who devoted his obvious brilliance to a philosophical defense of Calvinist doctrine, Nevin recognized that, without the nurture of the institutional church through its worship and pastoral care, Calvinist theology would not survive as a vibrant expression of the Christian religion. For that reason, Nevin deserves the nickname "high-church Calvinist."

13

While writing this book I have acquired a number of debts. Bruce Kuklick, R. Scott Clark, and Charles Hambrick-Stowe offered valuable comments after reading a first draft of the manuscript. Sally F. Griffith graciously allowed me to see her manuscript on the history of Franklin and Marshall College, which shed light on Nevin's college teaching and career. The coeditor of this series, Sean Michael Lucas, and my P&R editor, Allan Fisher, encouraged me to take on a project from which I have learned a great deal. Finally, the staff at the Evangelical and Reformed Historical Society in Lancaster, Pennsylvania, was helpful in making available its resources and in granting permission to use the picture of Nevin that graces the cover.

This book is dedicated to Bruce Kuklick, a fellow Pennsylvanian of German heritage who, although not thinking as highly of Nevin as I, has been a thoughtful guide to me on American religious and intellectual history, a valued friend and neighbor, and a source of hope during the dog days of August when the Philadelphia Phillies' futility is as obvious in the standings as it is on the field.

The old Presbyterian faith, into which I was born, was based throughout on the idea of covenant family religion, church membership by God's holy act in baptism, and following this a regular catechetical training of the young, with direct reference to their coming to the Lord's table. In one word, all proceeded on the theory of sacramental, educational religion.

—John Williamson Nevin

Introduction: Romantic or Reformed?

*J*ohn Williamson Nevin should matter to American Presbyterians and Reformed Christians more than he does. For starters, he has Princeton Theological Seminary's seal of approval, having graduated from the young school in 1826. So impressive was Nevin as a seminarian that when Charles Hodge, who was a classmate of Nevin, went to Germany for further study, Nevin filled in for the third professor at the first theological seminary of the Presbyterian Church in the U.S.A. In addition to teaching at Princeton, Nevin trained Presbyterian ministers in the fine points of exegesis and Calvinism at Western Theological Seminary, an institution established in 1825 to serve the presbyteries of western Pennsylvania and Ohio, a region of Presbyterian vitality comparable to the vicinity of Philadelphia and Princeton. In 1840 Nevin advanced to his third teaching post when he assumed instructional duties at Mercersburg Theological Seminary, a school located in south central Pennsylvania close to the Nevin family's home. At Mercersburg, Nevin's reputation grew not simply because as he matured he came to and articulated convictions that gained a national audience. Nevin's prominence within Calvinist circles increased also because Mercersburg was an agency of the German Reformed Church, a denomination with historic ties to the Palatinate region of Germany, the site of the Heidelberg Catechism's composition and greatest influence, and a church with close ties to Dutch Reformed congregations and their synod. That sort of pedigree should qualify Nevin as a theologian of some significance to Calvinists from Great Britain (Presbyterians) and the Continent (Reformed).

But since Nevin's death in 1886 he has been a neglected figure among American Calvinists. For Presbyterians in the mainline denomination, Nevin has had occasional appeal but usually as a historical oddity or one who helped to break down the tight grip of Scholastic orthodoxy at Princeton. His call for a churchly and sacramental Calvinism has occasionally been useful in undoing the alleged austerity of Puritan piety, but it has provided little assistance to the project of social justice. For conservative Presbyterians, Nevin's use of German idealism to enhance Calvinist teaching on the church and worship smacked of the same sort of German theological innovations upon which liberal Protestants would later rely in the late nineteenth and early twentieth centuries. In addition, Nevin's high-church sensibility was at odds with the revivalist-friendly forms of devotion among those Presbyterians outside the mainline. Dutch Reformed believers, who were in the process of assimilation themselves, had little to gain from Nevin, whose circle of reference was largely circumscribed by the ethnic provincialism of the German Reformed. Dutch Calvinists preferred a system of theology more precise and less abstract than the one that Nevin produced. Finally, among German Reformed themselves Nevin was damaged goods, having been a major player in a church conflict over worship in the late nineteenth century. What is more, the German Reformed Church itself vanished over the course of the twentieth century, going through a series of mergers and church unions that landed the denomination in which Nevin labored for over half of his life in the United Church of Christ. The United Church of Christ does exhibit minor ongoing interest in Nevin. A small group of United Church of Christ ministers, largely situated in eastern Pennsylvania, established the Mercersburg Society and founded a journal, the *New Mercersburg Review*, to recover and promote Nevin's teaching. Otherwise, so complete has been the disappearance of a German Reformed tradition and along with it Nevin's legacy that when David Wells, professor of theology at Gordon-Conwell Theological Seminary, assembled a collection of essays on the Reformed tradition in America, none of the contributors remembered that the Reformed faith had been confessed and practiced outside American Presbyterian or Dutch Reformed circles.[1]

As limited as contemporary interest in Nevin may be, he is a figure about whom Presbyterians and Reformed (whether North American or otherwise) should know. Some historical figures are worthy of study simply because their lives encapsulate the issues or tenor of an era. Others bear scrutiny because their ideas or actions have enduring significance beyond their own times. In Nevin's case, his significance qualifies on both counts. First, he was not the sort of historical subject who by virtue of popularity and recognition in his time may provide a basis for generalizations about a period, region, or institution. In fact, Nevin's instincts ran precisely counter to those of mainstream American Protestantism, and he was one of a few critics who recognized the difficulties attending Christianity in the New World and tried to defend and propagate Old World (even ancient Christian) teachings and practices. But because Nevin was a dissenter from the revivalist-inspired Protestant mainstream, to study him and his critique is to understand better the peculiar predicaments that confronted and continue to bedevil historic Protestant traditions in the United States (i.e., Anglican, Lutheran, Presbyterian, and Reformed) since the early nineteenth century.

Second, because of his critique and because the circumstances that he faced are still enormous, Nevin's ideas and arguments not only possessed relevance for his own age but also for contemporary Protestantism. In many respects the sociocultural environment confronting Protestants in the early nineteenth century was historically unprecedented. Not since the days before Constantine's conversion had Christianity been forced to leave the corridors of power without the blessing of emperor, monarch, or magistrate. At the same time, Protestants confronted a novel form of Christianity in the revivals of the Second Great Awakening that were directly linked to the sociopolitical transformations of the American republic and that threatened to eradicate older Protestant beliefs and practices. Nevin's arguments and solutions were certainly not always convincing. In fact, Charles Grandison

Finney, for example, Nevin's contemporary and foil, rode the wave of religious enthusiasm and social reform to preside over the period. But however offbeat Nevin's thought may sometimes appear, his assessment of popular Christianity in the United States was arguably the most astute from the perspective of historical Protestantism that any American Reformed or Presbyterian theologian ever formulated.

The Church and Democratic Christianity

Novus ordo seclorum ("a new order for the ages") is a Latin phrase that many Americans overlook when using United States currency. Yet, it is not only part of the nation's official rhetoric but was an inspiring ideal for the eighteenth-century political leaders who sought liberty for thirteen British colonies in North America. Although the secular millennialism suggested by this Latin phrase encouraged a historical ignorance that today takes no notice of the classical republican Greek and Roman roots of the American experiment, when it came to religion the new nation of the United States did represent something truly novel in the history of the West. When the original state legislatures adopted and ratified the Sixth Article and the First Amendment to the United States Constitution, which declared respectively that religion would not be a condition for holding national office and that the new nation was freed from a government-sanctioned church, they were indeed embarking on a new era of politics. Since the fourth century, Christianity had been the official religion of those kingdoms, city-states, and nations that eventually supplanted the Roman Empire. Even before Christianity's endorsement from the emperor, public leaders and political philosophers believed that religion was essential to a well-ordered society. With the disestablishment of religion, the United States was in fact engaging in an innovation of historic proportions, even if individual states continued to support ecclesiastical establishments. (For instance, Massachusetts did not disestablish what was left of the old Puritan Standing Order until 1833 and thus became the last state to uncouple the official connections between church and state.)

Of course, for churches accustomed to tax support, the break with government could mean a serious threat to survival. And one of the prominent features of American Christianity ever since the early nineteenth century has been the principle of voluntarism—meaning that for churches to exist they would have to attract members, donors, and clergy on the basis of voluntary assent; the state would not and could not force anyone to be baptized, belong to a parish, or participate in public worship services. But the hardship to churches was not as great as it might have seemed since most of the denominations in the new nation were of English descent and in the Old World had been religious dissenters. In other words, with the exception of Congregationalists in Massachusetts and Connecticut, Presbyterians, Baptists, Methodists, and Quakers had ever since their arrival in the New World been dependent upon a voluntary principle of religious association. Without the assistance of the state, most Protestants in the British colonies in North America needed to generate their own support, recruit new members and hold on to them, and find and train worthy church officers. In this respect, the reality of religious disestablishment that came with the American nation was not a complete shock to the way that many Anglo-American Protestants participated in the life of the church.

What was new with the American experiment in religious liberty (and implicitly in religious diversity) was the rationale used by both secularists and the devout for this new arrangement of religion and public life. For the former, such as Thomas Jefferson (a theist whose religious views were uniquely heterodox) and James Madison (a deist with great respect for historic Christianity), faith was such a delicate part of human life that entanglement with the state was sure to crush it. In other words, the instruments of statecraft were far too crude to regulate or oversee faith in all of its personal and affective dimensions. Government and law were inherently coercive, but for religion to be genuine it needed to spring freely from the human spirit. According to Madison, who studied with the Presbyterian John Witherspoon at the College of New Jersey (later Princeton University), religion would actually benefit from the loss of government support. This Enlightenment understanding of Christianity was not too distant from one commonly used by Baptists and Presbyterians in New England and Virginia, the two sites of the most entrenched religious establishment

(Presbyterian arguments were strong in Virginia, nonexistent in New England). Here the argument involved the notion that governments and their religious establishments sanctioned a formal or nominal version of Christianity, one that was merely external or civil but not personal and genuine. As Sidney E. Mead aptly puts it, "During the eighteenth century rationalists [i.e., secularists] and pietists [i.e., the devout] could easily combine forces on the practical and legal issue of religious freedom against the defenders of Establishment who took the traditional view of the matter."[2]

Perhaps the most significant consequence of the American Revolution was its hidden and ironic religious agenda. The First Amendment makes the United States government (specifically Congress) a neutral party in matters of faith. But unintentionally the disestablishment of religion gave the upper hand to informal expressions of Christianity over formal ones. The most obvious example of this unexpected support for religious informality was the growth of Protestant denominations for whom seminary training, ecclesiastical protocol, and prayer books were signs of bad faith—namely, Baptists and Methodists. In the nineteenth century, these two denominations outgrew Congregationalists, Episcopalians, Presbyterians, and Lutherans at an unprecedented rate, prompting one American historian to claim that evangelicalism was *the* religious establishment of the new nation.[3] What accounted for the expansion of these denominations was the reliance upon the techniques of revival, from fairly routine practices of itinerancy to more novel examples such as Finney's new measures, among which were the anxious bench, a seat designed specifically to intensify (some said manipulate) the experience of guilt and heighten the need for faith and repentance. Equally important to the success of these revivalists was the conception of genuine religion that undergirded America's founding principles. For those who promoted revivals, true faith was ultimately a question of the heart, not something that depended upon religious formalities—whether matters of doctrine, church government, or worship. By assuming that religion flourished most when free from the oversight and nurture of government, the American founders, although aiming to free the state from faith, implicitly paved the way for the advance of heartfelt faith, while frowning on those forms of religion for which external expressions and practices were crucial.

This is not to suggest that the rationale behind the disestablishment of religion was inherently opposed to Christian communions for whom word and sacrament were central in their self-understanding and practice. The point instead is that the American settlement of church-state relations gave greater plausibility to religious informality, thereby granting an advantage to forms of faith with fewer formal constraints. By making religion unofficial, Christianity became disentangled from notions about ministerial office, corporate practices and ceremonies, and formal teachings of creeds and catechisms. In other words, with religious disestablishment came a host of unofficial forms of faith, with the revivalist varieties of Protestantism taking the early lead in the new nation. Consequently, the new environment in which all churches competed on an even playing field for congregants, support, and leaders generated statistics of church growth—both in the number of denominations and in the numbers of religious adherents. The religious free market of the United States also privileged a specific kind of piety. This publicly plausible faith was spontaneous, informal, and enthusiastic because the logic behind the idea of religious liberty presumed that religion flourished when freed from formal constraints.

Of course, revivalism and its democratic and informal manner of piety was not new to the United States. The First Great Awakening of the 1740s had achieved widespread support from various Protestant communions thanks in part to the leadership and notoriety of the likes of George Whitefield and Jonathan Edwards. Religion of the heart or faith that plumbed the affections was thus a religious reality in the British colonies before they gained independence to form a new nation. What was different about revivalism during the Second Great Awakening (i.e., the 1820s and 1830s) in contrast to that of the First Great Awakening was that the older ecclesiastical establishments could no longer mount any form of suppression. In the new environment of religious freedom, churches would have to attract support and membership, and revivalism proved to be especially effective in doing so. In addition, the democratic or populist character of religion prompted a severe reduction in clerical status. If faith was a matter of the heart, a question of the individual's own experience and appropriation of Christianity, and so dependent on the mysterious workings of the Holy Spirit, ministers and church officers were merely supplemental. They might be useful at certain occasions and could sometimes provide worthwhile assistance. But the real action in American religion was among the people and the efforts to corral them into a cohesive religious public, not within the often stuffy walls of the church, where ministers held sway.

Any number of scholars have studied the effects of this reorientation of American Protestantism during the first half of the nineteenth century. The work of Nathan O. Hatch and Mark A. Noll is especially fruitful. Hatch's awarding-winning *Democratization of American Christianity* (1989) examines precisely the war for independence within the churches in which the laity achieved a coup for popular sovereignty in religious matters. Between 1780 and 1830, he argues, American Protestantism emerged with a peculiarly democratic and egalitarian ethos. "Many humble Christians," Hatch writes, "began to redeem a dual legacy. They yoked strenuous demands for revivals, in the name of George Whitefield, with calls for the expansion of popular sovereignty, in the name of the Revolution."[4] This democratic mix in turn toppled centuries-old order within the churches. Hatch demonstrates, first, how the new form of Christianity liberated the people from the oversight of clergy and the theological norms of creeds or confessions and, second, how this religious revolution took the spiritual insights and longings of the laity at face value, imbuing them with a worth and significance previously unimagined in settings dominated by ministers and the creedal statements to which they subscribed. Finally, the ideals of democracy and equality among Christians generated any number of utopian and millennial dreams of establishing heaven on earth. Although these changes yielded impressive statistics—more people professed faith than had done so during the colonial era—they fundamentally altered the character of Protestantism. No longer a faith led by ministers, priests, or pastors, it had become a religion dependent upon the consent of church members.

Where Hatch observes the outworking of American political ideals in the relations between ministers and laity, Noll sees similar results in the way that American Protestant ministers and theologians conducted the enterprise of theology. In *America's God* (2003), he argues that the transformation of American Protestant doctrine, owing to the influence of the political views that triumphed in the American Revolution, fundamentally altered the course of Protestantism. "It is not an exaggeration," he writes, "to claim that this nineteenth-century Protestant evangelicalism differed from the religion of the Protestant Reformation as much as sixteenth-century Reformation Protestantism differed from the Roman Catholic theology from which it emerged."[5] This new brand of theological reflection combined older Protestant convictions about the authority of Scripture with republican or Whig political ideals about the good society. The result was a theological orientation that "shared both a mistrust of intellectual authorities inherited from previous generations and a belief that true knowledge arose from the use of one's own senses." Americans thus assumed that "people had to think for themselves in order to know science, morality, economics, politics and especially theology."[6] Noll concludes that this outlook was responsible for giving Protestant theology a distinctly American accent. Most ministers and theologians continued to study questions that had animated their predecessors, such as the nature of sin, the work of Christ, and the duties of faith. But because of the imperative of independent thinking, the answers to such questions echoed less the classic utterances of Christian truth and sounded more like the idiom of American public officials.

But the Americanization of Protestantism in the United States did more than recast theological discourse or establish a new relationship between clergy and laity. These were clearly important factors that accompanied the changes that Nevin witnessed and tried to resist. But arguably the more significant alteration was one in which clergy and the services they performed were no longer considered central to the Christian life. The shift toward a democratic or informal Christianity, nurtured by revival and revolution, turned American Protestants' piety from forms and routines oriented around the church and the ministry of its officers to religious practices geared toward the experience of the individual, the reformist activities of voluntary associations, and small groups of zealous converts. Some who have written on Nevin

assumed that this change was much older, starting with the introspective and arduous piety of the Puritans. But in fact Puritan piety,
along with the devotion of the major branches of the Protestant Reformation (i.e., Lutherans, Anglicans, Presbyterians, and Reformed), was
distinct from the revival-inspired faith that became the dominant form
of Protestantism in the United States during the first half of the nineteenth. Noll well describes the difference between Puritanism[7] and
evangelical Protestantism:

> Although Puritans stood against Catholic and Anglican formalism,
> salvation for the Puritans was still mediated by institutions—family,
> church, covenanted society; in evangelicalism (at least in American
> forms), salvation was in principle unmediated except by the written
> Word of God. Puritans protested against nominal ecclesiastical life,
> but they still treated institutions of church and society as given; Amer-
> ican evangelicals created their own communities, at first ecclesiasti-
> cal, then voluntary. Puritans accepted authority from designated lead-
> ers; American evangelicals looked to authority from charismatic,
> self-selected leaders. Puritans fenced in enthusiasm with formal learn-
> ing, respect for confessions, and deference to traditional interpreta-
> tions of Scripture; American evangelicals fenced in enthusiasm with
> self-selected leaders, individualistic Bible reading, local grassroots
> organizations, and intuitively persuasive reason.[8]

In effect, American Protestantism entered a new phase during Nevin's
lifetime. It is not an overstatement or caricature to say that, no longer
regulated by the state and no longer administered by ordained officers, Protestant Christianity in the United States became a religion of
the people, by the people, and for the people.

One way to illustrate the transformation of American Protestantism
is to look at the difficulties faced by communions for whom clergy and
church life were central, namely, the Lutherans and Episcopalians. The
American Lutheran controversy took place during the 1840s and
1850s, and it concerned whether the ministry and witness of
Lutheranism in the New World could legitimately accommodate the
newer forms of Protestantism emanating from the Second Great Awakening. On the one side stood Americanizers such as Samuel Schmucker,

who taught at Gettysburg Seminary and whose book *The American Lutheran Church* (1851) stripped down Lutheran teaching and practice to make it conform to the more generic form of Protestantism promoted by revivals. Schmucker advocated the development of a Lutheran Church with an American character, and this included a communion in which the importance of sacraments, creeds, and clergy diminished considerably. One of Schmucker's chief opponents was William Julius Mann, born in Germany and pastor of one of American Lutheranism's oldest congregations in Philadelphia after his emigration to the United States. Instead of adapting Lutheran teaching and practice to the most popular forms of American Protestantism, Mann insisted upon the importance of Lutheran confessions, sacramental teaching, formal worship, and the office of minister. In the context of the 1840s and 1850s, when immigration patterns brought to the United States large numbers of Roman Catholics, the confessional Lutheran defense of the church and its ministry sounded to some revivalist Protestants like Romanism. But Mann and other conservative Lutherans believed and argued that Roman Catholic views of the church or revivalist distrust of official or churchly Christianity were not the only options. In between Rome's emphasis upon apostolic succession and the Great Awakening's altar call rested historic Protestantism's delicate balance of the church as God's ordained means of salvation.

Similar tensions between a churchly regard for creed, sacrament, and church office and a utilitarian search for effective methods to win large numbers of converts plagued the Episcopal Church in the United States. For the New World descendants of the Church of England, the danger that evangelical revivalism presented had more to do with church order and polity than with sacraments and creed, as in the case of Lutherans. In addition, fewer ties existed between revivalism and Episcopalianism, thanks to the formation of the Methodist Church, which drew away many pro-revival Protestants formerly in the Episcopal Church. For these reasons the question of Episcopalian identity in the mid-nineteenth century did not take on the proportions of a controversy. Even so, the emergence of revivalism and a low-church evangelical party in the Episcopal Church did raise the issue of Episcopalian essentials. In this context, what Robert Bruce Mullin calls the Hobartian synthesis became the position of a high-church party that challenged efforts to conform Episcopalianism to American (read: evangelical) realities. Named after New York Bishop John Henry Hobart, the Episcopal high-church outlook placed great emphasis upon the mediated character of the Christian faith and as such on the necessity of the church and its ministry. According to Mullin, this high-church position was characterized by the attempt to locate the reality of redemption not in the Christian state, as many evangelicals did, but in the "church as a visible society, 'made by Divine appointment the regular and ordinary channel by which the blessing of mercy, and grace, and eternal life, in Jesus Christ, are conveyed to a fallen world.'"[9] Like confessional Lutherans, high-church Episcopalians held out for a self-understanding that stressed the particular features of their Protestant tradition as opposed to the evangelical tendency to submerge historic Protestant differences for the sake of greater influence and efficiency. For those who followed the Hobartian synthesis, the Episcopal Church, because of its theology but especially its polity, "was an alternative to evangelical theology and culture and not part of it."[10]

In the second fifty years of the United States' existence, then, Protestantism faced a significant crisis of identity. On the one hand, a new form of Protestantism emerged that not simply adapted the faith to American realities but that also saw the new society as affording a tremendous opportunity for evangelism and mission. For neo-Protestants, revival and the altar call were symbols of the new form of faith. Accordingly, the appeal of revival was to rational autonomous individuals who could not simply vote for local and federal politicians but also choose for themselves whether to accept Christ. In contrast stood paleo-Protestants, such as the high-church Episcopalians and confessional Lutherans, who insisted on maintaining Protestantism's older ways and habits. For them creed, ecclesiastical office, and sacrament were symbols of an older and truer form of faith that depended less on the sovereignty of individual choice than on patterns of inheritance and nurture that embodied and shaped church members up in the faith. The trouble facing paleo-Protestants, however, was the very significant change from religious establishment to free-church system. Now that the people were sovereign politically, and so religiously sovereign as well, would they choose the paleo-Protestant ways? Could an older form of Protestantism persist without the patronage of the state, especially if its leaders could not secure the interest and support of the people?

Presbyterians and Reformed Christians did not escape these difficulties, and they also manifested a similar turn to the past for sustenance and guidance. One example is the case of the Old School Presbyterians, the branch of the mainstream Presbyterian Church that in 1837 broke with theological and parachurch developments trickling down to their communion from the Second Great Awakening. The Old School arguably exhibited a degree of theological reflection that has never been matched among Presbyterians in North America through the writings of figures such as Samuel Miller, Charles Hodge, Robert Louis Dabney, James Henley Thornwell, Benjamin Morgan Palmer, John L. Girardeau, and John B. Adger. They distinguished themselves for defending with great acumen the central tenets of Calvinist soteriology, the dignity of Reformed worship, and the wisdom of Presbyterian polity. What was not as evident in Old School Presbyterianism as it was in Nevin's corpus was an understanding of the mediated character of grace and of the church's centrality in dispensing the blessings of the gospel. To be sure, Old School Presbyterians could offer almost airtight exegesis for the special character of the minister's office or for the necessity of elders to church order. But less agile were these Presbyterians when it came to what might be called ecclesial Christianity or a sacramental view of the church.

Some blame Old School Presbyterian awkwardness with liturgical matters on the influence of Puritanism and its reaction against Anglicanism's formalism. Scottish Presbyterianism's liturgy and prayer books, however, might temper this argument. A better explanation for Old School Presbyterianism's reluctance to fall in line with high-church sentiments might be that these Presbyterians were heirs of New Side Presbyterianism, the colonial branch of the church that had favored revivalism and sought evidence of conversion experience for membership and ordination. Although the division among colonial Presbyterianism was healed in 1758, the terms on which both sides reunited clearly favored the revivalist experimental piety that would eventually dominate nineteenth-century American Protestantism. As such, Old School Presbyterians were not as critical of revivals as Nevin came to be. For them, good revivals needed to be distinguished from the excesses of bad ones; the sheep of Whitefield needed to be separated from the goats of Finney. Old Schoolers believed that the revivals of the 1820s and 1830s were seriously flawed, but that revivalism per se could be a boon for serious Presbyterianism. Unlike Nevin, high-church Anglicans, and confessional Lutherans, then, the Old School did not regard the populist Christianity sweeping the United States after the Second Great Awakening as fundamentally at odds with the churchly forms of devotion practiced by the historic Protestant churches.

This contrast between Old School Presbyterianism and Nevin's own evaluation of American Protestantism highlights the significance of the man mainly responsible for the Mercersburg Theology. Nevin represents a Reformed version of high-church Protestantism. Two aspects of his understanding of the church were especially important. The first was his recognition that the official ministry of church officers through worship was crucial to Reformed devotion. Participation in the formal ministry and instruction of the church was not a luxury, something that could supplement activity in parachurch agencies or small groups of devout believers. Membership and participation in the elements of worship and adherence to church teaching were in fact measures of genuine piety. This conception of Reformed piety clearly ran against the grain of mainstream American Protestantism. But because of its antithetical character it produced one of the most forceful critiques ever written of Christianity assimilated to American tastes and customs. Second, Nevin's thinking about the importance and necessity of the church was significant because it yielded an interpretation of the Reformed tradition that accurately reflected Calvinism's churchly and liturgical character. Nevin's project was not one of trying to include the Reformed faith in some form of high-church movement because it was fashionable. If Nevin were simply interested in becoming high-church, he could have left the Reformed faith for other communions—and for a time in his life he considered this alternative. But Nevin's study of the Reformed tradition indicated that churchly and sacramental concerns were not foreign to the Presbyterian or Reformed communions. What was odd, in his view, was a version of the Reformed faith in which questions of ecclesiology and worship had been jettisoned to fit better the sensibility of a popular and democratic Christianity taking hold in the United States. As such, Nevin became an effective critic not only of revivalism's subjective and individualistic faith but also of Reformed and Presbyterian expressions that minimized his tradition's inherently churchly outlook.

This work as critic turned out to be a difficult role to play. A man plagued throughout his life by dyspepsia, Nevin suffered constantly both physically and psychologically. His greatest years of anguish came after his most fruitful decade of theological reflection. After teaching at Western Seminary during the 1830s, he moved from Pittsburgh to Mercersburg to join the faculty of the German Reformed Church's seminary in that small Pennsylvania town. There he witnessed firsthand the oddities of the Second Great Awakening within his own congregation, an experience that prompted one of his most important works, a small pamphlet entitled *The Anxious Bench* (1843), in which he worked out the fundamental difference between church-based faith and revival-driven devotion. Nevin soon acquired help in his struggle to expound and defend the Reformed faith's churchly character when Philip Schaff joined him on the faculty at Mercersburg. Properly fortified, Nevin followed his critique of revivalism with *The Mystical Presence* (1846), a book that employed Calvin's own teaching and new currents in German philosophy to defend the real presence of Christ in the Lord's Supper. Nevin's tapping of historic Reformed wellsprings continued apace in 1847 with the *History and Genius of the Heidelberg Catechism*. His outpouring of writing on the church swelled with *The Anti-Christ; or, The Spirit of Sect and Schism* (1848), another critique of American Protestantism's novelty. Along the way Nevin continued to teach divinity at the seminary and moral philosophy at the German Reformed Church's Marshall College. The latter duties help to account for his many articles and essays on philosophical questions as well as the variety of articles he wrote for the *Mercersburg Review*.

The pace of activity during the 1840s and the controversy that ensued took a marked toll on Nevin. During the 1850s he retired from his duties at both the seminary and the college. Part of the explanation was poor health. But Nevin's theological explorations had also generated spiritual afflictions. As a result, his literary output slackened, and Nevin would never resume his former productivity. During the 1860s he came out of retirement to teach and preside over Franklin and Marshall College in Lancaster and to teach at the denomination's seminary across the street. His resumption of teaching and administration notwithstanding, the only notable literary achievement of the last thirty years of Nevin's life was *A Vindication of the Revised Liturgy* (1867), a book written to defend the work of the committee on which he had served to bring the German Reformed Church's worship into line with the churchly devotion for which he had argued during the 1840s. But the controversy in the denomination over those revisions indicated that Nevin's efforts had not been entirely successful. The case for a churchly brand of the Reformed faith had proved to be as unsettling for the German Reformed Church as Nevin's stomach was for him.

Assessing Nevin

In an essay on Charles Hodge's place in the history of ideas, University of Pennsylvania historian Bruce Kuklick concludes that the Princeton theologian has failed to interest intellectual historians because Hodge did not sufficiently "juxtapose the sacred texts of his tradition with his own life experience and the knowledge of his culture."[11] For Kuklick, Jonathan Edwards clearly meets this criterion, thus explaining the wide and ever-growing scholarly interest in the eighteenth-century revivalist-philosopher. Using roughly the same standard upon Nevin, religious historians generally evaluate the Mercersburg professor as a theologian who began to employ German philosophical and theological insights in what otherwise might have been a fairly dull intellectual task—namely, training Reformed ministers and serving an ethnic Protestant denomination. Hints of this approach come from Kuklick himself in his book *Churchmen and Philosophers*, where he asserts that the most significant piece of Nevin's legacy was his work in founding the *Mercersburg Review*, a journal that "gave

learned credibility to Hegelian theology."[12] Kuklick well summarizes
the standard treatment of Nevin: he was an intellectual innovator,
breaking outside the predictable ranks of Scotch-Irish philosophy and
the theological categories of Reformed Scholasticism.

To be sure, other assessments of Nevin have looked beyond questions of philosophical innovation to his contributions as a theologian
and churchman. For instance, Sydney E. Ahlstrom contends that Nevin
and Schaff "participated in one of the most significant movements of
theological renewal and church reform in nineteenth-century America."[13] But in the Yale historian's estimation, what made the Mercersburg Theology significant was its introduction of German ideas into
American Protestantism, thus prompting Ahlstrom to call Nevin the
"Romantic Church Reformer." For James Hasting Nichols, a mainline Presbyterian church historian who often searched the history of
American Christianity for a past to use against the rationalistic dogma-
tism that continued to bedevil his Presbyterian communion, Nevin's
"broad perspectives," "interdenominational friendships," and "pas-
sion for ecumenical unity" offered Protestantism in the United States
an attractive alternative from the domination of British theology and
philosophy. Nevin's use of German thought particularly placed him in
a "romantic current" that broke down "American intellectual provincialism" and opened "communications with the live currents of European theology."[14] In a similar fashion, historical theologian B. A. Gerrish sees in Nevin an American Protestant who wrestled more (and
perhaps more attractively for Gerrish) with Friedrich Schleiermacher
than with John Calvin. According to Gerrish, "for both Nevin and
Schleiermacher, the church was not—as rationalism and sectarianism
had come to suppose—a voluntary human association, but a divine
organism, the locus of the continuing life of Christ."[15] The impressions left by many who have studied Nevin, then, is one of an intellectual ahead of the curve of American religious and philosophical
development.

As accurate as interpretations are that stress Nevin's innovative
views, they slight his fundamental identity and contribution as a
Reformed theologian. As such, he was constantly in dialogue with a
doctrinal tradition begun by Ulrich Zwingli and John Calvin, refined

in creedal and catechetical standards such as the Heidelberg Catechism and the Westminster Confession of Faith, and perpetuated in those communions formed by Nevin's own Scotch-Irish Presbyterians and the German Reformed in which he served for most of his distinguished career. In fact, most of his original insights were forged in the context of developments within his own denomination, from the rise of Finney's new measures in his local Mercersburg congregation to his rationale for the revised liturgy of the German Reformed Church. Even his use of German philosophy is hard to disconnect from his work as a churchman since part of what made German sources more attractive to him was the very present reality of the German-Americans with whom he lived and worked. To look to German intellectual life for insights was not necessarily a highbrow endeavor to form the cutting edge of American religious and philosophical thought; instead it was simply one of the intellectual tools at Nevin's disposal by virtue of his work for a ethnically German communion.

To be sure, Nevin's application of German philosophy to Reformed faith and practice in North America may have generated theological novelties such that his significance may appear to be more creative than conservative. Clearly, ministers in his own denomination thought this, as well as any number of his critics from other churches. Still, what is important to grasp about Nevin is his genuine contribution to American Protestantism generally and to the Reformed tradition specifically. For the former he identified the fissure dividing historic Protestantism from a novel form that was dominating religious life in the United States. For the Reformed world Nevin recovered the older Calvinist regard for the church as a mediator of divine grace. These were no small accomplishments, and exploring their emergence, development, and significance is the aim of this book.

Presbyterian Provincialism

ad John Williamson Nevin never taught at Mercersburg Seminary, he would likely be confined to lists of nineteenth-century American theological education's also-rans. The United States' decentralized and unregulated educational system nurtured great spontaneity and creativity. One of the home-grown institutions in American learning was the seminary, formerly a Catholic structure that American Protestants co-opted. Without an established church or establishment universities, denominations turned to their own resources for pastoral training. As such, the nineteenth century teamed with seminaries, prompting one historian to refer to the period between 1820 and 1850 as one of "too many schools."[1] With these numerous schools went a bevy of faculty who even in their own time had trouble standing out from the pack. In the case of Princeton Seminary alone, an institution dear to American Presbyterians, faculty held long tenures whose names would be as unfamiliar to Presbyterian pastors and officials as those of the most important Baptist seminary. After Charles Hodge, Archibald Alexander, and Benjamin Warfield at Princeton came the likes of James Waddel Alexander, John D. Davis, William Brenton Greene, Frederick Loetscher, and George T. Purves. In the historical record, Nevin's life could well have turned out like one of these unrecognized figures in Reformed theological education. In fact, in the annals of Presbyterian theological education,

Nevin is one of those figures of slight significance, having taught at Princeton for two years, 1826 to 1828, filling in for Charles Hodge, and from 1830 to 1840 at the new Presbyterian seminary of the West in Pittsburgh.

Nevin's early life, in other words, had all the marks of what contributed to the making of second-rate or average theological acumen. Not even his time of study at Princeton Seminary established Nevin's reputation. His was an unexceptional youth and early career. To be sure, his family was well connected to some of the nation's military and political figures of note. Furthermore, as a young man who became a college graduate, Nevin was in a rare class of American citizens, since only approximately one percent of the population attended college. To study at a professional school like Princeton made Nevin even rarer. Even so, Nevin's upbringing and education among the Scotch-Irish of Pennsylvania were not responsible for moving him from the middle tier of the Davises, Greenes, and Purveses to the ranks of the Hodges, Alexanders, and Warfields. Indeed, Nevin's Presbyterian roots had no direct role in elevating him, as Yale church historian Sydney Ahlstrom did in his anthology of American theology, to a status comparable to that of William Ellery Channing, Nathaniel William Taylor, Ralph Waldo Emerson, and Horace Bushnell. For that to happen, Nevin ironically had to leave the world of Scotch-Irish Presbyterianism for the even more provincial one of German Reformed. But to understand what Ahlstrom calls Nevin's "second conversion," some attention to the circumstances before and after his first is necessary.[2]

A Different Sort of Cumberland Presbyterianism

John Williamson Nevin was born on February 20, 1803, in Franklin County, Pennsylvania, a rural, hilly terrain southwest of the state's capital in Harrisburg. His father, John, was a college-educated farmer of what one biographer calls "a quiet and studious disposition."[3] John Sr. was also the nephew of Hugh Williamson, a physician from North Carolina who cared for soldiers during the American Revolution, became a member of the Continental Congress, and was one of the drafters of the United States Constitution. A graduate of Dick-

inson College in 1795, the senior Nevin was self-conscious about public speaking and so declined a career in the ministry or law to become
a "Latin Farmer," that is, one who could teach his sons Latin and
Greek. Although John Nevin was so intimidated by speaking in front
of others that he declined leading assemblies in prayer, he nonetheless
was well respected and served briefly as a trustee at his alma mater
and was elected to the United States Congress from his district, an
office that death prevented him from occupying. Little is known about
John Nevin's wife, Martha McCracken, the mother of John Williamson
Nevin, though as a local girl she was part of the resilient Scotch-Irish
settlers who during the first half of the eighteenth century expanded
the sphere of western European influence and culture westward. John
and Martha Nevin had nine children in all, John Williamson Nevin
the oldest of them.

Although Nevin senior was half English, the Nevin family in
Franklin County was thoroughly enmeshed in the religious and cultural life of Scotch-Irish Presbyterianism in the Cumberland Valley.
Nevin was reared in the congregation at Middle Spring, three miles
outside Shippensburg, the oldest of the Presbyterian churches in the
Presbytery of Donegal, a jurisdiction that dated back to the turbulent
decade of the 1740s when the First Great Awakening divided Presbyterians into the Old and New Sides. Congregational life registered a
decisive impression on the young Nevin, so much so that at the age of
sixty-seven, when writing on his early upbringing, he would describe
the situation as the "Scotch regime" being "in full force."[4] What Nevin
meant by those phrases was a system of piety that grew out of the
church. Indeed, so deep was the impression left upon Nevin that the
biographer is tempted to interpret the trajectory of his career as a
project of preserving the faith of his boyhood.[5] As he described this
"Scotch regime," it was "the old Presbyterian faith, . . . based throughout on the idea of covenant family religion, church membership by
God's holy act in baptism, and following this a regular catechetical
training of the young, with direct reference to their coming to the Lord's
table."[6] Nevin also explained that this churchly Presbyterian faith was
"staid, systematical, and grave; making much of sound doctrine; won-

derfully bound to established forms; and not without a large sense for the objective side of religion embodied in the means of grace."[7]

James Hastings Nichols, in his otherwise capable and insightful study of the Mercersburg Theology, characterized the Middle Spring congregation as New Side.[8] Such a labeling undoubtedly adds irony to an interpretation of Nevin's own theological development, since the New Side was the branch of colonial Presbyterianism that favored revivalism and Nevin himself would emerge as American Protestantism's most forceful critic of revival. But the irony is likely more a mirage than a genuine instance of incongruity. Nevin's own description of the congregation as Scotch dovetails with other interpretations of colonial Presbyterianism that regard the Scotch-Irish, who comprised the Old Side, as generally more Old World and formal in their piety as opposed to the English Puritan influence among the New Side, where zealous intensity counted for true godliness, or what some label experimental Calvinism. One of the most significant indications that Nevin's congregation was Old Side comes from his own reference to the church's use of the Rous psalter, a book of psalms for congregational singing collected by Francis Rous, a member of the Westminster Assembly, heavily used by the Scotch and Scotch-Irish. As a sixty-seven-year-old, Nevin could still hear in Rous's psalter "a fond echo borne in upon my soul from the old stone church at Middle Spring."[9] The New Side churches were quicker to introduce the hymnody of Isaac Watts than the Old Side, which held on to Rous. Hymnals alone cannot settle the issue, but Nevin's own description of the churchly piety of the Middle Spring congregation, and the way it would later inform his own understanding of the Christian ministry, suggest strongly that the church in which he was reared was Old Side. This hunch receives support from Guy S. Klett's history of colonial Presbyterianism in Pennsylvania in which he describes the Presbytery of Donegal as overwhelmingly Old Side, except for the staunch New Side efforts of two ministers in the judicatory. These New Side ministers turned Donegal into one of the "chief centers of conflict" in the Old Side–New Side controversy.[10] But those New Side Presbyterians also appear to have left little mark on the practice of Reformed Christianity among Nevin's forebears.

During Nevin's youth Middle Spring witnessed the retirement of Robert Cooper and the call of John Moodey. Little is known about either man, except for what Nevin himself would recall. Cooper, who baptized Nevin just before retirement in 1803, was a 1763 graduate of the College of New Jersey and resisted preaching from a manuscript, both of which are signs that he may have sympathized with the New Side even though by the time of his ordination in 1765 the breach between the two churches in 1758 had been resolved. Cooper's successor, Moodey, born on the day the Declaration of Independence was issued, also studied at the College of New Jersey, graduating in 1796. He took a call to Middle Spring and ministered there for the remainder of his career. Moodey's understanding of and practice in the ministry was sufficiently impressive for Nevin, while acting as president of the German Reformed Church's Marshall College in the 1840s, to convince the school's trustees to grant his former pastor the honorary Doctor of Divinity degree. This is another suggestion of Nevin's approval of the formal and historic patterns of devotion that he experienced as a boy.

Yet, his inheritance of Reformed Christianity was not simply the product of an old-style ministry of word and sacrament. Nevin also gave credit to the piety of his parents. As soon as he could speak, he remembered, "I was put on simple Bible questions." After that followed the *Mother's Catechism*, a popular elementary form of instruction used by many English-speaking Protestants. When he mastered that instruction, Nevin's parents introduced their oldest son to the Westminster Shorter Catechism, "hard to be understood, but wholesome for future use."[11] Nevin recalled that all of this indoctrination at home received reinforcement at the parish school, where the teacher also drilled students on the Shorter Catechism. The purpose of catechetical training was to nurture the regular ministry of the pastor. Nevin also recollected that part of the duties of his own pastor, John Moodey, was a regular pattern of family visitation, one year going to every home in the congregation, the next holding larger meetings of several families in one area. In both cases the pastor and elders would examine children on the Shorter Catechism and adult members on the Westminster Larger Catechism. It is no wonder that Nevin would later speak of the system of the catechism as a rival form of devotion to that of the anxious bench.

Calvinist doctrine was not the only subject that Nevin learned at home. His father, a college graduate and lover of books, in many ways typified the gentleman farmer that Thomas Jefferson had said was the backbone of American democracy. From his father, Nevin junior learned first Latin and then Greek, the prerequisites for admission to college. This "country learning," as Nevin called it, was irregular. Sometimes his lessons occurred in the field, and at other times in the barn. "But the course was full," he conceded, "and the drill severe."[12] At the same time, this unlikely classroom proved, as he also admitted, to be "more worth to me in truth, as I came to know at a later day, than all I learned of these languages subsequently in passing through college."

At the apparently young age of fourteen Nevin left the hinterlands of rural Pennsylvania Presbyterianism for Union College, an outpost of New England Puritanism in upstate New York. The normal course would have been for Nevin to follow his father's footsteps and attend Dickinson College, only thirty-five miles or so from the Nevin farm. But Nevin's parents believed that Dickinson had slipped from its earlier brilliance. In addition, Union became an easier decision when John Williamson, a wealthy relative, stepped forward to assume responsibility for financing his namesake's college education. With advice from his brother, Hugh Williamson, then living in New York, Union became the place where the young Nevin would receive his training in the liberal arts.

If Nevin's provincial Presbyterianism was crucial to his own reflection on the nature of Christian devotion and the church's ministry, his time at Union proved to be equally significant since it turned out to be the foil for his conception of churchly piety. Schenectady, New York, the home of Union College, was not technically in New England but it was clearly in the cultural orbit and theological trajectory of the Puritan faith and outlook that had shaped the region to the east. For Protestants outside the Reformed tradition, spotting the difference between Puritanism and Presbyterianism may have been as hard as telling German and Dutch Reformed apart. Nevertheless, since its inception in the New World, Presbyterianism of the Scotch-Irish variety had uneasily cooperated with New England Puritans. These tensions were evident early on when the Scotch-Irish in southeastern Pennsylvania in the 1720s had insisted upon strict subscription to the Westminster Standards, and those Presbyterians from New England countered that such strictness was at odds with liberty of conscience. Antagonism between the Scotch-Irish and New Englanders surfaced again during the First Great Awakening as the former were critical of the revivals and the enthusiasm that characterized them, while the latter promoted revivals as a clear indication of God's blessing. In fact, the Old Side–New Side controversy and split, which lasted from 1741, the high water mark of the First Great Awakening, to 1758, reflected these differences between the Scotch-Irish in the middle colonies and the Presbyterians from New England who had migrated to New York and northern New Jersey. As a boy of fourteen, Nevin was undoubtedly unaware of these tensions. After his undergraduate studies at Union he would no longer be so naïve.

The young Pennsylvanian arrived at Union shortly after a significant change in the college's curriculum, thanks to the direction of its president, Eliphalet Nott. A native of Connecticut, Union's president was born in 1773 and reared in the religious and educational institutions of New England. Like most educators in antebellum America, Nott began his career as a minister, first pastoring a Presbyterian congregation in Cherry Valley, New York, and then First Presbyterian Church in Albany. New York Presbyterianism had great affinities to New England Congregationalism, and those ties became definite in the Plan of Union of 1801 between the Presbyterian and Congregationalist denominations. The plan provided a mechanism for the two churches to cooperate in home missions in western states such as Ohio, Indiana, Michigan, and Illinois and even parts of New York. The name of the college itself over which Nott presided was not simply a reference to the national union of the states but also to the united purpose of Congregationalists, Presbyterians, and Dutch Reformed. In fact, Jonathan Edwards, the son of Connecticut's greatest minister, theologian, and philosopher, drew up plans for cooperation between Congregationalists and Presbyterians while president of Union College.

Nott assumed office in 1804 and would not relinquish it until his death some sixty-two years later.

Despite Nott's reputation as a conservative Congregationalist minister, he was also responsible for establishing Union as a pathbreaking institution among America's colleges. He had come to the public's attention because of his preaching against dueling in the aftermath of Alexander Hamilton's death at the hands of Aaron Burr. But as a college president, Nott was hardly old-fashioned. Only two years before Nevin's enrollment at Union, Nott had instituted the so-called Laws of 1815, a curricular revision that made the college a trendsetter. The new course of study actually turned out to be the seeds of the elective system that would not become standard in American colleges until the late nineteenth century. Students could choose between two plans of study, one that replicated the traditional pattern of classical languages and humanistic learning and the other—a novelty—that stressed a practical curriculum that was less oriented to producing gentlemen. In both cases, Nott furthered Union's innovative ways by revamping the senior year of instruction and giving it over to training in the natural sciences, demoting many of the Greek and Latin ancients to the junior year.[13] As Nott's biographer puts it, the Union College president's vision of college education deserves to rank with that of Thomas Jefferson because Nott believed that "training in the physical and political sciences, not in the trivium, not in the theology of the Puritans, nor in speculative systems of thought, was the central concern of higher education in the America of his time."[14] Like the university presidents of the late nineteenth century at places like Johns Hopkins, Chicago, Cornell, and Stanford, Nott contended that the United States needed men of action and that such a need should be met by advanced learning.

On Nevin, however, Nott's innovations registered barely a ripple, at least in the short run. In his memoirs Nevin demonstrated little interest in the curricular reforms that Nott undertook. He recalled that the president "took only a very small part in [the college's] actual work of instruction, and this itself never amounted to much more than an empty form." So underwhelmed was Nevin with his undergraduate education that he also commented that Union "lived largely on the outside credit of its name." He admitted that he himself was partly to blame for the poor impression that Union made. Nevin reflected that he was too young; "I was the youngest and smallest student in my class, and a mere unfledged boy, I may say, on to the end of my college course."[15] After all, he was only eighteen when he graduated, and his health suffered to boot, the result of his unsteady digestion that no amount of diet or remedies could alleviate. He also suffered from bouts of depression that were undoubtedly connected to his chronic burning stomach, but telling whether the dyspepsia or depression was the chicken or the egg is not a conclusion that the historical record allows. Whatever the source of Nevin's melancholy, his memories of Union did not include much room either for Nott and his reforms or for one of Union's best known professors, Francis Wayland, later president of Brown University and one of the leading moral philosophers in the United States at a time when that subject supplied the capstone of the college curriculum. Nevin could look back on his college days only "as a sort of horrible nightmare, covering with gloom the best season of my life."[16]

The reason behind such a dire assessment is that the extra curriculum at Union, not the actual courses, were what proved to be decisive in Nevin's life. After having grown up in the rich church life of Pennsylvania Presbyterianism, he experienced a great lack at Union. Morning and evening prayers were required of students, as well as attendance of worship services on Sunday. But Union's Protestantism was generic; the college "was organized around the principle of representing the collective Christianity of the so-called evangelical denominations." As such, religion at Union was abstract and removed from the "spirit and soul" of the college. Nevin admitted that he did not recognize it at the time, but Union's Protestant faith was a serious "falling away from the educational and churchly scheme" upon which he had been reared.[17]

Nevin's religious naïveté became all the more apparent when during his junior year New England Congregationalist minister and revivalist Asahel Nettleton visited campus for a series of special meetings. At the time, the Hopkinsian Calvinist, who stood self-consciously in the revivalist tradition of Edwards and the First Great Awakening, had been recently ordained as an evangelist by the South Consociation of Litchfield, Connecticut. Nettleton was also leading a series of successful revivals at the invitation of various pastors in his home state and in Massachusetts. He had not yet seen the chief manifestations of the Second Great Awakening, namely, the revival crusades led by Charles Grandison Finney—mainly because Finney himself had yet to convert, doing so two years after Nettleton's visit to Union. But once Finney devoted his energies to revival and began to experience great success, Nettleton was not encouraged. In 1826, for instance, he wrote in one letter, "whoever has made himself acquainted with the state of things in New England near the close of the revival days of Whitefield and Edwards cannot but weep over its likeness to the present."[18] Such a reaction to Finney's methods suggests a fundamental difference between the First and Second Great Awakenings. Unlike Edwards, whom Nettleton followed, Finney believed and taught that revivals were not miraculous but scientific—that is—they could be planned, predicted, and executed with the right efforts and means.

The differences between Nettleton and Finney are important for understanding Nevin. Of course, much of Nevin's eventual modest fame would come from his critique of Finney in *The Anxious Bench* (1843). And when Nevin wrote that work he did appear to leave open the door to revivals of the right kind, those like Nettleton's where the anxious seat was never used, as opposed to Finney's "worked-up" variety. But this distinction between the good awakening of Edwards and the pernicious one of Finney (repeated often today by zealous Calvinists) fails to do justice to Nevin's overarching point about the character of nineteenth-century Protestantism in America and its departure from the faith and practices of the Reformation. Indeed, as Nevin learned at Union, the differences between the churchly piety of his Middle Spring Presbyterian congregation and the revivals of Nettleton, even if not manipulated, were profound. To say that the rest of his life's work was devoted to working out that proposition may seem like an overstatement. But it bears enough truth to turn an assertion of apparent exaggeration into one with plausibility.

As an impressionable lad seldom exposed to the excitements of revivals, Nevin was ripe for the picking. Compounding the situation was his failure to have made a public profession of faith by the time of his junior year. Furthermore, Nevin held Nettleton in high esteem, regarding the evangelist as "the impersonation of the apostle Paul." So he submitted himself to the pokings, proddings, and diagnoses of the revival's "miserable obstetricians." The results were not satisfactory. Nevin recalled:

> I, along with others, came into their hands in anxious meetings, and underwent the torture of their mechanical counsel and talk. One after another, however, the anxious obtained "hope"; each new case, as it were, stimulating another; and finally, among the last, I struggled into something of the sort myself, a feeble trembling sense of comfort—which my spiritual advisers, then, had no difficulty in accepting as all that the case required. In this way I was converted, and brought into the Church—as if I had been altogether out of it before— about the close of the seventeenth year of my age.[19]

Nevin added that the change in his life owing to conversion was not as radical as promised, but it was "earnest and thorough," the best that he could muster. His conversion was in fact the pivotal time of his life, not in the normal sense, for it did not deepen his appreciation for revivalism's piety. Instead, it set Nevin on a collision course with the dominant trend in American Protestantism. This was indeed an important lesson to learn—and the greatest one that Nevin took away from Union when in 1821 he graduated with honors, having won Phi Beta Kappa, and returned to his home in Pennsylvania. But it was a hard lesson, leaving his "whole constitution . . . in an invalid state, . . . dyspeptic both in body and mind."[20]

In such a physical and spiritual state, Nevin entered into a two-year period of convalescence. Nevin wrote that he "experienced all sorts of painful and unpleasant symptoms; was continually miserable and weak; had an intense consciousness all the time of the morbid workings of my physical system." In short, dyspepsia "hung on to me with a sort of death-like grasp." Nor did his recent conversion provide much comfort. To his shame he admitted that "the strength of Christ . . . was *not* made perfect in my weakness."[21] He attributed part of his spiritual woe to his physical state. But he would later also lay the blame at the feet of conversionist piety. Nevin called this form of devotion Methodistical, referring not simply to the form of Protestantism that grew up around the work of John Wesley, but also to the originally pejorative association of the term that linked it with mechanical and regulated procedures for instilling and remaining holy. This devotion, Nevin believed, because "intensely subjective and introspective," only increased his suffering. Instead of taking comfort from the objective promises of the gospel, Nevin thought he should constantly examine himself and how well he was progressing. "What could the result of such painful autopsy be," he asked, "(this everlasting studying of symptoms, this perpetual feeling of the spiritual pulse), other than the weakening of faith, the darkening of hope, and the souring of that most excellent grace of charity itself?" Here his own church did not provide the comfort for which he had hoped. Central Pennsylvania Presbyterianism itself was changing: "The catechetical system was passing away." And as a young man Nevin was divided over the change, split between his constitutional conservatism and the "would-be progressive tendencies" of youth.[22]

Still, these two years back at home turned out to be recuperative. First, Nevin's physical ailments led to inactivity—"hibernation" he called it—which afforded him time for study. Not surprisingly, he became familiar with a number of medical texts, especially ones having to do with dyspepsia. He also continued to learn French, a language he had begun at Union. Nevin dabbled in poetry, sometimes composing metrical versions of the Psalms, some of which were published in local religious periodicals. He also participated, with his father, in a debating society in nearby Shippensburg. All of these intellectual pursuits prevented the young scholar from losing his intellectual edge. Over time, his physical condition improved sufficiently for Nevin to help out with chores on the farm. An added sign of his renewed vigor was his joining a "crack volunteer company" of soldiers to assist in the defense of the community.[23] With his health improved, Nevin determined to pursue the vocation upon which he was intent "from the beginning," namely, the Presbyterian ministry. Family and community expectations were such that he knew he should at least go to seminary, though he was not certain of his calling to be a pastor. What he did know was that he could not pursue medicine or law. So with that bit of resolve, in 1823 he decided to enroll at Princeton Theological Seminary.

When Nevin arrived in the central New Jersey town in the fall of 1823, the seminary was still young: only eleven years old. Nevin's impressions before arriving were not positive. He wrote in his memoirs that "Princeton divinity students, so far as they had appeared among us yet in Shippensburg or Middle Spring, had a certain air of conscious sanctimony about them." He added that "they seemed to be rebuking all the time the common worldliness of these old congregations (especially on Sundays)." As a result, Princeton Seminary students gave off the odor of "a *Young Presbyterianism*, which was in a fair way to turn into old-fogyism soon all their existing religious life." As a seminarian himself, though, his tune changed. From the vantage of retirement, Nevin admitted that his days at Princeton were "the most pleasant part of my life."[24] The reasons for this memory had much to do with seminary's maturing academic program.

The Princeton Seminary to which Nevin came was still young, but its professors were not. The seminary's first professor, Archibald Alexander, a Scotch-Irishman born and reared in that part of Virginia where Presbyterianism and revivalism were strong, was by the time of Nevin's study fifty-one years old and at the peak of his abilities. Alexander had successfully pastored congregations in Virginia and Philadelphia before teaching at Princeton. Many of his strengths as a minister were the ones that distinguished him as a professor. Alexander taught courses in practical theology and preaching, and students usually remembered best his earnest devotion. His piety was also memorable in chapel and Sunday afternoon conferences, where the demands of revivalist zeal were on display for all to see. One graduate recalled that during preaching or lecturing, Alexander would explain a biblical passage or point of doctrine and then "seem to pause, and painful anxiety to be stamped upon his countenance, as though he were ready to say, I fear the Heavenly Father is not here! let us lay aside our helps and repair to him."[25] Aside from the fits of urgency behind the pulpit or lectern, Alexander also stamped Princeton with his decision to use Francis Turretin's *Institutio theologiae elencticae* as the primary theological text. The choice of a seventeenth-century Protestant Scholastic textbook helped to make Princeton an institution where, despite the soul searching encouraged by its piety, systematic theology's care and precision became a central feature of its education.

Samuel Miller joined Alexander on the faculty in 1813, only a year after the school's founding. The son of a Scotch-Irish Presbyterian minister in Delaware, Miller followed in his father's footsteps and ministered in New York City before leaving the pastorate to teach. Miller demonstrated a historical sensibility with the publication in 1803 of his *Brief Retrospect of the Eighteenth Century*, an ambitiously encyclopedic account of the advance of human knowledge during a century of "enlightenment." Appropriately enough, Miller taught church history and church polity, the two subjects that before academic specialization always went hand in hand in nineteenth-century seminary curricula. Miller himself received a junior colleague the year before Nevin arrived, when the seminary appointed Charles Hodge to teach Hebrew. Together the three Princeton professors taught a three-year curriculum that began with study of Scripture in the original languages; proceeded with exegesis, systematics, and church history; and culminated with more theology, polity, and practical theology. A further sign of the seminary's growing stature was Hodge's initiative in 1824, Nevin's junior year, to inaugurate the *Biblical Repertory and Princeton Review*. Over the years the name of this journal would change, but its editorial outlook seldom did, especially with Hodge as the editor, who used the journal to comment on any number of subjects religious, cultural, and political.

Student life at the seminary was rather dull but it proved to be a welcome tonic for the ailing Nevin. Thanks to his studies at Union he would have been accustomed to the recitation method of instruction. Here students read and prepared for the assigned reading and then in class were asked questions. The correct answers involved restating what seminarians had gleaned from their textbooks. Hodge recalled one student during his own time at Princeton who would "day after day be able to give the State of the Question—all the arguments in its support in their order, all the objections and answers to them, through the whole thirty or forty pages, without the professor saying a word to him." Hodge, who followed the same manner of instruction when on the other side of the lectern, wondered about the excitement of such methods but rested content that "it was definitely effective." "A man who had passed through that drill never got over it."[26] If classroom atmosphere was dull, town life was not much more dynamic. Princeton at the time, despite the presence of the College of New Jersey and the seminary, was still basically a sleepy farm town. The seminary had roughly ninety students in 1823, the college approximately the same. The only source of legitimate entertainment—students at the college had a history of generating their own illicit fun—was the patriotic celebrations that punctuated the daily routine. Patriotism came naturally to the town and its schools, thanks in part to John Witherspoon's having signed the Declaration of Independence and to Nassau Hall (College) being a temporary home for the Continental Congress during the Revolutionary War. One of the notable events during Nevin's student days was the visit of war hero Marquis de Lafayette during the fall of 1824, to receive a doctor-of-laws degree that in 1790 the board had conferred upon him in absentia.

As much as Nevin may have escaped the cocoon of gloom through his surroundings and studies at Princeton, the devotional character of seminary life left an unfavorable and unsettling impression. "Embarrassments, fears, doubts, with regard to my personal religion," he wrote, "attended me, more or less all the time."[27] Much of the problem for Nevin stemmed from Princeton piety at its best. He recalled that Alexander's "searching and awakening casuistry" was not easily forgotten. Nor was it easily endured since "it was by no means uncommon for students to go away from these meetings, in a state of spiritual discouragement bordering on despair." Nevin diagnosed the difficulty, again with the aid of hindsight and in tones that echoed his most important arguments, as a conflict between two forms of devotion: the "New England Puritanic theory" most evident in revivalism and "the old proper Presbyterian theory of the seventeenth century." Nevin admitted that as a seminarian he could feel but not articulate the difference. But his "constitutional affinity" was with the older Reformed faith. What is more, his own upbringing in Middle Spring reared him "in the bosom of the old Reformed order." Princeton was not thoroughly modernized. He explained:

> Our teaching at Princeton had much in it, that went against the new here, and in favor of the old. Dr. Miller was strong on certain ecclesiastical points especially, that would not square at all with the new way of thinking; while Dr. Alexander was always recommending the divinity and piety of the seventeenth century, as it was easy to see also, that they formed the element in which mainly his own piety lived, moved, and had its being. But with all this, the other unchurchly scheme also exercised over me a strong practical force, which I was not able to withstand. Our teaching was not steadily and consistently in one direction. . . . So it was that I found myself in a sort of strait between these two systems, and knew not how to adjust the one rightly with the other in my religious life.[28]

Just as studies had helped him endure during his two years between Union and Princeton, so academics—this time Hebrew—gave stability to Nevin's outlook and routine. Interestingly enough, the youngest faculty member, Charles Hodge, who taught oriental and biblical literature, proved to be an encouragement, both directly and indirectly. Hodge's course in Hebrew at first threatened to drown the young seminarian (as such first-year courses still do), and Nevin considered dropping out. But a seminary senior, Matthew L. Fullerton, intervened and persuaded Nevin to stay in the course by appealing to his potential service to the church. At first, Fullerton's argument was unpersuasive because Nevin believed that at best his ministry would be "in some out of the way country congregation, where Hebrew would be of no sort of use to me whatever." So Fullerton revised his case. He appealed to Christian duty. Nevin, being a good Calvinist, relented and actually found that with hard work "the lion which was in the way disappeared altogether."[29] Hebrew study even became "a pleasure," and he assumed the rank of "best Hebrew scholar" at Princeton. Nevin later interpreted this development as a major factor in his own devotion to exegetical study, an ironic reading of his life since philosophy more than exegesis stands out in his major works. Still, he was right to comment on the importance of exegetical theology during his time of study at Princeton because the ability to read and interpret the Bible in the original languages was one of the defining marks of the seminary's education.

Nevin's mastery of Hebrew was also important for the indirect assistance that Hodge gave the young scholar. Over the course of his seminary student days Nevin became no more resolved in his vocation than when he had first enrolled. His correspondence with family and friends indicated his doubts and fears of entering the ministry. At one point his father, in a manner that indicated exasperation with the son's quest for certainty in choosing a career, wrote:

> You have already been too long immured in schools and seminaries for the good of your bodily health; and it may be that the health of your mind would also receive benefit by your separating yourself from lectures and recitations. It is time for you to see the world as it is, and know your fellow creatures as they are. There is danger of your forming erroneous opinions of men and things; of your conceiving and brooding over ideas of duty and conduct altogether utopian and visionary—not to be realized.[30]

Teaching Hebrew to first-year seminarians was likely not what Nevin's father had in mind even if such students also have *real* lives. Even so, on the basis of Nevin's natural talent for language and Charles Hodge's two-year leave of absence for further study in Germany, in 1826 when the Cumberland native was graduated from Princeton he took over Hodge's teaching duties. The poignancy of Nevin's tenure at Princeton from 1826 to 1828 deserves comment no matter how small. Here was Nevin, who over the course of his life would eventually lose most of Hodge's confidence in him as a reliable theologian, substituting for arguably the most conservative Calvinist in nineteenth-century America. Moreover, here was Hodge, whose major critique of Nevin would be that his former student dabbled too much in doctrines German, going off to Germany to study in the presence of theologians whom Nevin would appropriate much better, even if only studying with them secondhand through their books and articles.

The two years of teaching at Princeton proved to be unremarkable for Nevin. They did afford him time to put off a decision on entering the ministry and give him duties to occupy his otherwise introspective morbidity. Nevin did manage to inaugurate his writing career with *A Summary of Biblical Antiquities*, eventually adapted for and published in two volumes in 1829–30 by the American Sunday School Union. Nevin later wrote that its production was in response to an urgent request that he felt he could not refuse. He also recalled, in his characteristically forlorn manner, "It cost me a heavy amount of work, for which I was very poorly paid."[31] As material for the training of the young, the book's coverage of the geography, climate, food, customs, legal structures, finances, and cult of the Israelites is by twenty-first-century standards impressive, bordering on doctoral. Even if antiquated by the research university's criteria for specialized knowledge, Nevin's presentation indicated a vast knowledge of the Old Testament and "the circumstances, natural and moral, of the time and country" in which it was written. Not only does the book reveal its author's own competency in the study of the ancient Near East as the scholarship then stood, it also reflects a recognition of the importance of the human characteristics of a book that Christians regarded as divine. As Nevin wrote in the preface, to understand the Bible properly

> we need to be conversant with the mountains, the plains and the streams; the beasts of the field and the birds of the air; the labours of the farmer and the habits of the shepherd; we need to walk, in fancy's vivid vision, through the streets of Jerusalem; to mingle with the inmates of the Jewish dwelling; to participate in their seasons of festive joy, and so to sympathize with their sorrow in the day of calamity and bereaving death; we need to go up to the temple, to unite in its worship, to behold its solemn rites, and to admire the beautiful grandeur of its scene.[32]

No doubt, its writing was therapy that many would have prescribed. It also helped distinguish Nevin among Presbyterian leaders who had recently launched another seminary in western Pennsylvania. That new school, Western Theological Seminary (now Pittsburgh

Theological Seminary), founded in 1825, was a shoestring venture, thus affording Nevin another period of respite at home on the family farm before the trustees could afford to pay for his services. But he returned to central Pennsylvania with Presbyterian papers of licensure, having been formally granted privileges to preach in the fall of 1828 by the Carlisle Presbytery. Nevin admitted that this fourteen-month period "was much in the same way as before, a general vacation from all regular study."[33]

While at home, Nevin provided pulpit supply, read in various subjects, and continued to battle and recuperate from physical maladies. The one academic discipline that caught his attention was political economy, a subject that had not made much impression upon him while at Union. He struck up a friendship with Henry Vethake, who taught the subject at Dickinson College. Nevin also wrote on scientific subjects, thus beginning to reveal some of the effects of Nott's curricular reforms at Union. But as he later confessed, "political economy" and other sciences, "starting from . . . merely natural and secular premises, cannot bring any positive aid to Christianity." Society, as well as individuals, ultimately needed "help from above—a strictly *supernatural* redemption."[34] Another subject that caught Nevin's attention was temperance, and he tried his hand at a sermon on abstinence from alcohol. One congregation that had been initially impressed by his preaching, when they heard his temperance encore, were greatly offended. Perhaps the forcefulness of this sermon stemmed not simply from its radicalism, but also from his newly adopted pulpit manner—recommended by his father—of preaching without a manuscript, what Nevin would call his "John the Baptist style."[35] He also used this time to take a trip to the new seminary in Pittsburgh on horseback, a mode of travel thought to be good for his health. Whether the excursion was successful remains a mystery, because soon after his arrival back at his parents' home, Nevin's father died unexpectedly. John Nevin had obviously been a great influence upon his son, even to the point of tinkering with pulpit mechanics. The son later wrote of his father, "Few men surpassed him in fine social and moral qualities. Earnestness and genial humor were happily blended in his spirit."[36]

Nevin's father's death forced a delay in his move to Pittsburgh. Not only did the business affairs of the homestead fall to the eldest son, but Nevin also became the head of his mother's household. He finally moved to Pittsburgh after the fall semester of 1829 and resided with Francis Herron, the pastor of First Presbyterian Church. Three years later his mother and sisters followed Nevin to Pittsburgh, at which point he found a new home in nearby Allegheny City. Then in 1835 Nevin was married to Martha Jenkins, the daughter of Robert Jenkins from Lancaster County, Pennsylvania, who owned a prosperous iron works. Fairly rapidly, Nevin went from the sole burdens of his own physical and spiritual condition to the main provider for his family and bride. How much the marriage owed to financial calculations is impossible to tell. But later in the 1830s, as Western Seminary fell behind in its professors' salaries, Nevin was able to maintain his household, perhaps through profits from the sale of his family's farm, perhaps through assistance from his prosperous in-laws.

What is curious is that with Nevin's newfound domestic and professional responsibilities, his own introspective misgivings subsided. Also of interest was Nevin's capacity for work beyond his home and the seminary. At the time Pittsburgh was a frontier town of only ten thousand residents, with a dozen churches, three of which were Presbyterian. It afforded lots of opportunity for a man with talent, and Nevin threw himself into his new surroundings, carrying a full load at Western, preaching most Sundays in local churches, serving on various humanitarian and religious organizations' boards, and even editing *The Friend*, the newspaper of the Young Men's Society of Pittsburgh and Vicinity, a forerunner of the YMCA. In almost a complete reversal from his student days, Nevin found in Pittsburgh a burst of energy that would carry him for the next two decades.

He later described Western Seminary in 1830 as having "no buildings, no endowments, no library, no prestige from the past, and only doubtful and uncertain promise from the future."[37] These were not ideal circumstances, but they did provide an ample outlet for Nevin's newfound energy. His duties in the classroom fell under the broad title of his appointment, the chair of biblical literature. Yet, little evidence survives of Nevin's instruction during his tenure at Western. No doubt, in addition to teaching Greek and Hebrew, he offered courses on the Old and New Testament that resembled his *Biblical Antiquities*. Some indication of Nevin's theological outlook comes from a number of sermons and lectures published during this time, such as "The Scourge of God" (1832), a sermon on an outbreak of cholera in Canada that many feared was headed for Pittsburgh; *The Claims of the Christian Sabbath* (1836), a report for the Presbytery of Ohio to address increasing instances of the desecration of the Lord's Day; *The English Bible* (1836), a pamphlet on the merits of the King James Version; "Personal Holiness" (1837), a lecture given at the beginning of the summer semester at Western; "The Seal of the Spirit" (1838), a sermon preached at Uniontown Presbyterian Church; *Party Spirit* (1839), an address given at the Literary Societies of Washington College; and "A Pastoral Letter" (1840), sent to members of the Presbytery of Ohio on the inadequacy of ministers' salaries. In addition, the publication of these sermons and addresses were signs of Nevin's emerging prominence as a theologian and churchman.

As conventional as some of these themes may have been, what caught the eye of his contemporaries as well as of later historians were Nevin's extracurricular activities. In addition to regular pulpit supply at the Hiland Presbyterian Church, just outside Pittsburgh, and editing *The Friend*, Nevin took an active interest in the debates over slavery while continuing to oppose alcohol and objecting to the theater in the city, the latter of which brought him threats of a "cowhiding." Nevin's father was an abolitionist, and the son followed in the father's footsteps. He editorialized in *The Friend*, preached sermons denouncing slavery as a "vast moral evil,"[38] and followed intently the abolitionist efforts of theological educators at Lane Theological Seminary in Cincinnati. Nevin's opposition to slavery hurt support for the seminary and *The Friend*. In 1835, under pressure he resigned from his editorial duties with a flourish:

> Slavery is a sin as it exists in this country, and as such ought at once to be abolished. There is no excuse for its being continued a single day. The whole nation is involved in the guilt of it, so long as public sentiment acquiesces in it as a necessary evil.[39]

55

In later life Nevin would express some embarrassment over his youthful idealism, not for his moral convictions, but for his poor ecclesiology. *The Friend* was a generically Christian effort, appealing to believers across the denominations. In retrospect, Nevin thought it inevitable that "this whole scheme of a high-toned Christian morality, holding in the power of Christian ideas supposed to be available for me in the world at large outside the narrower precincts of the Church," would result in "grief and failure."[40] But as a thirty-two-year-old man, such an outcome was not so obvious.

Only a few years later, when Presbyterians divided into the Old School and New School branches, slavery was one of the issues that caused the communion to fray. Indeed, the regional configuration of the division reveals that the Old School's excision of the northern and midwestern portions of the church, which became the heart of New School territory, also eliminated those parts of the denomination where antislavery sentiments were strongest. Consequently, the Old School was strongest in the South and Middle Atlantic States, with only Pennsylvania and New Jersey north of the Mason-Dixon Line, and the New School being the most populous in New York, New Jersey, Ohio, Indiana, and sections of Pennsylvania and New Jersey. Of course, New Schoolers could be found in the South and vice versa, but the regional representation of both sides indicated that slavery—and specifically whether slavery was a sin requiring church discipline—functioned as a source of disagreement and tapped other significant disputes.

Nevin's own antislavery sympathies, following the general rule, should have put him on the New School side of the 1837 division. In fact, his interest in Lane Seminary's affairs—a school that became a New School outpost—may have also indicated that his ecclesiastical ties were strongest with those Presbyterians booted from the denomination by the Old School. As it turned out, Nevin was ambivalent about the whole episode, but slavery did not appear to be the major factor. He later stated that his "theological sympathies were all along with the Old School."[41] His uncertainty stemmed from the extreme positions taken on both sides and from a sense that the controversy was confined to Philadelphia and New York, not one that really affected presbyteries like his own. This helps to explain Nevin's endorsement of Archibald Alexander's proposal to divide the church into regional and "relatively independent" synods where such controversies might be hammered out without implicating the national church. After the Old School decision of 1837 to excise those churches and judicatories that had become part of the Presbyterian fold through the Plan of Union, Nevin reacted negatively. He believed the action was unconstitutional. When his own, the Presbytery of Ohio, in 1837 deliberated a motion to ratify the Old School's decision, Nevin was one of ten presbyters (out of fifty) to vote no. The following year the presbytery proposed another resolution hoping to catch the dissenters from the previous year. The aim of this so-called adhering act was to declare allegiance to the Old School positions while also affirming the orthodoxy of those who, because they could not endorse all of the conservatives' actions, had voted in the negative the previous year. This motion succeeded by receiving unanimous approval. Even then, Nevin, who admitted that his fellow presbyters must have found him "somewhat wilfully scrupulous," needed to explain his vote. He did so at the next presbytery meeting in 1839 with a statement, signed by three other presbyters, that clarified that its author and signers could not consent to the proposition that the Old School General Assembly was the "only true and lawful succession of the Presbyterian Church in this country." Such a constitutional matter dare not be made "an article of faith either for themselves or others."[42]

Safe to say, Nevin was by the late 1830s much closer theologically to the Old School than to the New School, despite his pronounced views on slavery. The crusading zeal that opposed drunkenness, tobacco, theater, and desecration of the Sabbath was not the sole possession of the revival-friendly New School. It was a cultural sensibility that informed most Anglo-American Protestants, from Boston Unitarians to Baltimore Methodists. But slavery became such a divisive issue because economics and politics were also at stake in addition to questions of personal holiness or the church's duty.

After almost a decade of teaching at Western, and after the events of the Old School–New School controversy, Nevin was also growing weary of his tenuous existence in a frontier town where support for his seminary was flimsy. As he later characterized it, the seminary, "depending as it did on transient agencies and special collections among the churches, was subjected all the time to more or less financial difficulty, which in its way told seriously also on the comfort of those engaged in its service." With marked understatement, he added, "Altogether my situation in these years was no sinecure."[43] These circumstances likely led to Nevin's decision in 1840 to accept a call from the German Reformed Church to serve as theology professor at the denomination's seminary in Mercersburg. Because this decision fell so closely on the heels of the Presbyterian division, and because later historians would regard Nevin as the great proponent of ecumenism, the temptation is to interpret this move as an expression of disgust with Presbyterian polemics. But Nevin had actually been threatening to resign for at least four years because of financial uncertainties. What is more, the opportunity to return to central Pennsylvania, within thirty miles of his old home, provided additional incentive. Nevin may not have been German but, having grown up in a region of his home state, later called Pennsylvania Dutch because of its many German immigrants, he was accustomed to the culture of the communion calling him to Mercersburg. Even so, he admitted that the offer to teach at Mercersburg was entirely unexpected. "No movement was ever of more Providential account for my life; but I had nothing to do with it myself, and it lay at the time, in truth, altogether beyond the horizon of my knowledge."[44]

Nevin's Puritan Career

From the perspective of Nevin's entire life, his decision to leave the Presbyterian fold and join the work of the German Reformed Church appears to represent a major turning point. Indeed, considering his eventual critique of the Protestant churches of his day along with his program for establishing a churchly and liturgical expression of Reformed Christianity, his move to Mercersburg would appear to indicate in a highly visible and personal way a break with his Presbyterian past. Some might even be tempted to echo the verdict of Ahlstrom, who calls it a conversion, as if the world of the German Reformed and its Old World ways were so much more ecclesial than those of the mainstream Presbyterian and Congregationalist churches. Nichols, who wrote the best (and only) sustained study of Nevin and Schaff, in fact, categorizes Nevin's Presbyterian upbringing and early career as Puritan. This classification allows Nichols to interpret Nevin's later criticism of Puritanism, especially on the Lord's Supper, as a rejection of his Presbyterian past, with the terms *Presbyterian* and *Puritan* being synonymous.

This explanation of what was a significant development in Nevin's life is plausible. After all, Nevin himself said upon reflection on his transfer to Mercersburg that "no movement was ever of more Providential account for my life." To be sure, his new school, church, and religious community afforded opportunities that would not have been available among Old School Presbyterians. Still, to look at Nevin's German Reformed identity as a fundamental break with his Presbyterian past is wrong for the very important reason that he did not understand his life that way.

Here is where his autobiography is especially revealing and useful. If Nevin had wanted to indicate that the German Reformed Church allowed him to work out his frustrations with his Presbyterian youth, he could well have done so. He was not timid in objecting to inadequacies around him. But what becomes clear in his memoirs is how the rest of his life was a search to recover and bolster the churchly faith upon which he had been reared at the Middle Spring Presbyterian Church before having to endure the revivalistic measures of Congregationalism at Union College. As he described his experience during Union's revival, "this involved, of course—although, alas, I knew it not *then*—a very serious falling away from the educational and churchly scheme of religion, in which I had been previously born and bred."[45] In what comes across as a truly plaintive cry of the earnest soul, Nevin went on to write, "Alas, where was my mother, the Church, at the very time I most needed her fostering arms? Where was she, I mean, with her true sacramental sympathy and care?"[46] Rather than revealing a significant turning away from his Presbyterian congregation and boyhood home, more plausible is the idea that his boyhood Reformed faith set the course for his future theological development.

Ironically, then, Nevin's relocation to the German Reformed Church would turn out to be the means by which he attempted to reappropriate the churchly faith of his Presbyterian past. To be sure, this effort would involve a rejection of *a* Puritan career. But Nevin's Puritan past was different from his boyhood Presbyterianism; his Puritan career began in 1819 with his conversion, no matter how weak, at Union and would not end until 1846 with the publication of his reflections on the Lord's Supper. In between, Nevin tried to take sustenance from the revivalistic Protestantism that undergirded both the Presbyterian and Congregationalist communions. What he found was a spiritual diet rich in subjective experience but lean on the essentials of historic Christianity. Whether his Puritan phase was more painful than the period in which his views were labeled Roman Catholic is a question that likely only Nevin himself could answer. This query also suggests that the middle ground that Nevin hoped to stake out and defend, the one that he believed he had experienced as a boy at Middle Springs, was quickly disappearing in American Protestantism.

2

Becoming German Reformed

W hen Nevin decided to take the call to Mercersburg Seminary, a career development that surprised even him, he
sought the counsel of his former professors at Princeton.
Archibald Alexander responded that the move was no big deal. It was
merely a transfer from one branch of Reformed Christianity, "the
Scotch Reformed," to another very similar one, "the German Presbyterians."[1] For James Hastings Nichols, a mid-twentieth-century Presbyterian historian, Alexander's characterization of the difference
between German Reformed and Scotch-Irish Presbyterians revealed
more about Nevin than about his new communion. It indicated to
Nichols that Nevin would continue to work in lines sketched by the
Princeton theologians, until finally embracing the subtleties provided
by the German Reformed. Theodore Appel, Nevin's German Reformed
biographer and faculty colleague, also saw differences between Nevin's
new and old denominations that Alexander's characterization missed.
For Appel, Nevin's move into the German Reformed Church wore
away his rough Presbyterian edges, the "harsh" forthrightness of British
Calvinism, and replaced them with the "broader" and comprehensive
theology of the "Calvinistic-Melancthonian school."[2] While Nevin's
switch from his former professor's perspective was inconsequential,
for students of Nevin the change from the Presbyterian to the Reformed
fold was significantly a change for the better.

Evaluations of the German Reformed Church's influence on Nevin such as those of Nichols and Appel make assumptions about one of the less well-known branches of Reformed Christianity in North America. For instance, in *Reformed Theology in America* (1985), a collection of historical essays on the major branches of Reformed expression in the United States, the Princeton Theology, Dutch Calvinism, Southern Presbyterians, Westminster Seminary, and neo-orthodoxy all merit a section.[3] But the German Reformed Church receives no attention. Neither do the Huguenots (French Reformed), the Magyar tradition (Hungarian Reformed), or even the Puritans, so German Reformed need not feel blatantly excluded. Still, this book helps to illustrate the point that in the annals of Reformed Christianity the German contribution has not been recognized. Whether its contribution has been significant is an entirely different matter. In the case of Nichols and Appel, however, the German Reformed tradition made an important impact on Nevin, changing his theological orientation away from British sources and categories to the discourse and learning of the European continent, particularly in Germany.

A real temptation exists, as Nichols and Appel demonstrate, for students of Nevin to give credit to the German Reformed tradition for the Mercersburg theologian's eventual formulations of the Christian ministry, sacramental theology, and Reformed worship. American Christians so closely associate high-church Protestantism with things European (and conversely, low-church forms with Anglo-American culture) that explanations for Nevin's emergence as a proponent of sacramental and liturgical rigor automatically look to his association with the European theology and church life of the German Reformed Church. But closer inspection of both the German branch of Reformed Christianity in North America prior to Nevin's arrival at Mercersburg and his own theological development suggests that Alexander may have had the better interpretation of the situation than either Nichols or Appel, for the German Reformed Church before 1840 was hardly a monolithic expression of Old World Protestant faith and practice. Instead it had experienced the same pietistic and revivalistic forces that the Scotch Reformed had. Furthermore, the German Presbyterians exuded New World ways of being Christian as much as their Scotch-

Irish cousins, if not more so. At the same time, even before he received an offer to teach at Mercersburg, Nevin was reading and reflecting on German scholarship to the end that he grew dissatisfied with Anglo-American doctrinal formulations and church life.

Just as plausible, then, is an interpretation that reverses the influence that Nichols and Appel posit regarding Nevin's transfer to the German Reformed Church. Rather than his move providing him with an exposure to European theology and worship, Nevin's decision to join the German Reformed Church and teach at its seminary may actually have been a turning point in the German Reformed tradition. What had been a chaotic collection of immigrant congregations with a modicum of allegiance to the Heidelberg Catechism through Nevin's indefatigable efforts began to embody the Continental Protestantism that later historians would regard as characteristically Continental Reformed. In other words, without the leadership and theological direction of a disgruntled Scotch-Irish Presbyterian, the German Reformed tradition—as it came to be known—may not have become as distinct as it eventually did.

The Magisterial Reformation without Majesty

Like the Scotch and Scotch-Irish Presbyterians, German Reformed immigrants to colonial North America arrived and established their churches under difficult circumstances with depleted resources. The same could be said for New England Puritans, another immigrant group whose confident rhetoric about and eventual success in establishing a city on a hill for all the world to see has seemingly provided historical proof of Calvinism's world-transforming piety. To be fair, the Boston of 1630 was not Calvin's Geneva, and by the time Boston could rival Geneva as a city of international fame its Calvinist reputation had faded significantly. Even so, for the sake of comparison, the Puritans took only six years before establishing a college, Harvard, that would train their civic and religious leaders. Scotch-Irish Presbyterians, who in 1706 formed their first presbytery in Philadelphia, took forty years before in 1746 founding a college, the College of New Jersey (later Princeton University), that might be reasonably called their own. (New Side Presbyterians had founded the College of New Jersey, even if for all intents and purposes it functioned as an interdenominational institution in student body and donors.) In this race with Puritans and Presbyterians for securing educational leadership and the requisite resources, the German Reformed ran a distant third. The first federation of German Reformed congregations occurred in 1747, a year after the College of New Jersey started. But almost eight decades would pass before the German Reformed could flex their institutional muscles in 1825 to form their first seminary, originally located in Carlisle, Pennsylvania, relocating in 1829 to York, Pennsylvania, and then in 1837 to Mercersburg. A preparatory academy, established in 1829, blossomed into Marshall College by 1836 and took root where the seminary had in the small town of Mercersburg. By the standard of educational institutions the German Reformed Church did not make a grand entrance on the American stage.

What was true of German Reformed higher education was no less true of church life. The original membership of the German Reformed congregations consisted of migrants from the Palatinate and the German-speaking region of Switzerland. The former came to North America via England to escape wars of religion and empire that continued to disrupt life in the early eighteenth century. These Palatines settled in a variety of places, from Nova Scotia to what would eventually be North Carolina. But thanks to the liberal religious policy of William Penn and the Quakers, the German Reformed found the most hospitable environment in Pennsylvania, settling in the southeastern part of the colony, west and north of Philadelphia. Even though the German Reformed Church became known as a German communion, the Swiss element was sizeable, possibly even the majority at first. This explains why in later histories of the denomination Ulrich Zwingli, the great Reformer of Zurich, emerged as the patron saint of the German Reformed. The establishment of German Reformed congregations to minister to these immigrants was spotty and owed to a lack of ministers. A Swedish pastor laid the cornerstone of one of the first German Reformed structures, built in Germantown in 1719. The reason was that so few German Reformed ministers were available. The first ordained minister was Samuel Guldin, who lived in Berks County.

But he never had a settled charge and so preached in a variety of locations to the scattered German faithful. According to Joseph Henry Dubbs, who wrote the denomination's history for one of the first systematic efforts to chronicle the history of American Protestantism, "the religious condition of the Germans of Pennsylvania in the earlier part of the eighteenth century was certainly deplorable."[4]

A modicum of order began to emerge in 1725 when four congregations northwest of Philadelphia called Jacob Philip Boehm to be their pastor. Boehm had been a school teacher in Worms and Lambsheim but was rumored to have lost his post owing to pressure from Roman Catholic authorities. He subsequently emigrated to Pennsylvania in 1720 and soon thereafter the local German Reformed, desperate for some form of ministry, asked him to lead worship. The anomaly of calling an unordained man to be pastor prompted Boehm and his congregants to seek oversight from a Reformed church with the greatest affinities to the Palatinate. Dutch Reformed pastors recommended that Boehm's ordination and ministry be resolved by the Classis of Amsterdam (Holland). In 1729, after Boehm proved himself worthy, the Dutch Reformed ordained him in New York City. George Michael Weiss, a German Reformed pastor who in 1729 had come to Philadelphia and established a congregation in that city, attended Boehm's ordination. With the efforts of these two men the German Reformed Church had begun to take shape.

Throughout the middle decades of the eighteenth century individual pastors from Germany and Switzerland found their way to the German and Swiss settlers in the Philadelphia vicinity. The process of forming a communion was hardly systematic or impressive. Not until the arrival in 1746 of Michael Schlatter did formal plans for a German Reformed communion emerge. Even here the German Reformed depended mightily on the oversight of the Dutch Reformed. Schlatter, a native of Switzerland, taught in the Netherlands for a time and ministered in his native land before migrating to British North America with a commission from the Dutch Reformed church to establish a formal ecclesiastical organization. Schlatter's work was remarkably successful. He organized thirteen congregations, harmonized relations among rival pastors, and in 1747 established the first federation of churches, the Coetus of Philadelphia, all the while pastoring a congregation in Germantown. In 1748 further organization followed with the ratification and publication of the German Reformed churches' first book of order. Schlatter would also travel to Europe to recruit other ministers to labor in the New World. Still, for all of his success the German Reformed continued to experience a clergy shortage and at the same time depended upon the oversight of the Dutch Reformed.

The Coetus of Philadelphia persisted in effect as a mission work of the Dutch Reformed until after the American Revolution. With political independence firmly established as a cultural ideal, ecclesiastical independence soon followed. Not only did the German Reformed seek autonomy from the synods of the Dutch church, but the Dutch Reformed in the United States also gained independence from their Old World ecclesiastical overseers at roughly the same time. For the German Reformed, the spirit of independence emerged in 1791 when the coetus resolved that it had the power to examine and ordain candidates for the ministry "without asking or waiting for permission to do so from the fathers in Holland."[5] Two years later the first German Reformed Synod convened in Lancaster. The showing of pastors was meager. Only thirteen attended, and the clerk recorded nine as absent. Historians believe that many more German Reformed pastors were unable to attend, since the communion in 1793 counted roughly 15,000 members scattered over 178 congregations. Even so, the disparity between 178 and 22 gives some indication of the ongoing clergy shortage in the German Reformed Church, even if the absentees were twice as many as those listed in the minutes. German Reformed capital, both human and material, continued to be modest.

The denomination's resources were so meager, in fact, that in hindsight the decision to separate from Dutch Reformed oversight may have been premature. By the early nineteenth century the German Reformed Church was independent, but it functioned still like a dependent communion, now without recourse to help from an established church. For instance, as an American denomination the German Reformed had to find and recruit ministers from the United States. Europe was much less an option without formal ties to the Netherlands. But the German Reformed had no schools of higher learning at

which to train pastors. It is as if the enthusiasm for political autonomy from England blinded church leaders to the realities of what ecclesiastical independence would involve. So bleak was the situation that
again, according to Dubbs, "there is hardly a period in the history of
the Reformed Church which is more discouraging than the one that
extends from 1793 to 1825," the date of the denomination's seminary's founding.[6] Dubbs's reasons for this sour estimate had to do with
more than a shortage of ministers and limited mechanisms for addressing the problem. The denomination lacked "none of the institutions
which are now regarded as essential to success in the work of the
church," with the exception of a fund to assist widows of deceased
clergy. Even this, Dubbs remarked, "was so small that it was of little
use." The church had no theological school, no church paper, no board
of missions. All that could be said for the German Reformed Church
was that it had the bare bones of a Christian communion: rules of
church polity, a hymnal, and a confessional standard (the Heidelberg
Catechism). Beyond these skeletal elements the denomination was truly
on its own.

Without an institutional center, theological and devotional order
was hard to achieve among the German Reformed. The tradition of
Reformed church life in the Palatinate, with the inspiration it received
from the writings of Zacharias Ursinus, the embodiment of many of
John Calvin's reforms, and the efforts of Philip Melanchthon to achieve
unity between Lutherans and Reformed, connoted a Continental form
of Protestantism that possessed creedal, liturgical, and ecclesiological
resources for a rich Reformed witness. Certainly pockets of such
Reformed piety existed in German Reformed congregations here and
there in the United States. But just as common among the denomination's various churches and ministers was a low-church form of Protestantism, one readily associated with American traits of informality,
sincerity, and practicality. European Protestantism, especially in the
German regions, was partly responsible for this particular form of
church life. Pietism was a reaction within German Lutheranism against
the perceived formalism and irrelevance of Protestant Scholasticism,
that is, a faith built upon learning and perpetuated in the schools.
Pietists were not inherently anti-intellectual, and they even founded

important German universities. Still, their criteria for genuine Christianity were subjective and practical—a heart on fire for God, good deeds proceeding from sincere motives—and so pietists tended to disparage the established church's reliance upon formally educated ministers whose theology was precise and around whose ministry the life of the church revolved. Pietism was, in effect, one of the earliest expressions of a democratic zeal among the Protestant descendants of the magisterial Reformation. It was designed to allow the laity to appropriate the faith in terms that were meaningful to them, not necessarily to their university-trained pastors.

Some of the German Reformed immigrants to the British colonies in North America brought with them the influences of pietism. Philip William Otterbein, an eighteenth-century German Reformed minister in Baltimore, is one indication of a pietist strain among these Palatines and Swiss. Ordained in 1773, Otterbein was a hugely popular and successful local minister who promoted revivals in the regions beyond his city. Though the coetus frowned on some of Otterbein's practices, he remained in the German Reformed's good graces throughout his life. His congregation was a different matter; shortly after his death in 1813, they left the German Reformed Church mainly because the formal features of the denomination's faith were not compatible with the Baltimore church's evangelistic interests and religious zeal. Otterbein's appeal was not limited to Maryland. During the 1740s, before Boehm's and Schlatter's efforts to organize and consolidate a German Reformed church, the Moravians, through the ministry of Count Zinzendorf, had a considerable appeal to German immigrants in Pennsylvania. At the same time, German Reformed ministers of pietist leanings assisted George Whitefield in his itinerant preaching in Germantown and Springfield. Indeed, throughout the eighteenth century the German Reformed either lost members to other churches that were more pietistic or found ways to accommodate revival-friendly ministers such as Otterbein. (Two churches that broke away from the German Reformed in order to pursue revivalism without restraint were the Albrights [1803], followers of the German revivalist Jacob Albright, and the United Brethren in Christ [Otterbein's followers who in 1815 formed a separate organization].) In sum, the influence of pietism on the German Reformed was pronounced from the outset, and it was responsible for preventing a reproduction of formal European church life in the New World.

Pietism and revivalism, then, were not foreign to the German Reformed Church, and by the time of the Second Great Awakening in the nineteenth century the denomination was hard pressed to tell any difference between the awakenings of George Whitefield and Jonathan Edwards and those of Charles Grandison Finney. The first signs of the latter revivalist's influence upon the German Reformed came as early as 1827 with a Finney-style series of meetings in York, Pennsylvania, under the ministry of James R. Reily. From York, Finney's new measures spread first to other German Reformed congregations in the eastern half of Pennsylvania and from there south to churches in the Piedmont region and west beyond the Alleghenies. As John B. Frantz puts it in his study of the denomination, "By 1843, revivalism occupied a prominent position in the German Reformed Church . . . from Pennsylvania to North Carolina, from Philadelphia to Ohio."[7] Frantz cautions that to suggest that revivalism dominated the German Reformed would be to give the wrong impression. But conversion-experience-driven techniques of outreach, along with the individualistic and moralistic forms of faith that accompanied them, were by the 1840s well on their way "toward becoming the dominant method of evangelism in the Church."[8] As such, historic practices of confirmation and the observance of the Lord's Supper fell out of use.

Still, the most pressing problem facing the church was a shortage of ministers, an issue related to the infiltration of new measures among the German Reformed. With established pastors many congregations might be less susceptible to revivalist itinerants. For that reason an important development in gaining a measure of coherence within the German Reformed Church was the establishment of a seminary to supply a steady stream of pastors with a relatively uniform standard of learning and theological training. But a German Reformed theological seminary did not come without trauma. The first signals that some ministers were less inclined to support a school than to continue the informal theological training already being conducted by individual pastors came in 1820 in the form of a proposal to the synod that met in Hagerstown, Maryland. Had the plan simply been positive in seeking a new seminary it would have likely gone through without a hitch, although of course paying for the institution was another matter. But synod passed a resolution that indicated the denomination would not simply provide theological training through a seminary but also that "no minister shall hereafter have the privilege of receiving a young man in order to instruct him in theology."[9] The seminary in effect threatened the pattern that then existed of young men interning and reading theology with a local, recognized pastor. What is more, the plan would consolidate theological training in the hands of a small faculty—at the outset under the control of one man.

Opposition to the seminary emerged not from fears of denominational centralization but over location. F. L. Herman, a pastor in eastern Pennsylvania and the mentor to several ministerial candidates, objected to plans to establish the seminary in Frederick, Maryland. He believed this was too far from the churches in his region. He may have also felt slighted that synod passed him over for the first faculty position at the seminary. Two years later Herman led a not insignificant group of congregations out of the German Reformed Church to form the Synod of the Free German Reformed Congregations of Pennsylvania. At one point the Free German Reformed numbered as many as fifty-seven ministers spread out over one hundred congregations. In 1837 they reunited with the German Reformed Church. But the controversy showed how fragile the identity of the denomination was and how difficult the process would be of giving the church a measure of order and stability.

The seminary finally began in 1825, located in Carlisle, Pennsylvania, thanks to an invitation from the officers of Dickinson College. The first professor was Lewis Mayer, a native of Lancaster, Pennsylvania, and the first class of students numbered five in all. The school's financial footing was flimsy, and this prompted a series of moves as its overseers looked for less expensive conditions in which to conduct the work. In 1829 the school moved to York. But in 1831 German Reformed officers recognized that seminary students were deficient in classical learning and so laid plans to establish a preparatory academy. Thus the costs of theological education grew, but such growth was also essential if the church's ministers were to attain to that level of learning that had historically been the model for the Reformed pastor. In 1835 synod decided to locate the academy in Mercersburg, the town that the Pennsylvania legislature had also recently approved as the location of Marshall College, the German Reformed's contribution to American Protestants' seemingly limitless support for denominational liberal arts undergraduate institutions. In 1837 the seminary relocated to Mercersburg, thus consolidating the denomination's educational initiatives—the prep school, the college, and the seminary—all in one location.

But geographical consolidation and institutional might could not insure a well-ordered denomination with a clear and uniform theological and ecclesiological vision. When Nevin joined the German Reformed Church in 1840 its identity was still unclear. It had been an immigrant church, but in that capacity had never compiled the resources to achieve a consensus on what it meant to be German Reformed. Both revivalism and Americanization threatened to submerge the churchly and liturgical Protestantism of the Palatinate that had informed the church's earliest settlers. In effect, the German Reformed Church was in danger of losing its European confessional heritage at roughly the same time that Nevin decided to transfer his abilities and membership to the denomination. Seen in the light of the German Reformed Church's revivalistic and pietist past, much of the credit for the denomination's later recovery of its Old World heritage belongs to the Scotch-Irish Presbyterian from nearby Middle Springs.

A German Exposure

When Nevin decided to accept the call to teach at Mercersburg he did not likely know the fragile condition of the school or of the denomination for that matter. At the same time, he was not unfamiliar with working at a school on the margins. The Presbyterian seminary in Pittsburgh had not provided him with great security or confidence. In his letter of acceptance, Nevin wrote, "I go, indeed with fear and trembling; but I carry along with me my entire will. I give myself wholly to the German Reformed Church, and find no difficulty in making her interests my own. No church can boast of a better creed, or a better ecclesiastical framework."[10] Those were flattering words, to be sure, but Nevin would soon realize the hollowness of the part about the denomination's organizational health.

Still, he did not take his duties at Mercersburg in order to partic-ipate in a well-run and well-funded school. Nevin's finances are not fully clear, but he had inherited enough from his father so that he was not dependent upon a faculty member's salary for sustenance. If remu-neration was not responsible for Nevin's decision to join the Mer-cersburg faculty, its German culture and theological heritage were. In the same letter, Nevin asserted that his own training was "providen-tially ordered" for the new work he was to undertake. "Though not a German by birth," he disclosed, "I feel a sort of kindred interest in that people, which could hardly be stronger were I one of themselves."[11] Nevin noted that he had grown up in a region of Pennsylvania where "German manners and modes of thought" were common. In addition, he had while teaching at Western Seminary been studying increasingly the German language and German theological literature: "These have awakened in me a new interest in their favor, and brought me into more extensive fellowship with the peculiarities of the national mind."[12] Indeed, Nevin's own reading in German philosophy and theology dur-ing his time in Pittsburgh had predisposed him to look upon the appointment at Mercersburg as an opportunity to hone and deepen new insights learned from German sources. The question was whether his new denomination, owing both to institutional instability and to revivalism, was as prepared for German ideas as Nevin was.

Because his writing and teaching while in western Pennsylvania were somewhat haphazard—after all, he was busy preparing new courses at a young school and adjusting to family life in a three-generation home—Nevin remains the only and therefore the best guide to his intellectual developments during the 1830s. The most profound influence was Johann W. A. Neander, a church historian at the Uni-versity of Berlin who pioneered in applying the insights of German idealism and Schleiermacher's theology to the study of Christian his-tory. But even before Nevin began to experience the first glimmer of an awakened historical consciousness, his philosophical and spiritual inclinations conditioned him to be particularly receptive to the theological currents of German Protestantism.

From his own Presbyterian background and foray into New England Congregationalism, Nevin inherited a pietistic outlook that endeared him to the introspective devotion of seventeenth-century Puritans such as John Owen and Richard Baxter. This helps to explain Nevin's openness to the revivals that swept through Union College while he was an undergraduate. Puritanism was not overtly anti-Scholastic in the way that German pietism was; for Puritans the formal aspects of church life, such as doctrine, clerical authority, and systematic reflection, were not the impediments to personal devotion that pietists sometimes claimed these theological niceties to be. At the same time, Puritanism shared with pietism an indebtedness to the Augustinian variety of Christian introspection that encouraged believers, as a means toward godliness and holiness, to search themselves earnestly for signs of spiritual graces. Nevin admitted that his esteem for Puritan piety also made him receptive to German pietism. He held in high regard men such as Philip Jacob Spener, August Hermann Franke, Count Nicholas Zinzendorf, John and Charles Wesley, and George Whitefield: "Not to be in sympathy with [these men] must ever be taken as the mark of a more or less irreligious mind."[13] These spiritual predispositions also led Nevin to read the seventeenth-century Cambridge Platonists: John Howe, Archbishop Robert Leighton, and Henry Scougal. These devotional sources fed an otherworldly form of devotion in Nevin that many historians attribute to his chronic and at times severe poor health. Whatever the reason, Nevin's piety ranked the eternal over the temporal, the spiritual over the physical, the soul over the body. Furthermore, his Platonic streak resulted in an understanding of reality that was haunted by an awareness of the eternal; matter was not independent of the ideal but an embodiment of it, such that without reference to the eternal reality the world was void of significance. "We are never properly ourselves," Nevin wrote, "till we have waked within us the lively consciousness of our relationship to forms of truth and modes of being, of an immeasurably higher order than any with which we become acquainted through the medium of sense."[14] As such, faith and regeneration were means by which Christians became aware of the eternal realities informing earthly existence.

But Nevin became aware of the degree to which this form of piety could lead to subjectivism. So he looked for ways to ground it in realities outside the self, in effect to make the spiritual objective. Here his reading in German theology and philosophy proved to be fruitful. Recent developments in German scholarship were especially important for Nevin's effort to recognize the commingling of the supernatural and natural worlds. Some of his reading in German theology was simply the fruit of his teaching the Bible at Western Seminary. During the 1830s American theological educators were beginning to study and make use of newer lines of investigation opened up by German exegetes. Nevin himself read for profit the work of European scholars such as Robert Lowth and Johann Gottfried von Herder. They confirmed his sense that the true understanding of outward or external forms, in this case, the book of special revelation, was available only through the reader's identification with and involvement in the text. Again, the world of spirit was crucial to a right apprehension of the Bible, one that moved beyond the surface or historical meaning to one that also spiritually vivified and edified. English poet Samuel Taylor Coleridge was also responsible for mediating some aspects of German philosophical idealism to Americans such as Nevin, who demonstrated an awareness of and appreciation for the nineteenth-century romantic's writings.

Nevertheless, in 1837 when Nevin added to his teaching duties church history he encountered the thrust of German intellectual developments in a pronounced manner. In his autobiography Nevin wrote that what Neander was for Germany "on a large scale, this he became for me also in a private way, an epoch . . . a grand crisis or turning point followed by a whole era of new existence." He added that Neander's "magic wand" brought up "the dead past . . . in the form of a living present." Nevin's encomium was still incomplete: "How much I owe to him in the way of excitement, impulse, suggestion, knowledge, both literary and religious, reaching onward into all my later life, is more than I can pretend to explain; for it is in truth more than I have power to understand."[15] Nevin found in Neander two matters that were particularly influential. The first was an acquaintance with and esteem for the church fathers, a subject that Nevin had found to be a "puzzling mystery" before reading Neander's study of Tertullian. Second, the German church historian imparted to Nevin a theory of organic development in church history that confirmed the Mercersburg theologian's understanding of the spiritual and real worlds. As Nevin put it, the "key" to his own personal development was Neander's notion of the intimate connection between the supernatural and the natural, with the divine informing and directing historical development. After his acquaintance with Neander, Nevin described his ideas as moving "all along . . . in the same reigning direction . . . from the simply subjective in religion toward the supernatural objective; from the spiritually abstract to the historically concrete; from the Gnostically ideal to the Christologically real."[16]

Although he would eventually relinquish responsibility for teaching church history at Mercersburg to his capable and gifted colleague, Philip Schaff, Nevin retained a keen sense of historical development in his own theology. Here Neander's stress upon the resurrection of Christ was crucial for Nevin's most important insights about the church and its ministry. In Christ's rising from the dead the supernatural realm became a historical fact and real presence in the natural realm. As such, the resurrection functioned as the lens by which to see the meaning of history. But its significance was not merely interpretive, because the resurrection also, according to Neander, introduced a new form of life, a supernatural and spiritual one, into human history. The embodiment of this new divine presence in human existence was the Christian church. The church, in other words, was the manifestation in the natural world of the resurrected Christ, literally and supernaturally the body of Christ. In effect, Neander put flesh on the bones of Nevin's prior idealism. If the physical world were generally the embodiment of spiritual realities, through Neander Nevin came to understand the church, its officers, and ordinances as the ongoing presence of Christ's supernatural and resurrected life.

Nevin's theological preparation for the German Reformed Church acquired a fuller German accent upon his arrival in Mercersburg. Frederick A. Rauch had preceded Nevin to the small Pennsylvania town when Marshall College moved there in 1835. A recent immigrant from Germany, complete with a doctorate in philosophy from the University of Marburg, Rauch became the first American expositor of Hegel. He published that effort, *Psychology; or, A View of the Human Soul* (1840), just as Nevin was relocating to Mercersburg. Less than a year after Nevin began his duties for the German Reformed Church, Rauch died, thus leaving the editing of the second edition of *Psychology* to Nevin, along with many of the responsibilities for teaching moral philosophy at Marshall College, for which Nevin used Rauch's textbook. But the new Mercersburg professor did not appear to be burdened by the extra work, despite the loss of a budding friendship, for Rauch supplied Nevin with yet an additional means to articulate the idealist character of his mystical devotion.

Rauch's idealism was well suited to the American situation. It attempted to fuse the empiricist epistemology of Locke and the Scottish Enlightenment with the genius of Hegelian teaching on the mind. Even more pertinent for Nevin was Rauch's understanding of the relationship between the actual and the ideal. The basic reality of life, according to Rauch, was divinity, from which flowed the external world of matter and sense experience. The ideal was the life principle that invigorated and sustained the phenomenal world. Rauch's teaching was important to Nevin for two reasons. The first was that it provided an alternative to the reigning Anglo-American epistemology, which emphasized inductive observation of data and facts as the best route to true knowledge. Instead, Rauch's teaching emphasized the objective reality of ideals behind observable phenomena. Knowledge based on mere observation, accordingly, was partial. Genuine knowledge could come only through recognition of the ideal behind the real. This ideal world, however was not subjective or intuitive in Rauch, but in fact proceeded through universal or scientific laws that observers needed to grasp if knowledge was to be secure.

The second important influence that Rauch had on Nevin was to give expression to the idea of organic development. The latter appropriated the former's notion of the ideal becoming embodied or externalized in space and time to understand the relationship between Christ and the church and between Christ's resurrected body and the Lord's

Supper. In other words, the ideal (Christ), inaugurated in the incarnation, became manifest in the real (the church and its ministry). Such an understanding of embodiment implied that the church was an organic whole developing over time in which different periods, such as the Middle Ages or the Protestant Reformation, could not be isolated without dissecting the body of Christ. For Nevin, Rauch's ideas also suggested that the Protestant distinction between the visible and invisible church was a Gnostic abstraction that stripped the real church of its spiritual vigor.

Students of Nevin have written up the significance of his German intellectual interests in different ways. For some he is an early mediator of German philosophy and therefore on something of a cutting edge in American intellectual life. For others Nevin's appropriation of German thinking was mainly a tangent to deeper personal spiritual struggles; it provided the discourse in which to express his own unusual form of devotion. Whatever the significance of Nevin's reading in German theology and philosophy, it would have important effects upon his own theological development, setting him apart in marked ways from reigning paradigms such as either Princeton's or New England's. As William DiPuccio writes, the incarnational paradigm received from Neander and Rauch opened "a whole new world of theology and philosophy": "The Church, the sacraments, and the scriptures became for [Nevin] the very embodiment of Christ's glorified humanity in the life of the world."[17] Perhaps even more germane was how his reading in German sources made his transition to Mercersburg and the German Reformed Church a smooth one. It certainly made him more conversant with the German language and its literature, thus giving an ethnic outsider greater immediate credibility with his new denomination. Nevertheless, Nevin's German preparations may have created in him higher expectations for the German Reformed Church. As he was soon to learn after his arrival at Mercersburg, the gap between the ideal of what a predominantly German church might be and the reality of a marginal ethnic denomination surrounded by varieties of British Protestantism was great. Even so, in the effort to bridge that gap Nevin would make remarkable use of the insights he had learned from German sources.

German Independence

On May 20, 1840, Nevin delivered an inaugural address to begin his new work in Mercersburg. Included among its several noteworthy themes was the speaker's heightened awareness of the German Reformed Church's ethnicity. Some of Nevin's acknowledgment undoubtedly stemmed from his own efforts to put his best foot forward and not come across with an air of British superiority. "No people," he declared, "are more susceptible than the Germans of all the deeper and more spiritual emotions of our nature. None have a greater aptitude naturally to be wrought upon by music, by painting, and poetry, and all that addresses itself to the aesthetical faculty in the soul." To be sure, the German character had its blemishes, the flip side of its virtues, though Nevin believed that the New World helped to restrain those faults. Still, in none but the German people was "the instinct of religion more powerful, or the congeniality of the soul with all that is vast and awful in faith . . . more readily and strongly displayed."[18]

The unique mission of the German Reformed Church, Nevin continued, was to minister particularly to the German people. To be sure, he affirmed the catholicity of the Reformed faith and stated that the Reformed churches of Scotland, France, and Holland were "so many twin-sisters by birth, not merely of the Protestant Reformation, but of the Reformation in its purest form . . . under the gigantic spirit of Calvin." Nevertheless, the other Reformed communions could not minister to German-Americans because of differences in language and "national temperament." "Are our German Churches to merge themselves in the religious systems of England and Scotland?" he asked. "Are they willing to see their own missionary ground wrested from their hands?"[19] Nevin believed he knew the answer to his own questions. Nothing was clearer than that the German people had "not the least idea of thus quitting their national position at present." Perhaps to reassure his audience because of his own ethnic, denominational, and educational background, Nevin supported what he believed to be a popular sentiment. "I do not hesitate to say," he hammered away, "that the German Reformed Church ought not to lay aside her distinctive national character and merge herself in a foreign interest." Even clearer to Nevin was the case that the German Reformed Church needed to "adhere to her own standards." The denomination needed its own ministers, trained at the church's own institutions. The German Reformed Church needed to "cherish still her national sympathies, and the hallowed associations of her own faith and worship."[20]

These were inspiring words, and perhaps they also served to convince Nevin himself of his new church's outlook. But they soon took on a measure of hollowness. Early in his tenure at Mercersburg Nevin embarked upon a tour of the English-speaking churches in eastern Pennsylvania and Maryland. In turn he wrote up some of his experiences for the German Reformed Church's official publication, *Weekly Messenger*, including them in a history of the Heidelberg Catechism and the denomination. The tone of his initial remarks about the church changed dramatically. The German people may have possessed unique spiritual resources and a resilient national temperament, but their Reformed churches were suffering numerous afflictions. Nevin observed that the German Reformed congregations continued to lack an adequate supply of ministers, some churches hearing only one sermon a month, others lacking a constant ministerial presence. An unwillingness of German Reformed members to give voluntarily may have also been a problem in recruiting pastors. Baptism and confirmation took place mainly as formalities since they were removed from a regular ministry. Likewise, admission to church membership was routine with little examination of candidates.

As bad as these conditions were, they had unleashed according to Nevin an even greater difficulty. The lack of ministers had opened the German Reformed to various forms of "wild and irregular" religious experience.[21] Revivalism, at least of the Finneyite variety, was spreading its unchurchly influence among the Germans, gobbling up large sections of the Lutheran churches and spawning splits among the Reformed. One of the separatist German Reformed groups that Nevin singled out in this series was the Church of God, a denomination formed in 1825, centered in Harrisburg, Pennsylvania, and under the leadership of former German Reformed minister John Winebrenner.

The Church of God pastor heard about the reference in *Weekly Messenger* from an acquaintance, and subsequently the sparks flew. Nevin's German idealism was running directly up against the realities of German Reformed religion.

The dispute with Winebrenner came in two phases, and it functioned as a rude awakening for Nevin to the thinness of church life among the German Reformed during its first century of existence. During the first stage of the disagreement, Nevin and Winebrenner debated the virtues of the so-called new measures that Charles Finney had popularized during the Second Great Awakening. These methods included practices such as itinerant preaching, extended services sometimes for as long as a week, female exhorters, praying for persons by name from the pulpit, and, perhaps the most famous, the anxious bench, a pew at the front of the meeting place reserved for those under conviction to sit and receive counsel and encouragement. Winebrenner had used such means during the mid-1820s to great effect. But a conflict ensued when he questioned the faith of some of the men on his vestry when they expressed concern about his methods. Eventually the synods and classes of the German Reformed Church became involved and tried to work an amicable settlement between Winebrenner and his Harrisburg congregation, which was delinquent in paying his salary. At one point, Winebrenner had the support of one classis, while another classis sided with the congregation. Eventually, the 1825 Synod of Philadelphia settled the matter in favor of the congregation, which no longer wished to have the revivalist pastor. With that, Winebrenner severed his ties to the denomination and established his own.

When Nevin wrote unfavorably about Winebrenner in *Weekly Messenger*, the Mercersburg professor was unwittingly dredging up a sore point in the denomination's history. He had no intention of engaging the Harrisburg pastor in an extensive debate, but simply wanted to make a point about the relative health of German Reformed congregations. Nevin referred to the Church of God as a sect that gloried in "being the patrons of ignorance," railed "at hireling ministers," and encouraged "fanatical unscriptural disorder in their worship." For good measure Nevin threw in that doctrinally the denomination was, "of course," Pelagian.[22]

Winebrenner's response exhibited a mixture of indignation and condescension. He believed, rightfully so, that Nevin had slandered him and the church, and he demanded a retraction. Winebrenner also questioned Nevin's credentials, first as an outsider and second as a seminary professor. As a Presbyterian the Mercersburg professor was out of touch with the German Reformed Church, and as an academic he knew little of religious life in the pews. "To mix with the people," Winebrenner advised the German Reformed novice, "is the way to learn to understand their morals." He added:

> Had the German Reformed Church called you to the office of an evangelist—instead of calling you to . . . the Professorship of the Theological Seminary—and had you itinerated in the Church as an evangelist, half the days of years that I have done, you would have understood the true complexion of that Church much better than what you can possibly learn to understand it in your present situation. This knowledge can alone be acquired in the school of experience. It is not to be gained, in the Theological Seminary at Princeton—nor the Western Theological Seminary at Pittsburgh—neither in the . . . Theological Seminary at Mercersburg.[23]

Winebrenner's most telling point in the exchange over revivalism was to use some of Nevin's own observations about the German Reformed Church against the new Mercersburg professor. In the same series in which he questioned the intelligence of the Church of God, Nevin had written of the German Reformed that "experimental religion, in all its forms, was eschewed as a new fangled invention of cunning impostors brought in to turn the heads of the weak and to lead captive silly women."[24] Winebrenner did not use this description as he might have to vindicate the need for revivals like his. Instead, he argued that it demonstrated the German Reformed Church's lack of piety and faithfulness and so justified his decision to leave the denomination.

The exchange ended up sidestepping the differences between Nevin and Winebrenner. Instead, the issue became whether Winebrenner's name would be vindicated by some sort of publication, either a retraction by Nevin or a defense by Winebrenner, in *Weekly Messenger*.

Winebrenner did manage to assert that what Nevin considered fanaticism and spiritual quackery he held to be the power of God. Nevin countered that he considered Winebrenner's "system of religion" to be "radically defective and full of danger."[25] But Winebrenner wanted a public vindication, which he received when *Weekly Messenger* in the summer of 1843 printed his letter defending his actions. Nevin also conceded to have the entire thread of correspondence published in Winebrenner's newspaper, *Gospel Publisher*. By the end of the first round with Winebrenner, Nevin was trying to avoid any more controversy, since he had by that time started his own with the publication of *Anxious Bench*, a forceful and incisive critique of revivalism that took on Winebrenner as well as the German Reformed Church's taste for religious excitement. In fact, although the initial prompt for writing *Anxious Bench* was a revival in Mercersburg at which Nevin was uncomfortably present (see chapter 3), his dispute with Winebrenner was an additional factor. It alerted him not simply to the dangers of revivalism, but also to the darker side of the German Reformed Church.

Nevin's second dispute with Winebrenner would avoid the problems of the first. Instead of referring to the Church of God and Winebrenner's ministry simply on hearsay, Nevin reopened their differences with a review of a rather ambitious book from the Church of God minister: *A History of All the Religious Denominations in the United States* (1848). Although Nevin's comments in this round concerned material that was open to public inspection, he was no less scathing than in the first episode. For instance, he admitted to initially wanting to have nothing to do with the book, judging it not only by its gilt cover but also its glossy pictures and embossed sides. But Nevin's original disdain, upon reading the book, turned into sarcasm. He called the book a "valuable commentary" on the sect system prevailing in the United States, a "credit to the mind from which it sprang." Its value lay in giving "this moral Babel an opportunity of speaking for itself; and now that it has thus spoken, it is well to lend an ear to the cataract of discordant sounds that is poured forth from its tongue."[26] Nevin was clearly itching for another round with Winebrenner.

The reasons for the Mercersburg professor's scorn were numerous, none of them really personal. First, by 1849 when the review appeared, Nevin was in the thick of working out an understanding of the incarnation as the basis for the doctrine of the church. Here he drew on German idealism and notions of historical development to attribute to the church the ongoing presence of the resurrected Christ. Churches that recognized the continuity of the church through the ages—from antiquity, through the Middle Ages, to the Reformation—were properly catholic. Sects, in contrast, manifested the spirit of the antichrist by denying Christ's physical presence in the church and the vital force that invigorated Christian life and witness. Winebrenner clearly fell into the second category when he left the German Reformed Church to form what amounted in Nevin's estimation to a sect. Second and closely related, Winebrenner's Church of God was also guilty of the classic crimes of sects, namely, an exalted understanding of *sola scriptura* that resulted in an endless number of American Christians establishing their own churches according to their own private interpretation of the Bible. In effect, Winebrenner had walked right into the thicket of Nevin's troubled thoughts. While the former was innocently celebrating the Bible Christianity of his own and other denominations, the latter was beginning to doubt Protestantism's ability to represent the catholicity of the Christian faith.

In the end, Winebrenner would not be drawn into the fray. The best he could do was to express sympathy for his former colleagues in the German Reformed Church, while questioning their habit of going abroad "to buy up their professors in Germany or among the Presbyterians."[27] Still, Winebrenner let Nevin's criticisms pass, and he turned to the notions that he and the German Reformed professor shared. Winebrenner's tact may have been an instance of heaping coals on his enemy's head through kindness. But Nevin's distress was so great at this time (see chapter 5) that such coals, if they were, would have missed their target.

If Nevin's disputes with Winebrenner contained a personal aspect, it stemmed from the Mercersburg professor's own frustration with American Protestantism and the evidence of it that he experienced in the German Reformed Church. Winebrenner was, in effect, a German

Reformed foil to Nevin. The Church of God minister obviously was no longer part of the Reformed churches and so cannot be construed as representative of the German Reformed. But Winebrenner did represent an important and perhaps the largest part of the German Reformed Church's identity during its first century in the New World. The denomination into which Nevin had transferred in 1840 was imbued with the ethos of revivalism. In contrast, he was on a mission to recover the liturgical and churchly character of historic Protestantism in its Reformed branch. Consequently, Nevin was attempting to infuse his new church in the United States with liturgical order supplied by German theology and philosophy. That he eventually succeeded at least in part is a tribute to Nevin's genius and energy. But such success would come with a high price.

3

The Comforting Church

When Nevin wrote *The Anxious Bench* in 1843, Charles Grandison Finney may not have achieved the status of American Protestantism's elder statesman, but he was clearly in the mainstream of religious life in the United States. The previous year Finney had turned fifty and was doing the sorts of things to solidify and conserve the strides that in younger years struck many as bold if not radical. Since 1835 he had been teaching moral philosophy at Oberlin College in Ohio, while continuing to itinerate as an evangelist and to perform ministerial duties at a Congregational church near the school. If teaching at a liberal arts college was not responsible for making Finney more respectable, by the 1840s the revival techniques that many found shocking in the 1820s had lost their novelty. So tame had the so-called new measures of Finney's revivals become that the evangelist-turned-college-professor took on the heady duty of preparing a work of systematic theology. Almost ten years earlier Finney demonstrated his knack for systematic thought in his famous *Lectures on Revivals* (1836). Now at the peak of his influence, he moved from the practical concerns of soul-winning to the sometimes abstract arena of God and his nature, revelation, and relationship to humankind.

Finney's lectures on theology turned out to be relatively thin on the divine aspects of theology. Like many New England theologians before him, the relationship between divine sovereignty and human responsibility ended up occupying most of Finney's attention. His lectures on Christian teaching thus began with moral government and duty, ran through discussions of law and love, probed notions of depravity and inability, and developed the doctrine of sanctification. These subjects may have been germane for someone teaching the senior year college course in moral philosophy where college presidents had their last chance to instill virtue in their students. But it was an odd scheme for something bearing the title *Lectures on Systematic Theology*, for this particular set of instruction was far removed from the historic *loci* of Protestant dogmatics.

Finney's theology did make sense, however, from the perspective of his career in revivalism. His handling of sin, duty, human nature, holiness, and sanctification dovetailed precisely with his efforts to persuade and exhort sinners to become saints. Of course, one of the criticisms of Finney was that his theology left little room for divine activity, thus turning the work of changing men and women into agents of righteousness into a process of calibrating effective techniques of revival to the largest number of converts and the greatest amount of holiness. The chapters on regeneration underscore this point. Finney's own view of this aspect of salvation was the theory of "Divine Moral Suasion." Accordingly, regeneration "consists in a change in the ultimate intention or preference of mind, or in a change from selfishness to disinterested benevolence."[1] Finney added that this change was the work of the Holy Spirit, but when he explained the practical benefits of such an understanding of regeneration, he revealed his hostility to Reformed teaching. According to Finney, his own theory encouraged ministers because if regeneration came by "the influence of truth, argument, and persuasion, then [they] can see what they have to do, and how it is that they are to be 'workers together with God.'"[2]

Statements like these were sure to draw fire from Presbyterian traditionalists, especially those in the Old School Presbyterian Church who had dreaded the influence of Finney's theology on their communion through the Plan of Union (1801). Charles Hodge, professor at Princeton Seminary was one such critic, and his review of Finney's lectures testifies to the Presbyterian theologian's deserved reputation as a strict Calvinist. In his review of Finney's book Hodge balked at even granting that the publication was a manifestation of systematic theology. The book was in the Princeton theologian's judgment clearly a work of moral philosophy, and so he cautioned, "Let moral philosophy be called moral philosophy not Systematic Theology."[3] But aside from the question of classification, Hodge regarded Finney's teaching as emblematic of "the popular theology current in many parts of our country." Whether the source was Nathaniel W. Taylor of Yale's Divinity School or some general spiritual impulse among American Protestants, the chief assumptions were two: "that inability is incompatible with obligation, and that happiness is the highest good."[4] True to his Calvinist instincts and to his reputation for polemics, Hodge had little difficulty tracing Finney's views to that heretic against whom Augustinians had groused since the fifth century, namely, Pelagius. Hodge wrote, "It was, says Neander, the radical principle of Pelagius's system that he assumed moral liberty to consist in the ability, at any moment, to choose between good and evil." The Princeton divine also claimed that "no church, under the sun, unless that of Oberlin be an exception," had taken Finney's view of human power to choose contrary to fallen human nature.[5] Even so, Hodge was keenly aware that Finney's teaching was not only gaining in popularity but also making implausible the idea of the Christian doctrine of original sin.

The point about Finney writing a book of moral philosophy instead of systematics may help to explain why Hodge spent no time addressing the revivalist's doctrine of the church. The nature and mission of the church simply were not there in Finney's treatment of the law, duty, and human agency. Even so, when the Oberlin moral philosopher addressed the topic of regeneration, he added a discussion of its evidences. Here he spent several pages on the differences between "saints and sinners." While unregenerate persons were "without exception" selfish, Christians exhibited "disinterested benevolence."[6] The sinner, Finney continued, was governed by "feeling, desire, and impulse," but "reason, the law of God, or the moral law" held sway in the life of the Christian. "Saints are interested in, and sympathize with, every effort

87

to reform mankind, and promote the interests of truth and righteousness in the earth." But, "the sinner is never a Reformer in any proper sense of the word. He is selfish and never opposed to sin, or to any evil whatever."[7] As this series of contrasts piled up, one that stood out for its absence was church membership. A regular reader of Christian theology might plausibly expect Finney to use the church as one evidence of regeneration, suggesting that a creditable faith recognized by duly constituted church officers, along with habitual attendance upon the means of grace, would be one indicator of genuine piety and spiritual renewal. But the revivalist was silent on the church since he believed that sin was absent from the lives of saints.

Nevin registered an altogether different critique of Finney and the system of revivals associated with him. To be sure, the Mercersburg theologian was still worried about the preservation of Augustinian notions of sin and grace. But the effects of revival were just as palpable in the give and take of church life as they were in fine print of theological quarterlies. In fact, revivalism encouraged a form of devotion that undermined not simply the creeds of the Reformers but also the church reforms that they had endeavored to accomplish. Nevin opened this line of criticism in a little pamphlet that went under the title *The Anxious Bench*. It proved to be the initial foray in a series of articles and sermons in which he attempted to recover an Old World faith for New World Calvinists.

Anxiety in Action

To say that Finney's new measures took the sleepy little village of Mercersburg by storm at the end of 1842 would be an overstatement. Nevin had already encountered the effects of the Second Great Awakening among Presbyterians during his time in Pittsburgh. In fact, the Old School–New School controversy that split the Presbyterian Church in 1837 was the result in no small measure of the revivals of which Finney was emblem and for which Nathaniel Taylor's theology was the rationale. Having moved from Anglo-American Protestantism to its German-American variant, Nevin also knew that the religion and devotion of revivalism was drawing Reformed and Lutherans away to what he would categorize as sects. The two he had in mind when applying the modifier "ranting" to the German splinter groups were the United Brethren and the Church of God.[8] In the summer of 1842 Nevin singled out John Winebrenner, a German Reformed minister who under the influence of revivalism broke from the Reformed communion to establish in 1825 the Church of God (General Conference). Nevin noted fanatical elements such as groaning, crying, shouting, swooning, clapping of hands, female prayer in mixed assemblies, and frequent condemnation of ministers who would not support the revivals. Nor was Winebrenner's theology any better, in Nevin's estimation, conveying a Pelagian bias that supposed that the exhortations of Scripture implied a person's moral ability to do what the Bible commanded. He observed the increasing influence of revivalism upon German Protestantism through the likes of Winebrenner and feared for the scriptural order, disciplined devotion, and learned ministry upon which Reformed and Lutheran churches depended.

Later that year the contagion of revivalism spread all the way to Nevin's new home of Mercersburg when the German Reformed congregation there took up the search for a pastor. One of the men brought to candidate was an old classmate of Nevin from Princeton Theological Seminary, William Ramsay. A Presbyterian in background, Ramsay was fresh from a recent tour of missionary duty in China. By most indications he made a favorable impression on the congregation and the theological students in the town. In one of his sermons Ramsay displayed a level of emotion that disquieted Nevin. Then during the Sunday evening service, without consulting anyone and to Nevin's great astonishment and alarm, Ramsay decided to employ the device of the anxious bench. He finished the service by inviting sinners who felt themselves under conviction of their guilt and unworthiness to come forward to the altar, sit on the bench, and receive the benefits of prayer. The response was electrifying. A number of congregants, many of whom were elderly women and who were members of the church in good standing, went forward. According to Nevin's biographer, Theodore Appel, Ramsay "was evidently now in his element and showed that he knew how to manage a modern revival or religious excitement." Nevin, who observed all of this from the vantage of the

platform behind the pulpit was "amazed . . . with a flushed countenance." Appel's observation that this occasion "helped to furnish
[Nevin] with suitable phrases when afterwards he graphically described
similar but still wilder scenes in his Tract on the Anxious Bench" was
indeed an understatement.[9]

Once things had quieted down Ramsay called on Nevin for a few
words. The Mercersburg professor would not be steamrolled by the
situation. He warned the congregation not to mistake coming forward
to the altar with genuine faith and repentance. According to Appel,
Nevin even remarked that physical exertion of any kind, even creep-
ing "about from one corner of the church to the other until their knees
were sore and bleeding," would not edify.[10] Even so, the congregation
went forward to call Ramsay as pastor. Nevin was not entirely opposed
to the call since the congregation needed a pastor, since ministers were
in short supply in the German Reformed church, and since the church
had displayed an interest in piety seldom seen before. He also feared
for the seminary's relations with the church and town if he took concerted steps to block the will of the congregation. Nevertheless, Nevin
wrote Ramsay a letter indicating his misgivings about the Presbyterian's methods. In response, Ramsay declined the call and informed
the consistory that Nevin's letter was an important factor. Ramsay's
letter made life awkward for Nevin. He had intervened to keep the
congregation from its choice for pastor. For this reason—partly to
defend his own position in the local church and town and partly to
stop the spread of revivalist new measures among the German
Reformed—Nevin, who was lecturing on pastoral theology during the
semester, addressed the true methods of the Christian ministry with a
critique of the anxious bench.

When *Anxious Bench* appeared in 1843 it was a short pamphlet,
divided into six chapters published under the auspices of the German
Reformed periodical *Weekly Messenger*. At the outset Nevin conceded
that he was a tad late in responding to the new measures popularized
by Finney. The fires of the Second Great Awakening were by the 1840s
smoldering in those regions previously scorched by the New York evangelist. Nevin may have been overly optimistic in asserting that "the
Anxious Bench, after having enjoyed a brief reputation, has fallen into

discredit."[11] But his concern was for German-American Protestantism where the bench had recently been revived. Lutherans in particular had been duped by the "quackery" of the new measures. Here Nevin singled out the *Lutheran Observer*, whose editor believed a recent revival "to have been probably the greatest since the days of the Apostles."[12] So even if Finney's techniques had already been tried and discussed by other American Protestants, they were newsworthy to the German Reformed and thus needed sustained attention.

Nevin also admitted at the outset that he was treading on dangerous ground. Not everyone was comfortable with the new measures, but because they were apparently successful in producing a rich spiritual harvest, they were also apparently above reproach. "It is a serious thing," Nevin wrote, "to find fault with any movement, that claims to be animated by the Spirit of God." As such, criticism of the revival methods for many demonstrated hostility to genuine faith and the things of God, not a pious disposition. But Nevin would not yield to such spiritual "tyranny," employed "to repress inquiry or to silence objection." In fact, he insisted, "it is a mere trick unworthy of the gospel, for any one to confound with the sacred idea of a revival, things that do not belong to it . . . for the purpose of compelling a judgment in their favor." Nevin's aim, then, was "to show that the Anxious Bench, and the system to which it belongs, have no claim to be considered either salutary or safe, in the service of religion." Instead of "promoting . . . true vital godliness," the new measures actually "hinder[ed] its progress."[13]

With some of the preliminaries out of the way, Nevin began his critique by arguing against the popularity of the new measures as proof of their genuineness. First, he observed that "spurious revivals were common." As such, "hundreds may be carried *through* the process of anxious bench conversion, and yet their last state may be worse than the first." Even in those cases where the conversion turned out to be real, Nevin was unprepared to accept that this vindicated the use of the new measures. Here he countered the argument that used the conversion of even one soul to justify the bench: "If only *some* souls are saved by the use of the new measures, we ought thankfully to own their power, and give them our countenance; since even one soul is

worth more than a world." To this logic Nevin made the bold assertion that the new measures were so pernicious that the salvation of
even one sinner "may notwithstanding cost *too much*!" He added that
"if truth and righteousness are made to suffer for the purpose, more
is lost than won by the result." Gaining converts was not a sufficient
reason for "do[ing] *wrong*."[14] The history of the church proved as
much. Nevin here used the examples of Simeon the Stylite, monasti-
cism, Roman Catholicism, and Millerism. In each case, religious techniques recommended themselves for apparently godly reasons. In the
case of Rome, for instance, "her penitential system" had been so regulated "to produce *effect* by means of outward postures and dress, till
in the end, amid all the solemn mummery, no room has been left for
genuine penitence at all." The same was true of the anxious seat. It is
a "mere outward demonstration" lacking all "inward power . . . to
move a congregation."[15]

Nevin was not arguing from the abstract position of a seminary
professor. He recounted his own encounter with the use of the bench
to prove his point, though whether he was referring to his friend Ramsay's experience in the German Reformed congregation in Mercersburg is unclear. The passage is worth quoting at length as a firsthand
account of the new measures and as a indication of how Nevin reflected
on such circumstances:

A stranger, in a church, where a preacher of some little note in connection with the subject of revivals, had been introduced, under the
expectation and hope that something of the kind might be secured,
at the time, by his instrumentality. The congregation had but little
appearance of life at the beginning, and still less as the sermon drew
towards a close. The truth is, it was a very dull discourse, at the best.
The preacher was not well, and altogether he failed to make the least
impression on the great body of his audience. A number were fairly
asleep, and others were bordering on the same state. The preacher
saw and felt, that he had preached without effect; and took occasion, after the sermon was properly ended, to express his regret in
view of the fact, and to add a few valedictory remarks in the prospect
of his leaving the place the next day, without any thought evidently
of calling out the anxious, where not a trace of feeling had been dis-

cerned. But the new strain adopted at the close, served to rouse attention and create interest. The congregation put on a more wakeful
aspect, and something like emotion could be perceived in the coun-
tenances of a few. The preacher took courage, and after a few minutes dared to try the Anxious Bench. As usual, the hymn was started,
Come, humble sinner, &c., and carried through, with pauses, in
which sinners present were urged and pressed to seek their salvation
by coming forward. Soon a female was seen going to the place, then
another, and another; till at last a whole seat was filled. One old lady
rose, and moved around, trying to induce others to go forward. At
the close of the meeting, I retired, wondering within myself that educated men, as were both the preacher in this case and the pastor at
his side, could so impose upon themselves, as to attach any importance to such a demonstration, in such circumstances. It was
attempted to carry forward the work, by an appointment for the next
evening. But on coming together at the time, it was found that it
would not go forward, and so it was dropped altogether.[16]

As much as Nevin's account cast the bench in a negative light, it did
give the impression that something more was at work. After all, the
problem with the new measures was not that they were ineffective.
Otherwise, Nevin would have had no reason for his pamphlet.

Even if Nevin overemphasized the bench's weakness, one of his
strongest critiques was to break through the mystique surrounding the
new measures' effectiveness in generating new converts. Instead of
looking at the external pressure of coming forward at the end of a service as a positive method, Nevin unmasked its psychological assumptions to show just how manipulative such techniques were. He began
this part of his argument by demonstrating how the invitation to sit
in the bench actually supplanted the real issue before the person experiencing anguish for sin. The point of preaching to the unconverted is
in fact to call upon men and women "to acknowledge their guilt and
misery with true repentance, and to submit themselves by faith to the
righteousness of the gospel." So, Nevin continued, when sinners
become aware of their actual position before God, the preacher should
help them see "the true nature of the controversy in which [they are]
involved," lay down their "weapons of . . . rebellion," and cast them-

selves "upon the mercy of God in Jesus Christ." But the bench actually interfered with this crisis of conscience and distracted someone under conviction with an altogether different problem: "A new issue is raised, by which the other is obscured or thrust out of sight."[17]

To make this point clearer, Nevin illustrated it with the case of "a gentle girl, sixteen or seventeen years of age . . . in the midst of a large congregation," and at the end of the sermon the pastor issues the invitation to go forward to the bench. This girl has for some time been concerned about her spiritual state:

> She hears the invitation, but shrinks from the thought of doing what the minister demands. The call however is reiterated, and enforced by the most exciting appeals to the imagination. After a few moments there is a stir; one is going forward to the bench, and then another and another. She is struck, moved, agitated. A struggle has commenced in her bosom, which she herself is not prepared to understand. May she not be fighting against God, she asks herself, in refusing to go forward with the rest? . . . Already her soul has passed from the element of conviction into the element of excitement. The "still small voice" of the Spirit is drowned amid the tumult of her own conflicting thought. But, see, she yields. With a desperate struggle, she has thrown herself forth into the aisle. Trembling and agitated in every nerve, poor victim of quackery, she makes her way, consciously in the eye of that large watching assembly, from one end of the house to the other, and sinks, half fainting with the effort, into a corner of the magic seat.[18]

The end result of the whole affair is one where the convicted sinner, according to Nevin, "is farther off from God, than she was before this struggle commenced, in her father's pew." "Can the pastor be wise," Nevin asked, "who is willing to subject the lambs of his flock to such a process?"[19] He even compared the use of the bench to the high-church movement and Roman Catholicism's elevation of the sacrament of baptism. Nevin believed that in both cases "Christ is seriously wronged" by conflating an outward form with the genuine article of dependence upon the Savior. The only difference, he qualified, was that at least the Puseyites and papists used an external form "of divine prescription." Finney's techniques were "wholly of man's device."[20]

Nevin completed his attempt to rout the revivalists with a discussion of the disorder created by the new measures, obviously, an indication of their inferiority and error. He began the last chapter of the 1843 edition of the pamphlet with the assertion, "The Anxious Bench tends naturally to disorder."[21] Nevin's point was that once the churches started down the path of the seat and the call for those under conviction to go forward, soon any number of irregularities would follow. For instance, the style of preaching, aiming at a certain emotional response or religious experience, became "rude and coarse," and "the pulpit is transformed, more or less, into a stage."[22] Another example of revivalism's "coarseness" was female preaching and exhorting. Nevin argued from the Pauline Epistles that women were prohibited from leading or speaking publicly in worship. For this German Reformed theologian, "there can be no surer sign of grossness and crudeness in religion, than a disposition to tolerate this monstrous perversion, under any form."[23] He gave other examples, ones common to Finney's critics, of "fanaticism," such as the way songs were sung, prayers prayed, and emotions displayed, all lacking the decency and order that Reformed Christians prized. But beneath these objections was a subtle point about the nature of Christian piety. For Nevin, the proper response to the divine was not excitement and drama but quiet and order. Genuine faith produced sobriety. But the new measures thrived on frenzy. Nevin would not entertain arguments suggesting that Christianity permitted a diversity of styles. Superior Christianity was that form of faith that was serious, subdued, and orderly. Because the bench produced effects precisely the reverse, its religion was for "the most part of a dwarfish size and sickly complexion."[24]

In its initial iteration, *Anxious Bench* failed to accomplish what Nevin had set out in his introductory comments. He had hoped to reveal not simply his objections to the particular instances of the new measures' "quackery," but also to explore and expose the system of religion upon which the bench was constructed. Subsequent interaction both with critics and colleagues prompted Nevin to come out with an expanded edition in 1844, which did more of what he had originally set out to do. Here his analysis of the psychology undergirding the anxious bench paved the way for Nevin to make his most telling point in his critique of the new measures.

At the conclusion of the first edition of *Anxious Bench*, Nevin briefly sketched the difference between the system of religion implied in the new measures and the rival system signified by the catechism. By the catechism he did not mean simply the method of instructing children in the faith by question and answer, such as the German Reformed Church's own Heidelberg Catechism. The catechism did, though, point to a system of religion by which its adherents grew up into or inherited the faith, not unlike that of passing on the faith through the memorization of received Christian wisdom. For Nevin the catechism symbolized the regular ministry of the church, "sermons full of unction and light," "systematic instruction," an earnestness for holiness, pastoral visitation, catechesis, church discipline, and "patient perseverance in the details of the ministerial work."[25] These were the God-appointed means of growing the church and its members. And this was the system that was antithetical to the new measures. Nevin wrote:

> The spirit of the Anxious Bench is at war with the spirit of the Cat-echism. Where it comes decidedly to prevail, catechetical instruction, and the religious training of the young generally, are not likely to be maintained with much effect; and it will not be strange, if they should be openly slighted even, and thrust out of the way as an incumbrance to the Gospel, rather than a help.

Nevin then added a line that was crucial for the development of his own thinking about the church and its mediation of the Christian faith. "What is wrought in the way of the Catechism," he asserted, "is considered to be of man, what is wrought by the Bench is taken readily for the work of God."[26] But this way of looking at the matter was backward. Nevin's conviction that the ministry of the church was directly tied to God's work of salvation became a central feature of his subsequent teaching on the church.

In the meantime, in the expanded edition of *Anxious Bench*, Nevin tried to explain the reasons behind his contrast between the system of the catechism and the new measures. He did so by fleshing out the nature of the church's ordinary ministry. Nevin began by attributing the shallowness of devotion in the new measures to Pelagianism, a heresy that misconstrued the nature and extent of human sinfulness and consequently regarded conversion as "the product of the sinner's own will, and not truly and strictly a new creation in Christ Jesus by the power of God."[27] For Nevin, then, the Calvinist doctrine of original sin was key, the very foundation upon which the bench and the catechism differed. In the scheme of the catechism, sin was something more profound than the actual transgressions of the lone individual. It was "a wrong habit of humanity itself, a general and universal force which includes and rules the entire existence of the individual man from the very start."[28] From this conception of human guilt and misery proceeded the Christian understanding of salvation in which the organic union linking the sinner to the first Adam is reconstituted into "an inward living union with Christ." Just as particular sins of individual persons were manifestations of the estate in which the entire human race lived after the fall of Adam, so salvation was larger than the individual's decision to go forward or to believe in Christ. Salvation, according to the catechetical scheme, consisted of a new life emanating from this union with Christ, who is "the organic root of the Church."[29] If Nevin's ideas here reflected, which they did, the federal theology that he had learned at Princeton Seminary, they were no less a marked departure from the religious individualism that was beginning to characterize American Protestantism. For Nevin, the body of Christ and membership in the body took on greater significance than any single decision or intention by an autonomous rational agent.

By conceiving of Christianity in organic or corporate, as opposed to individualistic, categories, Nevin had an easy time explaining the churchly system of religion symbolized by the catechism. If men and women were to be saved, such restoration would have to occur from outside themselves. Here the ministry of the church came to the rescue. Salvation came to sinners through the "institutions and agencies" of the church "which God has appointed, and clothed with power expressly for this end." So, as Nevin's logic proceeded, "where the system of the Catechism prevails great account is made of the Church" because it comprehended the means of grace that God ordained for the accomplishment of salvation. "In this view the Church," he concluded, "is truly the *mother* of all her children. They do not impart life to her, but she imparts life to them." In other words, the church did not follow the dictates of individualistic Christianity but precisely the reverse was the case: "Christ lives in the Church, and *through* the Church in its particular members."[30]

As Nevin fleshed out the catechetical system, he revealed that his concern was for a pattern of inheritance or familial religion. Church life was ideally one where parents passed on their faith to their children, with the church performing those religious ceremonies and functions that mediated the Christian religion and supported the care of parents. Nevin asserted, "It is counted not only possible, but altogether natural that children growing up in the bosom of the Church under the faithful application of the means of grace should be quickened into spiritual life in a comparatively quiet way."[31] If the rearing of children were the natural way of producing Christians, as opposed to the mechanical and vulgar means of the anxious bench, then families were essential to the constitution of the body of Christ. The family was, he explained, "a vital and fundamental force in the general organization of the Church."[32] The family's importance in turn gave parents significant responsibilities, such as praying for their sons and daughters, family worship, catechetical instruction, and setting a "pious and holy example" in the home. The work of families in conversion was then an important part of the system of the catechism. In effect, the contrast between the bench and catechism was one of individualism and decision versus organic ties and nurture.

But as important as the family was in the catechetical scheme, Nevin devoted far more attention to the work of ministers and the institutional church. Word and sacrament were the most obvious duties of the Reformed pastor. But equally important was a sequence of pastoral visitation in the homes "to recommend and enforce the gospel [that the minister] is called to preach."[33] This work of pastors was like that of a caretaker, or even better, a mother's care for her children. Its aim was to build up and strengthen the flock. Unlike the system of the bench that made the conversion experience "the all in all of the gospel economy," the catechism was designed to care for believers over the entire course of their lives, from birth to death. Nevin's theory of the catechism did not hide the significant stylistic differences between the bench and the catechism, which involved contrasts such as the number of converts versus greater spiritual maturity or mechanical techniques for attracting converts versus natural and organic means of generating faithful devotion. "It is in the kingdom of grace," he explained, "as in the kingdom of nature; the greatest, deepest, most comprehensive and lasting changes are effected constantly not by special, sudden, vast explosions of power, but by processes that are gentle, and silent, and so minute and common as hardly to attract the notice of the world."[34] Or to put it another way, "The extraordinary," in the case of the catechetical system, "is found ever to stand *in* the ordinary, and grows forth from it without violence so as to bear the same character of natural and free power." As such, the catechism was not opposed to revivals. Rather, the system of catechetical religion involved a different notion of revival, one where the church enjoyed "special showers of grace" through the regular ministrations of the pastoral office.[35]

Nevin's model for the ordinary work of the minister was Puritan Richard Baxter during his work in the parish of Kidderminster. Nevin admitted that he could not think of a better example of "the true character and force of the system [just] explained and recommended."[36] When Baxter arrived in the village the parish had been neglected. It was in short a place where advocates of the new measures believed those techniques to be most effective and necessary. But that was not Baxter's tack: "He had no conception or expectation of any general good to be accomplished by his ministry, except in the way of a patient, constant attendance upon the work itself, in its most minute details."[37] Those details included regular Sunday services and occasional preaching, prayer meetings in his home and with the young people in the church, family visitations, and catechesis. As such, according to Nevin, constancy, regularity, and earnestness characterized Baxter's ministry, not "noise and parade." And over time, the parish of Kidderminster experienced a revival, not in the ordinary sense as "an occasional and

transient awakening in the history of the church." The church grew
in numbers and spiritual maturity; in Nevin's words, "the life of religion in the place was constantly progressive." The lesson drawn from
Baxter's example was obvious, and it formed the substance of Nevin's
conclusion to the revised version of *Anxious Bench*: "Most happy
would it be for our Reformed German Church if all her pastors could
be engaged to lay to heart the weight of this great example." But
Nevin did not have the last word. He let Baxter have it, asserting that
"churches either rise or fall, as the ministry doth rise or fall; not in
riches and worldly grandeur, but in knowledge, zeal and ability for
the work."[38]

Anxious Bench was a remarkable performance for several reasons. First, Nevin articulated a conception of inherited faith that was
comparable to Horace Bushnell's. Ironically, although Nevin's preceded Bushnell's publication by three years, the Hartford minister's
notion of children growing up in the faith of their parents, beginning with infant baptism, has attracted more interest, thanks especially to the religious education movement within mainline Protestantism in the early twentieth century. Yet, for all of Bushnell's
apparent genius in his *Discourses on Christian Nurture* (1847), his
thesis that "the child is to grow up a Christian" was already present
in Nevin's *Anxious Bench*.[39] Bushnell's argument also took aim at
the model of conversion as decision made popular by revivalism.
Thus, like Nevin, Bushnell was pointing out the inadequacies of
revivalism's presumed individualism. But where Bushnell stressed the
primacy of the parents' role in the rearing of godly children, Nevin
emphasized the work of pastors, with parents reinforcing the corporate faith of the congregation. Likewise, where Bushnell's concern
was for the character formation of children and the cultivation of
virtue, Nevin was interested in faith. For that reason, Nevin, unlike
Bushnell, put great weight upon the official ministry of the church
in word and sacrament. These were the ordained means by which
faith came, not the mechanical process of walking the aisle to the
anxious bench. Nevin himself would eventually review Bushnell's
Discourses on Christian Nurture, and although he appreciated the
Congregationalist minister's critique of revivalism, Nevin believed

that Bushnell had failed to escape the essential outlook of the new measures. At bottom, Nevin faulted Bushnell for working from a rationalist premise by which Christian nurture was a product of human psychology rather than a gracious provision, issuing from a "strictly supernatural system."[40]

A second important point to observe about *Anxious Bench* is that it contains the seed of the Mercersburg Theology. As James Hastings Nichols observes in his own study of that school of theological reflection, Nevin's critique of the new measures, combined with his own elaboration of the system of the catechism, was "the first enunciation of what was to become the Mercersburg doctrine of the church."[41] This was particularly evident in Nevin's rejection of revivalism's individualism in favor of Reformed federal theology. For the Mercersburg Theology, salvation was organic and corporate, a participation in and union with Christ through his body, the church. Nevin explained in the revised edition that "the sinner is saved . . . by an inward living union with Christ as real as the bond by which he has been joined in the first instance to Adam." The church, by the power of the Spirit, mediated this union between the believer and Christ. As such, "the particular subject lives, not properly speaking in the acts of his own will separately considered, but in the power of a vast generic life that lies wholly beyond his will, and has now begun to manifest itself through him."[42] As it turned out, this revised section of *Anxious Bench* was not only crucial in giving a positive message to his otherwise critical book, but the idea of Christianity's organic character expressed through the believer's union with Christ through the medium of the church, the body of Christ, also proved to be the notion that Nevin would continue to unravel over the course of his career.

Finally, as much as *Anxious Bench* looked ahead to the Mercersburg's Theology central theme and Nevin's interest in German theology and philosophy, it also rested squarely on Nevin's own Presbyterian past and his education at Princeton Seminary. For instance, Nevin revealed the grip that his own theological training still had on him by quoting his former professors, Archibald Alexander and Samuel Miller, on the dangers of enthusiasm and the ineffectiveness of the bench respectively.[43] The Mercersburg professor showed the influence of his former professors also when discussing the differences between the First and Second Great Awakenings. Following the argument developed by the Princetonians, who tried to harmonize the pro-revival sympathies of the eighteenth-century New Side Presbyterians with the anti-Finney instincts of the nineteenth century's Old School Presbyterians, Nevin applauded the results of George Whitefield and Jonathan Edwards while distancing them from Finney and company. In answer to the charge that the colonial revivalists also used new methods, Nevin responded that although they "tolerated . . . new things in the worship of God," they "*needed* nothing of this sort to make themselves felt." "What was new," he explained, "was not sought; it came of itself, the free natural result of the power it represented."[44] Here Nevin showed himself to be still under the influence of Princeton's understanding of requirements for the pastoral ministry. One of the issues that divided the eighteenth-century church was whether those being ordained needed to give an account of a conversion experience. The Old Side argued that membership and subscribing the Westminster Standards were sufficient, while the New Side demanded an account of the man's religious experience, because without that reality of grace in his life his ministry would be ineffective. The Princeton Theology, though Old School Presbyterian, was yet New Side in its affirmation of the need for evidence in ministers of a conversion experience. Although Nevin would eventually modify his views on the nature of pastoral ministry, *Anxious Bench* reflects an unmistakable New Side Presbyterian perspective when its author writes, "Let the power of religion be present in the soul of him who is called to serve at the altar, and no strange fire will be needed to kindle the sacrifice."[45] In other words, the new measures were unnecessary as long as the old New Side standards prevailed.

Perhaps the greatest evidence of Nevin's dependence on his Presbyterian past was his use of Baxter as the model of the catechetical system of religion. The English Puritan must have struck some German Reformed readers as an odd choice. And eventually Nevin would take a much more critical view of Puritanism, while also turning to John Calvin for an alternative to the prevailing low view of the sacraments among Reformed and Presbyterians. But in 1844 Nevin was still sufficiently comfortable with his own Presbyterian background to use one of the standard authorities on the nature of the Reformed ministry. The compelling question that *Anxious Bench* raises in the development of Nevin's theology is the degree to which his search for an alternative to the system of the bench could bridge his past and his future. Could the system of the catechism incorporate his revival-friendly Princeton mentors and the sacramental teaching of older Reformed divines? With the publication of *Anxious Bench* the answer appeared to be yes.

Reinforcements at Mercersburg

With the arrival in Mercersburg of Philip Schaff in 1844, the better known of the two Mercersburg theologians, Nevin's ideas about the church became something more than the peculiarities of an out-of-the-way seminary professor. A native of Switzerland, Schaff was clearly Nevin's junior, having been born in 1819, sixteen years after the American. But despite his youth—Schaff was twenty-five upon taking up his duties at the German Reformed institution—he made up for it in educational experience. He had studied first at Tübingen, the center of biblical criticism, for half his university education. There he came under the influence of Isaak Dorner, who attempted to appropriate the theology of Schleiermacher and the philosophy of Hegel for pious ends. From there Schaff transferred to the pietist center of Halle and its university. At Halle, Friedrich A. G. Tholuck made the greatest impression on Schaff through his close interaction with students and his obvious Christian devotion. (Tholuck turned out to be something of a foretaste of Schaff's American career; the German professor had instructed and become friendly with several American theologians during their student days in Europe, for instance, Charles Hodge, Edward Robinson, Henry B. Smith, and George L. Prentiss of Union Theological Seminary in New York and Edwards Amasa Park of Andover Theological Seminary.) The theological influences on Schaff were not confined to the universities where he matriculated, however. He also managed to attend the lectures of University of Berlin faculty, such as Ernst W. Hengstenberg and Johann A. W. Neander. Neander's use of the idea of evolution or development in the study of church history had the most obvious influence on Schaff, who in addition to distinguishing himself as an ecumenist was arguably the greatest nineteenth-century church historian in the United States.

Throughout the course of his studies and his initial work as a *privatdocent* at the University of Berlin, Schaff formulated a doctrine of the church—some call it "high church" for lack of a better designation—that dovetailed neatly with Nevin's. In his inaugural address at Mercersburg, delivered on October 25, 1844, entitled *The Principle of Protestantism*, Schaff showed precisely why his was a crucial appointment in bolstering Nevin's sense of American Protestantism's defects and need for reform. Prominent in Schaff's lengthy address is a notion of historical development that he would use in his work as a church historian and that mediated German ideas about the evolution of human history to America. To be sure, these thoughts were not unrelated to Schaff's efforts as an ecumenist. The controversial idea that the Protestant Reformation had evolved from Roman Catholicism implied the possibility not only of finding unity even among traditions considered antithetical but also among the various branches of Protestantism. According to Schaff, "*The Reformation is the legitimate offspring, the greatest act of the Catholic Church.*"[46] Such an assertion, uttered at a time when Catholic immigration to the United States was large and when the Protestant majority in America responded with hostile demonstrations of anti-Catholic bigotry, was sure to stir up trouble. Indeed, one of the constant charges hurled at the Mercersburg Theology was that it was soft on Rome and so in danger of repudiating the gospel.

But aside from the merits of Schaff's theory of historical evolution, his address proved to be the second of a one-two punch, with Nevin's *Anxious Bench* being the first, that put the church question before American Protestants. In the second section of *Principle of Protestantism*, after defending the material (justification by faith alone) and formal (the sufficiency of Scripture) principles of the Reformation, Schaff turned to Protestantism's chief defects. The first was rationalism, and it manifested itself in theological or moral reductionism in which Protestants boiled down the Christian faith to its doctrinal or ethical core. The second was sectarianism in which genuine faith, freed from external or outward forms, gave itself over to unstinting zeal and holiness. Here Schaff singled out Puritanism as one manifestation of sectarianism's various weaknesses. "Inflamed against the despotism of bad forms, and the abuse of such as are good," he declared, Puritanism "makes war upon form in every shape, and insists on stripping the spirit of all covering whatever, as though the body were a work of the Devil."[47] In addition to this hostility to form, Puritanism also exhibited a hostility to history and tradition. Schaff went on to blame the general character of American Protestantism on Puritanism because it formed "properly the main base of our North American Church," thus injecting "an unhistorical and unchurchly" tendency "into the inmost joints of our religious life."[48]

The hope for the church in North America, then, according to Schaff, was for Protestant theology to shift from its Anglo-American orientation to a distinctly German one. "The land which gave birth to the Reformation," he averred, "stands pledged by that movement itself, not to rest till the great work shall have been made complete; when the revelation of God in Christ shall be apprehended in full, and the contents of faith shall be reduced to such form as to carry with them also the clearest evidence and most incontrovertible certainty in the way of knowledge."[49] Such optimism coming from someone new to the American scene did not mean that German theology and philosophy were free from problems. Schaff also hoped that American Protestantism might escape the struggles that German rationalism created. He also sensed that "believing science" had triumphed in Germany, "over both the popular and speculative forms of Rationalism," and had confidence that this "better form" of theology could be transplanted in the New World and "enter organically into our religious life."[50] And although Schaff was short on the specifics of how this improved theology could secure American Protestantism's "full reconciliation with the objective idea of the Church," the concluding pages of his address hinted that the path forward involved turning away from English philosophy (e.g., Locke) and following in the footsteps of German idealism. As Schaff indicated in the penultimate of the 112 "Theses for This Time" that he appended to his address, the

American churches needed "a thorough, intellectual theology, scientifically free as well as decidedly believing, together with a genuine sense for history."[51]

Because both Nevin and Schaff taught at Mercersburg and their views constituted the theology that bore the school's name, students of American church history assume that their views were basically interchangeable. Although they affirmed a similar understanding of the church and the relationship between Protestantism and Roman Catholicism, each man came to his views and executed them in different ways. The most obvious divergence was that each worked in different theological disciplines, Nevin in theology and Schaff in history, though making this a firm distinction is difficult since the former's theology relied heavily on historical consciousness and the latter's historical awareness sprang from certain theological convictions. Nevertheless, Schaff's major contribution to the Mercersburg Theology was *Principle of Protestantism* and its implications for the catholicity of the Reformation and the value of tradition. After he left Mercersburg in 1865 to teach at Union Seminary in New York City, Schaff would establish his credentials and an identity separate from Mercersburg as an advocate and architect of ecumenical relations among Protestants and as one of the most productive theological scholars of the late nineteenth century. In the latter capacity he oversaw authoritative reference works in theology, edited a series of English translations of the Nicene and post-Nicene fathers, chaired the committee responsible for the Revised Standard Version, and wrote a seven-volume history of the Christian church. As Nichols puts it, "No other American theological scholar of the century rivaled this production."[52]

But if Schaff's later scholarly output was prolific, Nevin produced the lion share of duties in formulating the Mercersburg Theology, and his reputation was bound up with that school's brief burst of theological creativity. Nevin articulated the centrality of the incarnation in Mercersburg's thought. He also worked out a sacramental theology that had important repercussions for his teaching on the Christian ministry. What is more, Nevin attempted to give coherence to these strands of theological development and defended them polemically, whereas

106

Schaff was more or less content to fill in with teaching and the occasional theological article. In fact, Schaff's contribution to the Mercersburg Theology was chiefly supplemental to Nevin's, because the former Presbyterian had set the tone for the seminary and its relations to the German Reformed Church. Consequently, Schaff's views received a reading colored by Nevin's original argument in *Anxious Bench*.

Nevin and Schaff also had markedly different temperaments, perhaps owing to differing degrees of health. Schaff tended to be more optimistic and less defensive than Nevin, who brooded at times to the point of despair and was not blessed with a cheerful disposition. Indeed, Schaff himself once described his Mercersburg colleague as possessing an "almost gloomy seriousness" that contributed to Nevin's criticisms of American Protestantism. As Schaff's son put it in his biography of his father: "The wonder is that, with their sharp differences of original temper and education, these two men should have stood together for a score of years in friendly cooperation. It will appear, however, that this very relation put Dr. Schaff more than once in a position where his real views were subjected to serious misconstruction."[53]

In many respects, that these men wound up teaching together at a small remote village in Appalachia is one of the remarkable coincidences of providence. Had they not worked together at Mercersburg, they would each have written similar things and been part of the nineteenth century's high-church renaissance. But without a common school their contributions would hardly have constituted a distinct variety of American theology. In the end, the revision of the German Reformed Church's liturgy was the closest that Nevin and Schaff came to sharing a common project, aside from the more general one of teaching at the same seminary. Like most academics, each man labored on separate theological and historical topics, working out the distinctive features of their scholarship under the umbrella of the Mercersburg school.

The response to Schaff's inaugural address had significant ramifications for Nevin; in fact, Nevin was deeply implicated in his colleague's inaugural address. The elder Mercersburg theologian translated Schaff's *Principle of Protestantism* into English for publication

in 1845 and edited the monograph by supplying an introduction and
a sermon that Nevin had preached in 1844 before a joint gathering of
German and Dutch Reformed pastors. Although such collaboration
necessarily implied agreement between the two men responsible for
developing a separate school of theology called Mercersburg, this Mercersburg Theology was still very much in its infancy. An important
factor in the evolving maturity of Nevin's and Schaff's views was the
degree to which they would turn away from Anglo-American philosophical and theological sources and norms to German insights. Nevin
himself, if his introduction and supplemental sermon were any indication, was not yet following Schaff in appropriating German philosophy and theology. To be sure, he stressed the organic character of
Christianity and affirmed Schaff's notion of historical evolution played
out in the life of the church. But these were themes that he had already
developed in *Anxious Bench* with much support from Puritan and
American Presbyterian sources. Even in his sermon entitled "Catholic
Unity," Nevin continued to work in categories familiar to Westminster Calvinism. Instead of discussing the union between Christ and the
church in accents distinctly German, as he would eventually do, Nevin
used instead the notions of the visible and invisible church to make
the point that unity needed to be not simply spiritual (i.e., invisible)
but also physical (i.e., visible).[54]

Even if the trajectory of the Mercersburg Theology was uncertain
by the time of the publication of *Principle of Protestantism* in 1845,
Nevin and Schaff had staked out the fundamental issue that their school
of theology would develop. As Nevin put it in his introduction to
Schaff's inaugural, "The great question of the age undoubtedly is that
concerning the Church. . . . Its issues are of the most momentous nature,
and solemn as eternity itself."[55] Nevin and Schaff came to this issue
from fairly different circumstances. Schaff came to the church question with the state of German churches in mind and the formulations
of German theology readily at hand. Nevin arrived at the issue of ecclesiology by a different route, one that bore the markings of Protestantism in the new environment of America's religious free market.
The trick for him would be how to recover the Reformed doctrine of
the church in ways that might make sense and gain support from fel-

low Americans in his own communion and other Reformed and Presbyterian churches. For the moment, though, Nevin had registered a critique of the damage done by revivalism to American Protestant piety that was arguably the most penetrating of its time because of his insistence upon a choice between either the church or the bench.

4

Reformed Catholicism

lmost from the start the Mercersburg Theology was a controversial school of thought. Disputes soon followed Schaff's address and its publication with Nevin's introduction and supplemental sermon. And this occurred even before Nevin formulated some of his more unusual positions. In fact, one plausible interpretation of the subsequent development of his thought after 1845 is that it became less conciliatory thanks to the opposition that Nevin encountered from both within and outside German Reformed circles.

The initial criticism of the Mercersburg Theology came from German sources, both Reformed and Lutheran. Joseph F. Berg, a prominent German Reformed pastor of an established congregation in Philadelphia and editor of the *Protestant Banner*, was among the first to complain. He would continue to be a ready critic of Nevin and Schaff, bringing charges against the Mercersburg professors to the Classis of Philadelphia. Nevin also drew fire from nearby Pennsylvania Lutherans. Benjamin Kurtz, editor of the *Lutheran Observer*, had been a proponent of the new measures and so received an unfavorable mention in Nevin's *Anxious Bench*. In both cases Nevin's call for an older form of Protestant devotion, one rooted in the official ministry of the church, sounded Roman Catholic. So hostile to churchly forms of faith—thanks to the influence of the new measures—were many American Protestants, that to take a high view of the sacraments and the authority of clergy was to approve of Rome's understanding of the church and its authority. Schaff's own conception of the relationship between Protestantism and Roman Catholicism, as one of continuity rather than a fundamental rupture, did not help matters.

Because Nevin had mentioned the paper that Kurtz edited, *Lutheran Observer*, by name in his critique of the new measures, Kurtz was quicker to respond than Berg. His main objection to Nevin's views was that the Mercersburg theologian had not grounded his rejection of revivalism in Scripture. Without a "thus saith the Lord," Kurtz charged, Nevin's accusations were based on "mere human reasoning," not the "most conclusive source of proof." The question in Kurtz's mind was not whether Nevin accurately represented the revivals but whether his views actually reflected those of Scripture.[1] For Berg, Nevin's critique of revivals, along with the emerging tendencies of the Mercersburg Theology sketched at Schaff's inaugural, revealed a softening of resolve against Roman Catholicism that for the Philadelphia pastor was truly alarming. Since 1840, when Berg published *Lectures on Romanism*, he had been on the lookout for signs of Protestant sympathy for Rome. Schaff's understanding of continuity between Catholicism and the Protestant Reformation clearly departed from Berg's understanding that the Reformers were recovering the truths of the ancient church, with medieval Catholicism functioning as the darkness that hid the light of early Christianity and Protestantism. But Nevin's sermon on Catholic unity, appended to Schaff's address, also showed Mercersburg's infidelity since Nevin articulated an understanding of Christ's presence in the Lord's Supper that moved substantially beyond Ulrich Zwingli's symbolic view. Indeed, for the German Reformed of Berg's persuasion, Zwingli was the fountainhead of the denomination's confessional tradition. To assert as Nevin had that Christ was present in the sacrament was a clear break with the German Reformed way.[2]

Of the two sets of criticism, Berg's turned out to be the more serious. In 1845 the Classis of Philadelphia passed six resolutions that expressed alarm over the recent teaching of the Mercersburg professors. These reinforced the impression that Nevin was engaging in theological errors that departed from historic Protestantism and moved in the direction of Rome. The first affirmed the formal principle of the Reformation in its teaching that the Bible alone is the "only rule of faith and practice." This was a clear rebuke to Schaff's apparently favorable attitude to history and tradition. The next four resolutions all concerned the sacraments. The nature and efficacy of baptism and the Lord's Supper had been barely mentioned in Schaff's inaugural or Nevin's introduction and supplemental sermon. But in the ensuing exchange between Berg and Nevin, the latter had affirmed the real presence of Christ in the Lord's Supper as a way of showing the disparity between contemporary German Reformed such as Berg and the teaching of sixteenth-century Reformers. Consequently, the second resolution contended that faith in Christ is "the life-giving principle of Christianity," and as such the sacraments were not "superior to . . . faith." The third resolution denied that the sacraments could be effectual without faith. The fourth resolution clarified the nature of the sacraments' function in the believer's life. Christians drew their life from Christ through the work of the Holy Spirit, and the sacraments worked mainly as "channels through which spiritual blessings [were] conveyed" and so could not "confer religious life."[3]

The final substantive resolution (the last of the six was a generic one affirming all of the above) was one clearly aimed at Nevin, and that would prove momentous for his theological development. It read:

> We hold that Christ is not bodily present with his people in the celebration of the Lord's Supper, in any other way than symbolically, but is spiritually present with them to the end of time, and that this institution is intended to remind us of his death, till he come the second time in his glorified body; that we cannot admit that the presence of Christ in the Lord's Supper is corporeal as it was in the days of his flesh, because his presence with his Church on earth is no longer human, but divine and spiritual, and that in all cases in which the flesh and blood of Christ are said to be received in the Sacrament of the Supper, the language is to be understood symbolically and not literally.[4]

As convincing as the Classis of Philadelphia's case was in the city, it was not adequate when the topic was taken up by the Synod of East. In the fall of 1845 synod met at York, Pennsylvania, to hear both sides in the dispute. Its ruling, by a vote of forty to three, exonerated the Mercersburg professors of all charges. Synod resolved specifically "that the Professors in our Theological Seminary are deserving and should receive the affectionate sympathy and cordial support of every friend of the Church in their earnest and untiring efforts to build up our Institutions and to advance the honor and welfare of the Church."[5] Not only did Schaff and Nevin deserve the church's encouragement, but synod's resolutions also included a vindication. The Mercersburg men had not "depart[ed] from the true protestant standpoint" but had actually "promote[d] the true interests of religion."[6]

Despite gaining acquittal from the German Reformed Church's regional authorities, the question of Nevin's affinities for Roman Catholicism would not go away. Consequently, the nature of Christ's presence in the Lord's Supper would be the next topic to which Nevin applied his churchly concerns. This subject was much bigger than the fairly precise (though mysterious) one of the relation of the second person of the Trinity to the bread and wine in the sacrament. It also concerned the relationship of Christ to his body, the church, as well as the character of the church's dependence upon its Savior. As such, the presence of Christ in the Lord's Supper, the doctrine to which Nevin devoted great attention after *Anxious Bench*, was directly connected to the argument that he had fleshed out in his critique of revivalism, for the nature and function of the Lord's Supper was a crucial element in the system of the catechism that Nevin had contrasted to that of the bench. This sacrament, though increasingly neglected by American Protestants, was at the heart of the lifelong care that the church provided to Christians. Convincing his fellow Protestants of that point, however, was another matter.

Mercersburg Polemics

The Mercersburg Theology—shorthand for the views of Nevin and Schaff—did not emerge after a time of ongoing reflection and instruction or as a program of pastoral training for church renewal. It did not have a chance to develop and mature as a tradition of theological reflection as, for example, the way the New Divinity in New England did as a legacy of Jonathan Edwards's theology or as the Princeton Theology did as the combined effort of generations of Presbyterian ministers. Instead, the Mercersburg theologians from the outset had no time to test their views first in the classroom and then try doctrinal variations in theological quarterlies before delivering a full-blown school of theology. Mercersburg Theology was from the start a polemical theology; it developed in many respects as a defensive system of doctrine in response to the criticisms of opponents. Because twentieth-century Protestant ecumenists would look back to Mercersburg for inspiration to soften the barriers dividing Christians, the historical image of the Mercersburg theologians has been one of charity and tolerance. But often overlooked is that the very catholicity of Mercersburg developed in the crucible of theological controversy, and it initially alienated as many Protestants as it pleased or persuaded.

A good indication of Mercersburg's positive teaching on the churchly and sacramental character of Christianity was Nevin's next significant publication: *The Mystical Presence: A Vindication of the Reformed or Calvinistic Doctrine of the Holy Eucharist*. Published in 1846, only two years after the revised edition of *Anxious Bench*, *Mystical Presence* was the fruit of seeds planted in Nevin's critique of revivalism. His explication and defense of older Reformed teaching on the real presence of Christ in the Lord's Supper drew directly upon the catechetical piety that Nevin had contrasted with devotion nurtured by the anxious seat. At the same time, *Mystical Presence*, like so many of the major publications of the Mercersburg Theology, was a book written to parry the doctrinal thrusts that were flying fast and furiously from east of the small Pennsylvania village.

Joseph Berg was again part of the instigation for the Mercersburg Theology. After failing to persuade synod of the seminary professors' errors, he continued his attacks in the pages of the *Protestant Banner*. As a pastor of a congregation in the heart of Philadelphia, Berg had to deal with the reality and presence of Roman Catholics in ways that

Nevin, who lived in a small rural town, did not. Like many American Protestants, Berg believed that the growing number of Roman Catholic immigrants, especially from Ireland, would fundamentally alter the character of American society. Here Protestant anti-Catholic prejudice drew less upon the doctrinal quarrels of the sixteenth century than upon the close overlap between Protestant and American ideals of religious freedom, a proximity that regarded religious liberty as the foundation for civil liberty. As such, Berg was overly sensitive to rhetoric or gestures that would weaken Protestant resolve against Rome's tyranny. Obviously, the Mercersburg professors were guilty of such Protestant softness. Nevin did not help matters when during 1845 he wrote a series of articles on what he called pseudo-Protestantism. In particular he singled out the anti-Catholicism that Berg and other Protestant communions manifested, as a break with historic Protestant understandings of Rome as part, even if in error, of the visible church. As Nevin put it, even if popery were the antichrist, "the Man of Sin, and so on," the proposition that Roman Catholicism "is without Christianity" did in no way follow.[7] In this series Nevin also addressed the question of the sacraments, specifically Protestant and Roman Catholic teaching on the presence of Christ in the Lord's Supper. Again, Nevin appealed to history, arguing that Protestants like Berg had veered from the Reformed consensus of the sixteenth and seventeenth centuries, which clearly affirmed a more objective conception of the sacrament than the symbolic one common among American Protestants. Interestingly enough, this series defending Mercersburg from Berg's attacks provided the basis for Nevin's next two major literary efforts, *Mystical Presence* and *Anti-Christ* (1848).

Nevin's Philadelphia nemesis made the mistake of attacking the Mercersburg professor on historical grounds. Berg held essentially to the "Waldensian theory" of Reformed church history. According to this understanding, the antiquity of the Reformation stretched back to the Waldensians, a group of twelfth-century French Christians who were intent on reforming the Roman Catholic Church in part through the translation of the Bible into the vernacular, lay preaching, and vows of poverty. In Berg's conception of Protestant development, a steady stream of such reform groups had existed in the West, stretching all the way back to the apostles. As such, the Reformation was no innovation but a continuation of a persistent stream in Christian history. But to appeal to history was to play precisely into Nevin's and Schaff's hands. For however good or bad their theology, their history was markedly superior to any of their contemporaries. And although Schaff established his reputation as the greatest church historian of the nineteenth century, Nevin scored his highest marks for the Mercersburg Theology by appealing to the original Protestantism of the sixteenth and seventeenth centuries.

Indeed, Nevin's chief contribution in *Mystical Presence* was to contrast the views of the past to those of contemporaries such as Berg. After a preliminary essay by Carl Ullmann, professor of theology at the University of Heidelberg, that Nevin himself translated and that would provide sustenance for his understanding of the incarnation and its relation to the Lord's Supper, *Mystical Presence* began with a basic statement of Reformed teaching that went straight to the sixteenth century, in particular to Calvin. According to Nevin, "to obtain a proper view of the original doctrine of the Reformed Church on the subject of the eucharist, we must have recourse particularly to Calvin." The French Reformer was nothing less than "the accredited interpreter and expounder of the article, for all later times."[8] (For reasons perhaps more personal than scientific, Nevin's understanding of historical development did not work so propitiously for Finney as an interpreter of Protestantism.)

Nevin knew well that to begin with Calvin played to his strength. But he also recognized that many in his own denomination regarded Ulrich Zwingli, another Swiss Reformer, who was older than Calvin, as the founder of the German Reformed tradition. And with a high regard for Zwingli came a justification for regarding the Supper as a symbol instead of a real means of grace, since Zwingli's teaching tended to be the favorite of low-church Protestants. Even here, however, Nevin made the intriguing point, one assisted by Schaff's own conception of historical development, that Calvin's view was actually more authoritative than Zwingli's. The reason was that Calvin was later and so benefited from the doctrinal debates that went on after Zwingli's premature death in 1531. As such, for Nevin, Calvin's doctrine was the mature reflection of the original Reformed church, thus making him the "theological organ" of the Reformed doctrine of the mystical presence.[9]

Although working from the perspective of the Reformed tradition's historical origins, Nevin introduced the section in which he surveyed sixteenth-century and seventeenth-century worthies with a contrast between Reformed teaching and rationalism on one side and Romanism on the other. As opposed to the symbolic view (synonymous with rationalism), Nevin declared that Christ's presence in the Lord's Supper was "not figurative merely and moral, but *real, substantial* and *essential.*"[10] At this point he emphasized that the sacrament was both a sign and a seal, underscoring the latter aspect to counter the common Zwinglian tendency of looking only at the sacrament's significance or meaning, rather than its objective force and activity. The Lord's Supper accomplished more than assisting "the memory and heart . . . in calling up what is past or absent, for the purposes of devotion; as the picture of a friend is suited to recal [*sic*] his image and revive our interest in his person, when he is no longer in our sight."[11] Moreover, the sacrament was more than simply a pledge of "our own consecration to the service of Christ, or of the faithfulness of God as engaged to make good to us in a general way the grace of the new covenant; as the rainbow serves still to ratify and confirm the promise given to Noah after the flood." If the Supper were no more than a sign, then, it would "carry with it no virtue or force, more than might be put into it in every case by the spirit of the worshipper himself." It was much more than an occasion to excite believers to "pious feelings and desires" because, Nevin countered, it "embodies the actual presence of the grace it represents in its own constitution." What is more, this grace was not merely the promise of God to encourage troubled souls but "the very life of the Lord Jesus Christ himself."[12]

Having underscored Christ's real presence in the Supper to correct the rationalistic view, Nevin next needed to demonstrate that his position, though sounding Roman Catholic, was not. Here he stressed the Supper as sign, in contrast to seal, but in a way that nevertheless affirmed Christ's real presence in the sacrament. Consequently, Nevin explicitly rejected Rome's teaching on transubstantiation. The bread and wine did not literally become the actual flesh and blood of Christ as Roman Catholics believed. In fact, Nevin referred to Rome's view as a "gross superstition," for Reformed teaching "admits no change whatever in the elements."[13] Nevin's critique of transubstantiation led inevitably to a condemnation of Lutheran teaching on consubstantiation, which affirmed that Christ's flesh and blood was "in, with, and under the outward signs" for all those partaking, whether believers or unbelievers. In each case, Roman Catholics and Lutherans missed an essential point about Christ's humanity that the Reformed position had always maintained, namely, that Christ's ascended body "remains constantly in heaven, according to the scriptures." Because of Christ's ascension, the participation of his flesh and blood in the Supper could be "*spiritual* only, and in no sense corporal." Furthermore, the partaking of Christ's body and blood was not oral but by faith. As such, Christ's presence requires faith on the part of the recipients. Unbelievers observing the Supper "receive only naked symbols, bread and wine, without any spiritual advantage to their own souls."[14]

With the errors of rationalism and Romanism delineated, Nevin briefly expounded the classic Reformed view on Christ's presence in the Supper. The Reformed church maintained that Christ's person was present in the sacrament "so far as the actual participation of the believer is concerned." Nevin noted that Calvin was even willing to use the phrase *real presence* as long as it was understood as "*true* presence," meaning a "presence that brings Christ truly into communion with the believer in his human nature, as well as in his divine nature."[15] *Real* too often designated a "local" or "corporal" presence, and consequently the Reformed church also spoke of a "*spiritual* real presence." According to Nevin this phrase meant that "the body of Christ is in heaven, the believer on earth; but by the power of the Holy Ghost, nevertheless, the obstacle of such vast local distance is overcome, so that in the sacramental act, while the outward symbols are received in an outward way, the very body and blood of Christ are at the same time inwardly and supernaturally communicated to the worthy receiver, for the real nourishment of his new life."[16]

From the spiritual real presence of Christ in the Lord's Supper followed two important points. The first was that the sacrament carries "with it an *objective* force, so far as its principal design is concerned."

It was not simply suggestive of a greater reality: "It is not a sign, a picture, deriving its significance from the mind of the beholder." For the sacrament to be efficacious the receiver needed to have faith, thus guarding against the "mechanical" view of Rome's notion of "*opus operatum,*" the idea that the sacrament worked whenever it was administered by priests in fellowship with the Bishop of Rome. But the Supper contained within itself spiritual grace: "The signs are bound to what they represent, not subjectively simply in the thought of the worshipper, but objectively, by the force of a divine appointment."[17] The second point was harder to grasp, and it would consume the last third of the book: partaking of Christ's body and blood involved a "real participation in him as the principle of life *under this form.*"[18] Nevin tossed out this assertion in the opening section of the book as if an eminently reasonable implication of Reformed teaching. But it would prove to be the hardest part of his argument to decipher.

From this explanation of what might have looked like a minor point in sacramental theology, Nevin had little trouble finding Reformed sources from the sixteenth and seventeenth centuries to show that the tradition was on his side, not on that of the likes of Berg. What was most impressive about Nevin's performance as a historian was the wide representation of his sources, as well as the weight he assigned to creedal statements as expressions of the church corporate, not simply the view of solitary individuals. Consequently, rather than beginning with Calvin in his survey and rather than filling up page after page with quotations from the Geneva pastor, Nevin began with the First Confession of Basel and worked his way through Calvin, William Farel, Theodore Beza, Peter Martyr, Gallic Confession, Old Scotch Confession, Belgic Confession, Second Helvetic Confession, Heidelberg Catechism, Zacharias Ursinus, Rudolph Hopsinian, Synod of Dort, Westminster Standards—all the way down to Thomas Hooker and John Owen. The collective voice of the Reformed churches, as Nevin tallied it, was decidedly against the unchurchly form of piety that had grown up around the anxious bench.

All of the citations he selected were weighty, so much so that someone like Berg would be hard pressed to explain them away as peripheral or the exception that proved the rule. Indeed, the overall force of

Nevin's historical evidence must have been shocking to those Reformed Christians who conceived of the Lord's Supper as a symbolic way of remembering Christ's death and showing collective unity. For instance, the First Helvetic Confession stated that although the bread and wine in the Supper "remain unchanged," "Christ himself is the food of believing souls unto eternal life." It went on to affirm that the believers' souls "are made to eat and drink the flesh and blood of Christ" to be nurtured to eternal life.[19] The Old Scotch Confession also declared Christ to be "so united to us as to be the very nutriment and food of our souls." This did not involve any notion of transubstantiation, but the Supper, through the operation of the Holy Spirit, "who carries us by true faith above all that is seen, and all that is carnal and terrestrial," enabled recipients "to feed upon the body and blood of Jesus Christ."[20] That Nevin could even marshal Owen for his argument was important since the Mercersburg divine conceded that the seventeenth-century nonconformist sometimes tended toward "an incorporeal spiritualism in religion, that might be counted particularly unfavourable to a right estimate of the sacraments." Even so, Nevin found Owen writing that "as truly my brethren as we do eat of this bread and drink of this cup, which is really communicated to us, so every true believer doth receive Christ, his body and blood, in all the benefits of it, that are really exhibited by God unto the soul in this ordinance, and it is a means of communicating to faith." Nevin conceded that Owen fell short of "the firm, clear utterances of Calvin." But considering that he wrote during the age of Cromwell and the English Commonwealth, Owen's teaching had merit. At least he conveyed "in strong terms, the sense of an objective force, a true exhibition of the thing signified."[21]

As Nevin had established in *Anxious Bench*, his theological method involved not simply positive declaration—in this case from history—but also contrast with what he called "pseudo-Protestantism." But while he had been critical of Finney's methods and the system of the anxious seat, in *Mystical Presence* his object of attack shifted from revivals to the Puritans. After showing the wide consensus among Reformed theologians and creeds on the objective and grace-communicating nature of the Supper, Nevin turned to a section entitled "The Modern Puritan Theory." He began with long and damn-

ing quotations from Jonathan Edwards, Samuel Hopkins, Joseph Bel-
lamy, Timothy Dwight, and John Dick. For good measure he threw in
Presbyterian stalwarts such as Ashbel Green and Albert Barnes, an
arresting combination since these ministers were antagonists in the
Old School–New School Presbyterian division. But this made his point
all the more poignant since it suggested that, however much the Old
and New Schools might have disagreed on the imputation of Adam's
sin, they were likely in agreement on the presence of Christ in the Supper, thus indicating how far even the conservative Old Schoolers had
departed from the Reformed tradition.

Furthermore, just as Nevin had contrasted the piety of the bench
with that of the catechism in his critique of Finney, so he explored the
different understandings of the Supper for Christian devotion. Those
differences were not simply "formal or accidental" but systematic.
"The modern Puritan view," Nevin concluded, "involves a material
falling away, not merely from the form of the old Calvinistic doctrine,
but from its inward life and force." The difference went precisely to
the matter of whether "the union of the believer with Christ [can] be
regarded as the power of one and the same life, or as holding only in
a correspondence of thought and feeling." Were believers "united by
means of [the sacrament] to the person of Christ, or only to his merits"? Did Christians "communicate in the ordinance with the whole
of Christ, in a real way, or only with his divinity"? Because, Nevin
warned, the doctrine of the Supper lay "at the very heart of christianity [*sic*] itself," the "chasm" separating the historic and modern Puritan views was "wide and deep." Churches claiming to stand in the
succession of the Reformed tradition could hardly "allow themselves
to make light of it."[22]

Nevin was not finished with drawing contrasts in Christian history. As if the case against the "modern Puritan theory" needed help,
he added a section on the early church. This passage of *Mystical Presence* would prove to be a foretaste of studies in which Nevin would
engage during the 1850s while he weighed the merits of Rome's claims
to authority based upon the antiquity of the papacy and apostolic succession. In the meantime, his overview of the church fathers' teaching
on the Supper had the cumulative effect once again of demonstrating

the novelty of contemporary American Protestantism. As Nevin put it, the "modern Puritan doctrine," when compared to the Reformed view, "may be said to be of yesterday only in the history of the Church," while the Calvinist doctrine "has been the faith of nearly the whole Christian world from the beginning."[23] By this Nevin was not claiming anachronistically that Calvin's views had a wide circulation among the Greek and Latin fathers. Instead, he was asserting that the early church held that Christ was present in the Supper and so gave no room for a symbolic understanding of the sacrament. The ancient church also, like the Reformers of the sixteenth century, understood Christianity in sacramental terms. The church's mission in part was to mediate divine grace through its ministry of the sacraments. "From the beginning," Nevin wrote, the sacrament was "not simply a memorial of Christ's sacrifice" but "an exhibition immediately of the offering for sin made once for all by Christ's death; in the participation of which, the believer was considered to receive the full benefit of it, as of a living atonement brought before God at the time."[24]

Had Nevin stopped with a historical treatment of the doctrine of the Lord's Supper, the Mercersburg Theology would likely have generated less excitement then and less interest by later church historians. But Nevin was the theology professor at Mercersburg, Schaff the church historian. Consequently, Nevin drew upon his skills as a theologian to attempt what he called a statement of the doctrine in its proper scientific form. At this point, he not only turned more theological but also more philosophical; this part of the book showed clearly his interaction with and appropriation of recent German theological developments. The German phrasing put off many of his Anglo-American critics, and it continues to create difficulty for those unfamiliar with the vicissitudes of nineteenth-century German intellectual history. Still, for all of the Germanizing, Nevin also drew upon specific parts of the New Testament that helped him bolster his case for the spiritual real presence of Christ and the doctrine of the incarnation that undergirded it.

On one level *Mystical Presence* was simply a fleshing out of the point made previously in *Anxious Bench*. But it also turned out to be much more. Nevin had started out with a critique of low-church, revivalist-driven Protestantism, the kind popularized by Finney. Clearly, to recover a sacramental piety, one in which baptism and the Lord's Supper were integral parts of Christian devotion, was to show how far that contemporary American Protestantism had departed from its roots. Yet, Nevin's quest to bolster the catechetical system of ecclesial Calvinism turned into a significant theological argument about the meaning of the incarnation and its place in Christian truth. He tipped his hand in the preface, where he reasoned that if the incarnation were "the principle and source of a new supernatural order of life for humanity itself, the Church . . . must be a true, living, divine-human constitution in the world." The church and its ministry, against which the anxious bench vied for the souls of American Protestants, was no organizational "contrivance" for performing certain work. It was instead the "essential form of Christianity, in whose presence only it is possible to conceive intelligently of piety in its individual manifestations." In other words, the life of the individual Christian "can be real and healthful only as it is born from the general life of the Church, and carried by it onward to the end."[25]

To make this understanding of the catechetical system stick, Nevin developed the idea that the visible or external church "is the necessary form of the new creation in Christ Jesus, in its very nature."[26] Here Nevin went beyond the basic question of whether Christ was present in the sacrament to what it meant for believers to commune and feed upon Christ in the Supper. As much as Nevin appreciated Calvin's sacramental theology, he also believed it was hampered by several difficulties. The main one concerned the way in which Christ's life was communicated to those partaking of the sacrament. If the Savior's life was really present and really conveyed to recipients, not simply a spiritual influence, Nevin insisted that Christ's presence needed to be both divine and human, both body and soul. But because Calvin resisted any notion that located Christ in the bread and wine, thus denying the actual presence of Christ's ascended body at God the Father's right hand, the French Reformer used the Holy Spirit, in Nevin's words, "as a sort of foreign medium introduced to meet the wants of the case."[27] What Nevin proposed instead was an organic conception of the human race that made Christ and the incarnation "a new *Life* introduced into the very centre of humanity itself." This life source is what allowed the Apostle Paul to speak of a new creation in which all things have become new. It also helped to explain how the church was the body of Christ, because this new life infused into humanity in the incarnation was not merely individual but corporate or organic. As Nevin explained it, "Christ communicates his own life substantially to the soul on which he acts, causing it to grow into his very nature. This is the *mystical union*; the basis of our whole salvation."[28] This union began at regeneration and continued to the resurrection. Obviously, its relevance to the doctrine of the Lord's Supper was that the sacrament became the means for sustaining and invigorating believers in their life source.

By exploring the meaning of the incarnation as a mystical union between Christ and the church, Nevin was doing more than trying to locate an adequate grounding (or as he put it, a "scientific statement") for the Reformed doctrine of the Lord's Supper. He was also attempting to make sense of biblical language about the new life that Christians experience in regeneration. Here scriptural metaphors—such as the Johannine image of Christ as the vine and the church as its branches, or the Pauline figures of Christ as the head and the church as its body or Christ as bridegroom and the church as bride—symbols that the biblical authors used to describe the union between Christ and Christians, were ones to which Nevin appealed. This part of Nevin's argument had a degree of plausibility. Even the classic federal theology of the Reformed tradition, which taught a union between Adam and the whole human race and between Christ and the church, indicated that Nevin's idea of mystical union was not as bizarre as it might at first have sounded. Just as Adam, he explained, "was at once an individual and a whole race," and just as "all his posterity partake of his life, and grow forth from him as their root," so with Christ believers "spring from [him], so far as our new life is concerned" and "stand in him perpetually also as our ever living and ever present root." Nevin added that this union did not involve Christ's "ubiquity or idealistic dissipation of his body."[29] But this participation in Christ's humanity did occur through the work and power of the Holy Spirit: "There is no other medium, by which it is possible for us to be in Christ, or to have

Christ in ourselves."[30] Nevin also indicated that the mystical union required faith, another reason why the work of the Spirit was essential.[31] This life, begun in regeneration, grew and developed over the course of the Christian's life, just as an oak tree grows from an acorn, and became complete or full in death and resurrection when believers would be "set free from the first form of existence entirely, and made to supersede it for ever in the immortality of heaven."[32]

Nevin closed the book without great fanfare. He restated the Reformed doctrine of the Lord's Supper and included a number of vignettes that used biblical material to support his case. The impression left was almost like that of a painting where the author, contrary to the intellectual analysis implied by his appeal to a "scientific statement," offered a variety of images that implied and hinted at the larger import of the incarnation. In a statement that carried even more weight than Nevin understood, he indicated that his demand in formulating an objective and forceful sacramental theology was fairly simple. "All" he wanted was "to make . . . a true sacrament . . . the *seal* as well as the *sign* of the invisible grace it represents." If this demand could be met, then "we should have a true and full persuasion of the supernatural character of Christianity itself, as a permanent and not simply transient fact in the history of the world." But the Protestant world of nineteenth-century America had only a partial view of Christianity's power, one reflected in its understanding of the sacraments. "Low views of the sacrament," Nevin deduced, "betray invariably a low view of the mystery of the incarnation itself, and a low view of the Church also, as that new and higher order of life, in which the power of this mystery continues to reveal itself through all ages."[33] So Nevin let Calvin, a theologian who held no such low view of the Supper, have the last word:

> They are preposterous . . . who allow in this matter nothing more, than they have been able to reach with the measure of their understanding. When they deny that the flesh and blood of Christ are exhibited to us in the Holy Supper, *Define the mode*, they say, *or you will not convince us.* But as for myself, I am filled with amazement at the greatness of the mystery. Nor am I ashamed, with Paul, to confess

in admiration my own ignorance. For how much better it is that, than to extenuate with my carnal sense what the apostle pronounces a high mystery![34]

As Nevin would soon learn, hiding behind Calvin would not prevent critics from taking swipes. Berg continued his attacks for a time, but soon he grew impatient with the German Reformed Church's tolerance of the Mercersburg men and transferred to the Dutch-American communion, the Reformed Church of America. As it turned out, Berg was not needed to supply theological pressure to Nevin because Nevin's former professor, Charles Hodge, assumed that responsibility. Indeed, the Princeton professor's review of *Mystical Presence* became one of the many decisive readings on Hodge's compass of orthodoxy in the United States that showed Nevin to be veering off course. At roughly the same time that Hodge was filing papers against Finney's errors, he also took aim at Nevin. Ironically, Finney and Nevin, who were poles apart on the spectrum of Protestant devotion and worship, came off as equally unworthy of ascending Princeton's holy hill.

Many of Hodge's points were telling. Nevin's views on the union of believers with Christ were often vague, less than scientific (read: systematic). For instance, if the incarnation made Christianity a historical fact and became the basis for the invigoration of the human mass with a new spiritual force, what about Old Testament saints?[35] In addition, what about the division in humanity between the saved and the lost? If Christ's incarnation injected a new spiritual leaven into the lump of humankind, in the way that all men and women shared in Adam's life, did all people, by virtue of their humanity, participate in Christ's life? Nevin had not addressed the doctrine of election, and *Mystical Presence* could sound universalistic with its appeal to a generic humanity, both of Christ and of the race. Another difficulty in Nevin's view was the implication that the union between Christ and believers became the means by which Christians participated in the deity or Christ's divine nature. The Reformed tradition had historically insisted that union with Christ, while legal, real, and vital, and the result of the indwelling of the Holy Spirit, never involved sharing divinity or becoming divine.[36] One further hurdle that Nevin had not cleared in

Hodge's estimation was to blur the imputation of Christ's righteous-ness with the doctrine of mystical union. Imputation was crucial to the doctrine of justification, and Nevin's metaphysical rendering of salvation as a life force that transformed the human race did not do justice to the legal categories inherited from the Reformation's teach-ing about Christ's satisfaction of the law as the basis of Christian hope. According to Hodge, whose pithy classifications of the nineteenth cen-tury's theological flora infuriated his opposing Protestant horticultur-alists, "the theory unfolded in this book . . . is in all its essential fea-tures Schleiermacher's theory."[37]

Such a summary put-down did not do justice to Nevin's point about Christ's presence in the Lord's Supper—whether it was the larger or smaller message is hard to say since his view of the incarnation, though limited in pages, was a large serving of theological reflection to digest. With the same apodictic certainty with which he challenged Nevin's teaching on the mystical union, Hodge also dismissed the Mercers-burg theologian's handling of the Reformed view of the sacrament. In effect, Hodge conceded Nevin's marshaling of the historical evidence when he noted that two views had been present in the church from the beginning, one that located the benefits of the Supper in "the sacrifi-cial virtue" of Christ's body and blood, the other in the mysterious and supernatural "efficacy flowing from the glorified body of Christ in heaven." Hodge held to the former view and interpreted the latter, the one articulated by Calvin—and, as Nevin also saw, by most of the Reformed confessions—as simply a concession to Lutherans during the give and take of the sixteenth century. As much as Nevin qualified his view by saying that it was a spiritual, not a physical presence, that its efficacy depended on the work of the Spirit and the faith of the recipient—in effect affirming exactly what his boyhood catechism taught (i.e., Westminster Shorter Catechism 91)—Hodge still heard a Roman Catholic or Lutheran hedging on a real physical presence.

But the Princetonian showed his true colors when he heard the same echoes in Calvin, calling them "extreme," "peculiar," and "dubi-ous."[38] When Hodge concluded that Calvin's view had died out in the Reformed churches by 1590 on the basis of his reading of John Craig's catechism, written at the request of the Scottish Kirk's General Assembly, his condescension toward Nevin's view was complete. To add insult to injury, Hodge even appealed to the kind of developmental notion of history that made Mercersburg tick:

> There is . . . a great difference between a doctrine's being lost by a process of decay and by the process of growth. It is very possible that a particular opinion may be engrafted into a system, without having any logical or vital union with it, and is the more certain to be ejected, the more vigorous the growth and healthful the life of that system. The fundamental principles of Protestantism are the exclusive normal authority of scripture, and justification by faith alone. If that system lives and grows it must throw off every thing incompatible with those principles. It is the fact of this peculiar view of a mysterious influence of the glorified body of Christ, having ceased to live, taken in connection with its obvious incompatibility with other articles of the Reformed faith, that we urge as a collateral argument against its being a genuine portion of that system of doctrine.[39]

Of course, Nevin had claimed that Calvin's views were not peculiar but in fact the culmination of early Protestant deliberations. He also had attempted to show that Calvin's views took root in a variety of other Reformed theologians and creeds. In this respect, the debate between Nevin and Hodge was little more than a skirmish about history: whose account of the Reformed past was superior? The verdict of modern historians is almost unanimous in declaring Nevin the victor on historical points. Indeed, the record indicates that, as Roman Catholic as it may have sounded, Reformed and Presbyterian ministers in the sixteenth and seventeenth centuries, almost to the man, affirmed an objective efficacy in the consumption of the Lord's Supper that truly communicated, in the words of the Westminster Shorter Catechism, "benefits of redemption." As the Westminster divines put it, "the worthy receivers are, not after a corporal and carnal manner, but by faith, made partakers of [Christ's] body and blood, with all his benefits, to their spiritual nourishment and growth in grace" (Westminster Shorter Catechism 96). Nevin's attempt to improve on Calvin did not help his case. In fact, his views in *Mystical Presence* were not clear. But had he limited his argument simply to the historical point that American Protestants had departed from the sacramental and churchly conceptions of historic Protestantism, he would likely have been no more successful, for those same American churches had moved so far from older views, as Nevin had shown in *Anxious Bench*, that a rendering of the church and its ministry as a medium of salvation would inevitably be dismissed as beyond the pale of Protestantism, if not Roman Catholic.

Push Comes to Shove

In retrospect, as condescending as Hodge's review of Nevin was in places, it also functioned as the sort of peer review that the Mercersburg theologians needed. Aside from Schaff, Nevin had no theological equals in the German Reformed Church. The denomination was still primarily an immigrant communion without a sustained tradition of theological reflection. The seminary at Mercersburg was an attempt to alleviate this problem. In contrast, the Presbyterians that sponsored Hodge's seminary and his theological journal were still ethnic in some ways, but by the mid-nineteenth century they had several colleges and seminaries and still had strong ties to universities in Scotland and Northern Ireland. Hodge was by no means the czar of Reformed orthodoxy in the United States, but he was close to the top in the hierarchy of Reformed academics. His review of Nevin clearly indicated that he believed *Mystical Presence* may have been good enough for Pittsburgh or Lancaster but was not ready for inspection at Andover, New Haven, or Princeton; it was the kind of response a theologian today might receive from the anonymous reader of a manuscript submitted to a publisher. Because the German Reformed Church did not possess a wealth of theological academics and because theology in America had still not professionalized, polemics of the kind that often result in better arguments and tighter prose today were on display, like closeted skeletons, in America's many theological quarterlies.

What also needs to be observed is that Hodge was not the raving anti-Catholic that American Protestantism sometimes produced during Nevin's day. Although the Presbyterian Church U.S.A. was not persuaded by Hodge's logic, in 1845 he had argued vigorously at its General Assembly and in print that Roman Catholic baptism was valid, thus not requiring Presbyterian churches to rebaptize converts from Rome. Hodge's argument for the validity of Roman Catholic baptism actually betrayed the low view of the church as a medium of salvation—he reasoned on the basis that Rome was part of the invisible as opposed to the visible church—that would come through in his review of Nevin. Even so, he was not necessarily suspicious of anything that sounded like Rome's sacramentalism. Of the leading nineteenth-century theologians in America, then, Hodge would have been among the most congenial to tolerate an argument that appeared to concede some points to Roman Catholicism.

Yet, when authors receive evaluations that correct their writings, the tendency of human nature is to fight back. This was no less true in Nevin's case. His response to Hodge particularly indicated the way he handled criticism and what such critique was doing to his own theological development. Nevin's first response was indirect and came in the form of a longish pamphlet called *The Anti-Christ; or, The Spirit of Sect and Schism*, published shortly after Hodge's review. As part of Nevin's own theological development this short work functioned as a bridge between his views on the Supper and his formulation of the doctrine of the church. His point in *Anti-Christ* was simple and provocative. The text for his discourse was 1 John 4:1–3 in which the apostle writes, "every spirit that confesseth not that Jesus Christ is come in the flesh is not of God." A simplistic reading of the pamphlet could have interpreted Nevin to be saying that all who disagreed with his own understanding of the Supper and the conception of the incarnation that informed the nature of Christ's presence were guilty of being the antichrist. Indeed, Nevin used this short work to put more flesh on his understanding of what the coming of Christ in the flesh actually meant for the church. "Thus, central and fundamental to the whole idea of Christianity and the church," he wrote, "do we find the mystery of the incarnation to be, not as a doctrine simply, but as a supernatural world-embracing fact, revealed in the person of Jesus Christ."[40] Conversely, the "great characteristic of all false Christianity" was the refusal to admit that Christ had come in the flesh. This was the source of all heresy and schism in the history of Christianity, according to Nevin.

Although he did not attribute directly the spirit of the antichrist to spiritual or symbolic views of the Supper, he did mention that a low view of the church's ministry, sacraments, and worship was a mark of the antichrist: "Sects clearly betray their rationalistic, Gnostic spirit, by making the Lord's Supper to be a simple sign or monument, and denying all power to holy Baptism." In fact, he saw the "Baptistic principle" to lie behind such low-church Protestantism. Here Nevin began to unravel the web that would unite the course of his career, from a critique of revivalism to a new order of worship:

> Sects have no sense for the objective and liturgical, in worship; hold all this rather to be at war with the idea of devotion; and aim accordingly, on principle, to clothe the entire service of God as much as possible with just the opposite character. Their hymns, and the tunes to which they are sung, their prayers, and of course also the whole tone of their preaching, bear the same impress of extreme subjectivity. This is supposed, indeed, to constitute their highest excellence and worth; as it seems to place the worshipper in direct personal juxtaposition with the spiritual world itself, and carries with it oftentimes a great show of earnestness and life, in its own form. But the transition here again is most easy, nay, necessary, as all experience proves, from the region of clouds downward to the region of clods. All Sect worship, fanatical and extravagant at first, sinks finally into the dullest routine of empty ceremony.[41]

Still, Nevin's concern was much more on the incarnation and the church as a medium of Christ's continuing ministry. The incarnation as the "central fact" of Christianity did not threaten the atonement, imputation, or justification, he argued, but provided for them "a suitable basis in the deep christological reality which lies beyond."[42] Consequently, *Anti-Christ* deepened his theology of the mystical presence more than it pertained to the doctrine of the Lord's Supper.

Even so, Nevin did use the preface to initiate his response to Hodge. To the Princetonian's charge that Nevin was guilty of Eutychianism (i.e., confusing the divine and human natures in Christ), the Mercersburg theologian shot back that, if true, Hodge was guilty of Nestorianism (i.e., so dividing Christ's two natures as to render him two persons). Nevin did not mean by "life" the same thing as "nature," and so Hodge had ham-fistedly become bogged down in Trinitarian minutia, missing *Mystical Presence*'s larger incarnational point.[43] Nevin also responded briefly to Hodge's complaint that he had "surrendered" to German modes of thinking. "Am I not," Nevin asked, "a teacher in the German church, and as such bound, in common honesty, to cultivate a proper connection with the theological life of Germany, as well as that of Scotland and New England?"[44] Finally, he conceded Hodge's criticism that his incarnational theology was different from Calvin's. Nevin had, in fact, admitted as much in the original publication when he tried to "cast" Calvin's doctrine in "scientific form." His reason for doing so was to try to overcome the "difficulties and contradictions that are acknowledged to accompany it as usually stated." So, yes, Nevin was guilty as charged of not keeping "in full" with Calvin's entire position. Even so, if the scientific statement were unsuccessful, "the old doctrine itself" of Christ's mystical presence still stood as "a matter of pure history." Hodge may have been able to skewer Nevin, but he had not "shown at all" that Calvin and the Reformed creeds "do not teach a real participation of believers in the life of Christ, by the Lord's Supper."[45]

Nevin's fuller response to Hodge continued in the vein of this last point, namely, the matter of history. In 1850 Nevin published in the recently founded *Mercersburg Review* a lengthy, deft, and intelligent historical survey of Reformed theology from the sixteenth and the seventeenth centuries. It showed amazing facility with the leading figures and background of the major and minor creedal expressions. Indeed, the bulk of Nevin's response was to lay out the history of Calvinist orthodoxy behind the numerous quotations that he had assembled in *Mystical Presence*, from the First Helvetic Confession down to John Owen. As impressive as his historical treatment was, even more stunning was his response to Hodge's argument about the peculiarity of Calvin's view, one that according to the Princetonian the Reformed faith eventually outgrew. Nevin's history actually showed the reverse; Calvin's understanding of the mystical presence did not wither and die but took root and bore fruit. At the same time, in a section called "Counterstatement," Nevin exacted from Hodge's concession regarding the difference between Calvin and the rest of the tradition a wedge through which to drive a decisive critique of contemporary American Protestantism and its nonsacramental faith.

Nevin sounded exasperated when summarizing all those points upon which he and Hodge concurred, mainly because the Presbyterian Hodge read either a sacramentalist or Schleiermacherian meaning into the German Reformed's prose. "It is agreed all around," Nevin explained, "that the Reformed doctrine allowed no local presence, no oral communication, no material contact, no physical transmission of Christ's flesh and blood into the bodies of his people, no mechanical virtue in the sacramental elements, no magical power belonging to them in any way to confer grace apart from the action of the Holy Spirit."[46] So then, what was the problem? The issue appeared to be what Nevin meant when going beyond these negations to the positive teaching of what transpired in the Supper, specifically, "the single clause, touching our participation in the *human life* of Christ."[47] Here Nevin let Hodge's own distinction do Mercersburg's holy work. In some statements Reformed churchmen spoke of the sacrament's "sacrificial efficacy" (e.g., sacrament as sign) while at other times they elaborated its "life-giving power" (e.g., sacrament as seal). According to Hodge, Calvin fit in the latter category, and that conception, also according to the Princetonian, died off in the Reformed tradition. Nevin countered by wondering why these two conceptions were at odds, why Calvin's "extreme" view needed to expire in favor of the symbolic or Puritan understanding. "How such a man as Calvin could have failed to see and feel the contradiction," Nevin wondered sarcastically, "is indeed surpassingly strange." And he piled on by offering an explanation for the contradiction from Hodge: "It only goes to show how little regard was had to the logical unity of doctrines, in the theology of the sixteenth century."[48] Nevin's rejoinder to Hodge, then, involved the assertion that no contradiction existed between the Supper's sacrificial efficacy and its life-giving power. Both aspects were true because the Bible taught both, and the tradition had affirmed them as well. In effect, Nevin's teaching was more catholic than Hodge's because he made room for both, while the Princetonian excluded Calvin's teaching as extraneous and a concession to Lutherans. Good history required as much.

But Nevin's argument for greater tolerance also involved revealing the consequences of understanding the Supper without its life-giving qualities. Simply put, Hodge's scheme denied not only the mystical presence but the sacrament's mystery. As merely a memorial or symbol, the Supper became wholly dependent on the believer's mind, "whether the relation between the sign and the thing signified shall be of any force whatever in the transaction." If faith is "so exercised" in the observance, then the general truth of the atonement is exhibited; "otherwise the institution will stand shorn of its celestial significance."[49] In effect, Hodge reduced the Supper to another sermon or lesson. By "robbing the Reformed doctrine of this conception of the objective grace in the sacraments," Nevin declared, Hodge had stripped the Supper of "all mystical character; since in such view no significance belongs to any institution of the sort, other than what the truth of the gospel carries with it in its general form." He summarized accordingly:

> The faith of the Reformed Church in the beginning, no less than the faith of the Lutheran Church, saw in the Lord's Supper the presence of a heavenly mystery—something more in this respect than the high nature of the truth here represented, under its general form; something different from the word, in no connection with such solemnity. An inward bond was acknowledged to hold, by the power of the Holy Spirit, between the visible and invisible sides of the holy transaction. It was allowed to carry in it thus a mystical force—a meaning above sense and natural reason—to which especially faith was encouraged and required to have regard in using it as a medium of worship.[50]

Nevin concluded his response by turning Hodge's argument against itself. For Hodge, at the heart of the Reformation were the doctrines of *sola scriptura* and justification by faith alone (the formal and material principles of Protestantism). Nevin did not dissent from this view, but questioned why Christ's mystical presence threatened either of those doctrines, especially justification, as if an affirmation of the Supper's internal efficacy undermined the external imputation of Christ's righteousness. But was this not a form of Pelagianism, Nevin asked, because it denied a "real union" between the believer and the grace of redemption.[51] Instead, "justification, to be real, must be also concrete—the force and value of Christ's merit brought nigh to the sinner as a living fact." Strange, he insisted, was it that Hodge would find any contradiction between "the grace which we have by Christ's death, and the grace that comes to us through his life." "Could the sacrifice of Calvary," Nevin continued, "be of any avail to take away sins, if the victim there slain had not been raised again for our justification, and were not *now* seated at the right hand of God as our Advocate and Intercessor? Would the atonement of a *dead* Christ be of more worth than the blood of bulls and goats, to purge the conscience from dead works and give it free access to God?" The difference made by Christ's resurrected life and its impartation to the elements of the Supper was in fact what distinguished the Supper from the Old Testament sacrifices and what prompted Calvin, in his comments on 1 Corinthians 10:4, to indicate that Christians did in fact partake of something different from that in which the Old Testament saints participated in their sacrifices. (Nevin quoted Calvin: "In our time, the manducation is *substantial*, which it *could not be then*.")[52] Christ's sacrifice was once for all because it reached "through all time," continuing to "live and make itself felt." In other words, the Reformers would not allow the sundering of Christ's merits and benefits from his living person: "What Christ does or has done, must ever be conditioned certainly by what he is; and it is hard to see how the force of his righteousness forensically taken can ever be impaired, by its being allowed to be in truth a part of himself and in union always with his own life."[53] That had been Nevin's point all along—an effort not simply to have a higher and more historic view of the Supper but to ground the life of the church in the mystery of the incarnation both before and after the resurrection. And that was the point on which he ended his defense against Hodge's accusations.

The Princeton theologian tussled with many of the departures from Reformed orthodoxy that he saw bedeviling the churches in the United States. Hodge's debate with Nevin does not rank as high in the standings of nineteenth-century major-league theology as does his critique of Finney, Horace Bushnell, or the long-winded contest with Andover Seminary's Edwards Amasa Park. Part of the explanation could be that Hodge did not fare as well with Nevin as he did with New England theology's strange concoctions. While Hodge was one of the few theologians of note to take pride in his conservatism, in Nevin, contrary to his own reading, he may have in fact encountered someone who stood to his theological right, a theologian who believed that even the theological neanderthal Charles Hodge had capitulated to modern conceptions of piety and faith. To be sure, Hodge had a point when observing that Nevin leaned so heavily on German philosophy that he sounded innovative if not wayward. But the Princeton divine also could not understand Nevin's point about the sacramental character of the Christian life, even among older Reformed expressions. In that sense, as much as Hodge joined Nevin in condemning Finney's new measures, he did not grasp in Nevin's diagnosis the nature of the church and its ministry. Here the reason likely stemmed from Princeton's close reliance upon a subjective and individualistic form of devotion that, from Nevin's churchly perspective, carried flaws similar to Finney's.

No matter how much Hodge and Nevin talked past each other, the Princetonian's rejection of Nevin's teaching would be profound for the trajectory of Reformed faith and practice in the United States. Nevin was trying to steer the Reformed churches back to the older Calvinist piety, but the gatekeeper of Presbyterianism in America had rejected his efforts as novel. As such, Nevin's ideas and influence became confined to the German Reformed Church, where he had few theological equals and so easily shaped a part of the denomination's next generation of ministers and theologians. But outside the German communion, thanks in large part to Hodge's verdict, Nevin's ideas became synonymous with a failure to resist Roman Catholicism's bewitching charms. In effect, after debating Hodge, Nevin could no longer be included in the mainstream of Reformed thought in the United States. Left to his own devices and the smaller pond of German Reformed life, Nevin sought a wider communion of saints than his own time and place. That search would prove to be agonizing.

Between Lancaster and Rome

*F*rom 1829 until 1853 Nevin was the most productive of any time during his surprisingly long life. He went to teach at Western Seminary in Pittsburgh as a young man of twenty-six. By the time he had turned fifty he had resettled on native turf in central Pennsylvania, established Mercersburg Seminary as one of the most creative theological schools in North America, and was also wrestling with issues that some today might consider a midlife crisis. In 1853 the trustees of Marshall College (the German Reformed school in Mercersburg) and the trustees of Franklin College (a Lutheran school in Lancaster) agreed to a merger that resulted in a new merged institution: Franklin and Marshall College. The overseers of each institution also agreed to locate the new college in the more populous city of Lancaster, arguably the capital of Pennsylvanian German culture, which embraced Lutheran, Reformed, and Anabaptist subgroups. Although Nevin worried about the control of the Lancaster college, as president of Marshall College since 1840 he was also intimately involved in the negotiations and supported the move. The plan held out the possibility of setting Marshall College on a securer financial foundation. But it also opened the possibility of a new board and administration that would allow anti-Mercersburg elements in the German Reformed Church to oust Nevin. Nevin decided not to make the move to Lancaster. In 1852 he tendered his resignation as president of

Marshall College (though he served until 1853), the same year that he stepped down as chief contributor to and informal editor of the *Mercersburg Review*. The previous year, 1851, Nevin had resigned as professor of theology at Mercersburg Seminary. The golden anniversary of his birth, in other words, brought a return to those melancholy days of bodily and psychological torments he had experienced as an adolescent and young man. Instead of coming into his own, at midcareer Nevin was entering a period characterized by religious doubt, illness, and spiritual gloom.

As Nevin explained to a fellow Marshall College faculty member, the man who would eventually write his biography, "the main difficulty . . . that lay in the way of further official duty of any kind in the Church, was the precarious condition of his health, which was very much broken down."[1] In that admission Nevin summoned up basic realities of his own life. His health was still a problem; not one day passed without physical pain from his stomach and liver. Nevin was also exhausted. After thirteen years of presiding over Marshall College, teaching full-time at the seminary, participating in the assemblies of the German Reformed Church as one of its most gifted officers, and after four years of writing for and assisting in the production of a new theological journal, he had exerted himself beyond the capacities of most men even in good health. Nevin was also the head of an extended family for whom he cared and was wont to make ample provision. A move to Lancaster would involve not simply the relocation of his own library and papers, but also the entire Nevin clan, the thought of which undoubtedly made him even more tired.

As significant as these physical factors were in Nevin's resignation, the spiritual were more so. Nevin's exposure of the vapid state of contemporary American Protestant church life had taken a severe toll. Like other nineteenth-century Protestants who found in Roman Catholicism a balm for Protestantism's rootlessness and cacophony, Nevin's understanding of Christianity as churchly and sacramental caused him to look with disgust upon American Protestantism. Many, even his wife, wondered if Nevin was also headed to Rome. To one family friend, Nevin explained that he was "greatly troubled with the claims of the Catholic Church. . . . It has become for me a question of life and death. One great object of disengaging myself from all past responsibilities has been that I might be more free to examine it."[2] At the same time, the religious question was intimately bound up with Nevin's deteriorating health. His biographer, Theodore Appel, later explained that Nevin thought he was going to die. Settling the issue of whether to remain a Protestant or convert to Catholicism involved a decision about where to be buried.

In the end, after a two-year soul-searching theological crisis Nevin did not convert to Rome. He believed that historic Protestantism could still be recovered in the German Reformed Church. But it was a close call. Furthermore, Nevin's crisis over the church question did not resolve unambiguously the doctrinal trajectory he had plotted by his own teaching on the incarnation and the nature of the church and his later efforts to trace lines of continuity from the early church, through medieval Catholicism, to Protestantism. Even so, to grapple with the issues with which Nevin wrestled is to understand even better his frustration with the form of Protestantism that was emerging as the mainstream in the United States. That Nevin did not convert, given his doubts and attempted solutions, may owe as much to that tethered thread connecting him to the Presbyterian Church at Middle Spring of his youth as to his impressive efforts to understand the latest European scholarship and supply Protestantism with a less wooden theological foundation.

Weary in Doing

To say that Nevin single-handedly carried the German Reformed Church for thirteen years on his back would be an overstatement. But the assertion is sufficiently accurate to suggest how hard the Mercersburg professor worked during the most productive period of his life—likely to the point of burnout. Of course, Nevin was not alone— the Mercersburg Theology itself was a two-man effort involving the labors of Philip Schaff almost as much as Nevin's. At the same time, the American half of the theological team was at the center of German Reformed institutional life all the while he was trying to work out the doctrines of the incarnation and the church.

Since 1840 Nevin had been teaching the major portion of the curriculum at Mercersburg Seminary, which included Bible, theology, church history, and practical theology. The call to Schaff to join the faculty in 1844 lessened Nevin's burden, relieving him of church history, but he still had plenty to do. He served as president of Marshall College since 1841, when Frederick A. Rauch, the president upon Nevin's arrival to Mercersburg, suddenly died. This post involved a seemingly endless list of responsibilities, including fund-raising, plans for buildings, curriculum oversight, and teaching moral philosophy to undergraduates. For many denominational college presidents, administering a school and teaching the senior year capstone course was a full-time job. But in addition to constant labor of trying to secure the college on a firmer financial footing and enhance its facilities, Nevin also served as the president of Marshall College's board of trustees, a duty that gave him greater exposure throughout the Eastern Synod of the German Reformed denomination but also made him the target of criticism and the scapegoat for perceived and actual failures. Had Nevin been more successful as a fund-raiser he would not have been forced to brush up on the algebra he learned at Union College. For when Marshall College's science professor in 1848 decided he could not endure the school's financial uncertainties and resigned, Nevin added mathematics to his many teaching duties.

Not to be forgotten are Nevin's responsibilities as a minister, an office he was required to hold if he were to oversee the college and teach at the seminary. He preached regularly at the Mercersburg German Reformed congregation that had almost called Presbyterian revivalist William Ramsay, who had employed the anxious bench. Here Nevin's success backfired, with his arguments against Ramsay's methods being sufficiently effective to prevent the call to Ramsay and forcing Nevin to conduct supply preaching. Being a minister in a Reformed communion involved not only these responsibilities in the local congregation, but also attending classical and synodical meetings and participating in the variety of committees that oversaw the affairs of the denomination.

In addition to his professional duties, Nevin had plenty to keep him busy at home. He and his wife, Martha, produced eight children in addition to providing a home for Catherine Jenkins, Nevin's mother-in-law. During their years in Pittsburgh the Nevins had three children. The first, Wilberforce (or Willie), was born in 1836 (died 1899) and went on to a distinguished career as newspaper editor and engineer, while also doing a stint of military service during the Civil War as a captain in the northern army. Following Wilberforce by a year was Alice (1837–1925), who remained single her whole life and served in a variety of church and cultural organizations in Lancaster through-out her adult life. Robert (1839–1906) was the last of the children born in Pittsburgh, and he became a priest in the Episcopal Church. Of the remaining five children, three lived short lives: George Herbert's was the shortest, dying only a year after his birth in 1840; Richard Cecil, born in 1843, died prematurely at the age of twenty-four; and John Nevin Jr., born in 1846, lived only two years longer than Richard, dying in 1872. Nevin and his wife had two more children, both daughters. Blanch (1841–1925), the fifth in sequence, also remained single and became a noted artist, poet, and sculptor in Lancaster's cultural circles. The only one of Nevin's daughters to marry was Martha Finley (1845–1935), who became the fourth wife of Robert Sayre, a prominent industrialist in Bethlehem, Pennsylvania. Clearly, the early deaths of three of Nevin's five sons undoubtedly contributed to his melancholy spirit. At the same time, the birth of all eight children during the ten years between 1836 and 1846, by no means an easy feat for Martha, meant that Nevin's period of greatest literary output coincided with the natural tumult of seven children varying in ages between one and eleven. No matter how much Nevin deferred domestic duties to his wife and mother-in-law, overseeing such a large home undoubtedly brought an extra range of duties that makes his writing from 1846 to 1852 all the more impressive.

How Nevin found time to work out and write his thoughts on the church is a puzzle. At the same time, his bibliography of published work was not obviously impressive. Compared to his colleague, Philip Schaff, or to his chief rival, Charles Hodge, Nevin's writings appear meager. *Anxious Bench* and *Mystical Presence* were not long works, the former a lengthy pamphlet, the latter a more substantial work of close to two hundred pages. On the surface, these titles appear to be the high point of his publishing career. The sheer originality of his 1840s' books is in and of itself remarkable given all the responsibilities that Nevin had. But one could easily reach the conclusion that his writing suffered because of administrative work.

This conclusion needs to be modified, however, once another important piece of Nevin's several duties is factored into the equation. In 1848 the Alumni Association of Marshall College sponsored a new theological quarterly, *Mercersburg Review*, as an indication of the school's intellectual stature and to provide an outlet for the nascent theological perspective associated with the town and seminary. The publisher, Henry A. Mish, an attorney in town, tried to persuade Nevin to add the journal to his responsibilities. He declined, but did agree to be what Appel terms "the leading contributor."[3] That phrase was apt but also was a huge understatement. Most readers assumed he was the editor because he wrote so many of its articles and reviews. Over the course of *Mercersburg Review*'s first six years Nevin contributed close to half of the journal's contents: 306 pages in 1849, 269 pages in 1850, 334 pages in 1851, 306 pages in 1852, and 334 pages in 1853, the year he stepped down as its primary correspondent. In and of themselves, these writings could by their length alone qualify as at least four if not six books, a prolific amount in so short a time.

Nevin's contributions to *Mercersburg Review* were not, however, simply padding to make up for a short list of book titles on his bibliography. The essays he wrote and published during the six years after *Mystical Presence* was published proved to be the chief means by which he endeavored to work out the implications of his theology. Even more, the writings from these years also plumbed the depths of Nevin's unstable faith. At first, Nevin continued to explore the ecclesial character of Christianity through the doctrine of the incarnation. He also extended his critique of contemporary American Protestantism with historical studies of the early church and the development of Christian creeds. But as the idea of the church as an organism increasingly involved the related notion of historical continuity throughout Christian history, Nevin was forced to come to terms with Joseph Berg's original complaint—namely, that the Mercersburg professor was becoming increasingly unable to defend Protestantism against the accusations of Roman Catholicism.

James Hastings Nichols, whose study of the Mercersburg Theology is as good an account of nineteenth-century American theological developments as exists, correctly observed that the organizing principle of Nevin's theology was "unmistakably" the doctrine of the incarnation. Nichols added that the christological emphasis of Mercersburg differed markedly from the other two dominant schools in American Protestant divinity—namely, the Princeton Theology and New England Congregationalism. In both cases, the debates and assertions of Old School Presbyterians and New Englanders centered on soteriology: the nature and extent of human depravity, the requirements of divine law, the imputation of Adam's sin and Christ's righteousness, and the efficacy of the atonement.[4] Where Nichols engages in excess is when he concludes that these classic lines of analysis in Reformed theology were to Nevin stale and worn out. What is easier to argue is that for Nevin Reformed orthodoxy as it had been mediated by the Puritans and their Presbyterian cousins was incapable of providing an adequate account of the church and its sacramental life. With the exception of Old School Presbyterians such as Louisville's Stuart Robinson or South Carolina's John B. Adger, whose writings did not appear to catch Nevin's attention, the dominant schools of American Protestant theology demonstrated little interest in the church question that Mercersburg's theologians were asking. That may also explain why these Presbyterian critiques of revivalism missed the issue of what such piety was doing to the church. As a result, Nevin had been compelled to turn in new directions, in this case to the incarnation and the church as the body of Christ, in order to find an adequate theological footing from which to launch a reorientation of American Protestantism.

The import of Christology continued to be a significant theme in Nevin's writings for *Mercersburg Review*. In an 1850 review of Robert I. Wilberforce, an Anglican priest, Nevin wrote with some optimism that "on all sides" the christological question, "embracing the true idea of the Church and its relation to the Savior's living person, is in truth the great question of the age, and carries in itself a power by which all the interests of religion are to be moulded hereafter into new shape."[5] Of course, this may have been wishful thinking, since it had been Nevin's own point in *Mystical Presence*, which in turn had helped to provide a theological justification for his extensive critique of American revivalism in *Anxious Bench*. Still, he looked for assistance wherever he could find it. And through reviews for Mercersburg's journal of record, Nevin continued to read up on and develop his own notions about the doctrine of Christ.

Three review essays in particular stand out from this period of soul-searching. The important question facing him in his christological formulation was the relationship between the newfound interest in the incarnation and the old Protestant divinity: was the idea of Christ's ongoing living presence in his church a supplement to the older teaching about his vicarious death and sacrifice for sin, or should it replace the older Reformed emphasis? At issue precisely was the relationship between creation and the new creation in Christ. Would Christ have taken human form if the fall had never happened? In other words, did the incarnation elevate the creation to an even higher plane than its originally sin-free constitution? In a review of R. C. Trench, a colleague of F. D. Maurice at King's College (England), whose lectures on the incarnation argued for contrast instead of continuity between the old and new approaches, Nevin appeared to find support for his own conception of Christ's humanity introducing a fundamentally new source of life to creation. Accordingly, the incarnation was not simply a mechanism for the atonement. Instead, as Nevin summarized Trench's teaching, "some of the profoundest teachers of the past . . . have rather affirmed that the Son of God would equally have taken man's nature, though of course under very different conditions, even if he had not fallen—that it lay in the everlasting purposes of God, quite irrespective of the fall."[6] Another review essay, this time of K. T. A. Liebner, a German Lutheran theologian who attempted to avoid the pitfalls of the Lutheran tendency toward Docetism and Reformed lapses into Ebionitism, also appeared to confirm Nevin's high estimate of the incarnation as the culmination of God's original design in creation. Liebner contended that the divine purpose in creation was full communion between God and humanity, and as such humanity was incomplete, even apart from the fall, until the coming of Christ.[7]

Nevin concluded his ongoing study of and reflection on Christology with a third article, this time on the writings of Julius Müller, another German Lutheran theologian. In Müller, Nevin encountered a strong rebuke to the views of Trench and Liebner. Müller believed that the two main views under consideration, the modern German and idealist one, which regarded Christ as the completion of the original creation, and the older soteriological one, which taught that Christ took human form to remedy the curse and consequences of human sin, could not be reconciled. He also argued that the idealist understanding tended toward the deification of humans and inevitably resulted in pantheism. The proper answer to the question "why did God become human?" then, was the soteriological problem introduced by sin, not the stunted condition of the original creation. Nevin summarized Müller's position by stating that it was "only the fact of sin in truth, apprehended in its world-vast solemnity and significance, that furnished an adequate reason for the highest act of God's love." A proper understanding of sin and human need alone could account for every effort "to understand or interpret the christological mystery."[8]

This was virtually the last time that Nevin would address the significance and nature of Christology in a sustained way, a subject that had absorbed his interests since at least 1846 with the publication of *Mystical Presence*. And it was an unsatisfying culmination of theological development. Nevin was not entirely clear which of the two views he favored. As it stood, by giving Müller the last word the Mercersburg theologian could be read to be saying that the older soteriological view was the right one. Still, even more curious is why the topic would fade from Nevin's horizon. Nichols even goes as far as to conclude that with this review of Müller the Mercersburg Theology's whole doctrine of the incarnation "ran out into a question mark and remained unresolved."[9]

One explanation for Nevin's silence on the incarnation was that at roughly the same time as this review of Müller was published, the Mercersburg theologian was plunging into the depths of despair. The Müller review appeared in the spring 1851 number of *Mercersburg*

Review. The very next issue (July) contained Nevin's reflections on the Gorham case in the Church of England. By practically all of his contemporaries' and biographers' reckoning, this was the forum in which the question of Roman Catholic claims for the antiquity and authority of the church caught up with Nevin. In particular, the Gorham case involved the theological question of baptism's efficacy. Not only that, it was also bound up with church-state relations and the prerogatives of church power. George C. Gorham was a vicar in the Church of England who ran afoul of his bishop, Henry Phillpotts. When Gorham became eligible for a promotion and increased salary, Phillpotts refused to endorse the vicar on the grounds that Gorham's views on baptismal grace were heretical. Gorham held that baptismal regeneration, a notion championed by Anglo-Catholics, was at odds with the teaching of the Church of England. Eventually, he appealed the ruling of Phillpotts to the civil courts, a process that led to the vindication of his views. The court ruled that Gorham's teaching fell within the bounds of the Thirty-Nine Articles. Occurring as it did during the peak of the Oxford Movement, when high-church Anglicans were reconsidering Rome's claims of authority and when the Church of England appeared to be losing its own spiritual powers to Parliament, the Gorham case was the proverbial last straw. Many high-church Anglicans interpreted this episode as a clear sign of the Church of England's deficient ecclesiology and used it as a justification for converting to Rome.

The Gorham case had a similar effect on Nevin. It shook him to the core by raising the question whether Protestantism owned a doctrine of the church sufficient for Christianity's comprehensive truth. "The force of the question in the end is nothing less than this," Nevin opined, "whether the original catholic doctrine concerning the Church, as it stood in universal authority through all ages before the Reformation, is to be received and held still as a necessary part of the christian [*sic*] faith, or deliberately rejected and refused as an error dangerous to men's souls at war with the Bible?"[10] For six years German Reformed ministers like Philadelphia's Joseph Berg had been warning that Nevin's views would result in capitulation to Roman Catholicism. It is no wonder that, with the weight of the Gorham case pressing down on his weary and painful frame, in 1851 Nevin began to withdraw from his official duties in the German Reformed Church.

The Search for Mother Church

Over the next three years, while Nevin backed away from his educational responsibilities, he also tried to address the question raised in the Anglican crisis. In many respects this period of reflection was a further outworking of Nevin's doubts about low-church Protestantism that he had exhibited in *Mystical Presence*. Moreover, it resulted in a similar line of investigation, namely, contrasting the past with Protestant practices in the present. In his earlier work on the Lord's Supper Nevin enjoyed the safety provided by defense for his views from sixteenth-century and seventeenth-century Protestant sources. On the matters of church authority and sacramental grace Nevin's studies moved back to early Christianity, a subject he had broached in *Mystical Presence* but ever so slightly. Now he felt compelled to evaluate the entire sweep of Christian history, not simply the recent differences between Catholics and Protestants, but also those between ancients and moderns. Nevin had to know that such investigation would further alienate him from mainstream American Protestantism of the Puritan and Baptistic variety. This explains why so many of those intimately associated with Nevin believed his conversion to Rome was inevitable. But his historical investigation was designed not simply to store up more ammunition against revivalistic Protestantism. Its aim was also to discover the true nature and capacity of the Christian ministry.

In many respects, the Gorham controversy turned out to be the case of the anxious bench all over again. Nevin regarded Gorham as another example of low-church Anglicanism in which sacramental grace had to be abandoned in order to avoid the dangers of Rome. He declared that the Puritan party in the Church of England with its "Baptistic tendencies" had taken ground that rendered the prayer book's teaching on baptism "a pure superstition."[11] By making the grace of baptism conditional upon the faith of the recipient, Gorham had raised poignantly whether "baptism is to remain a sacrament at all for Protestantism, in the old universal church sense."[12] Just as Nevin's critique of revivalism had pushed him to develop an alternative, namely, the system of the catechism, which in turn led to his study of the gracious character of the Lord's Supper, so the Gorham case illustrated anew the nonsacramental and nonchurchly character of modern Protestantism, what Nevin referred to as Puritan. "Evangelical Puritanism under the drapery of Episcopal forms," he wrote, reduced the divine element in Christianity to "the way of precept" rather than conceiving of it as "in the very bosom of the system itself."[13]

But instead of leading to a systematic exposition of baptismal grace, akin to *Mystical Presence*, Nevin isolated the more basic question of the church. Faith in the church, he explained, was not simply a persuasion and confidence that "certain arrangements" in polity or liturgy were of divine appointment. The question of sacramental grace went deeper. Was the church a "living supernatural fact, back of all such arrangements, having its ground and force in the mystery of the Incarnation, according to the order of the ancient creed, and communicating to the marks and signs by which it is made visible through every particle of virtue that is in them for any such end"?[14] Nevin believed the answer had to be yes. "We must believe in a divine church," Nevin insisted, "in order to believe in divine sacraments, or in a divine ministry under any form."[15] Indeed, without a conviction and understanding of its divine constitution, the institutional church became nothing more than the American Tract Society or "any other outward league of evangelical sects!" Baptism, in other words, was the husk, and the church was the kernel in the Gorham case: "All turns here on the *idea* of the Church. . . . Is the idea of a really supernatural constitution under this name, as it once universally prevailed, a sober truth for Christian faith, or has it become a dangerous though beautiful *fiction*?"[16]

This question of the church's status as a divine institution led Nevin once again to an investigation of Christian history. Was this notion of the church as a mediator of supernatural grace present in Christianity from the start? Or had Roman Catholicism foisted it onto Western Christianity, with the Protestant Reformation recovering the ancient church's purer teaching (the position of Mercersburg's critics as early as Schaff's inaugural address in *Principle of Protestantism*)? During the torment of his indecision about moving to Lancaster and his growing frustration with unchurchly Protestantism—now not simply in the United States but even infecting the Church of England— Nevin set out to study the church fathers and the earliest forms of Christianity.

Of course, Nevin's quest for the historical church had begun as early as *Mystical Presence*. One section of that book prefigured his later studies by comparing Puritan understandings of Christ's presence in the Lord's Supper with those of specific church fathers. He followed that initial foray with a series of articles in *Mercersburg Review* on the Apostles' Creed. In a manner similar to his book on the sacrament, Nevin explored the historical origins of the creed, the later attestation by Catholics and Protestants alike to its binding address, and its articles' meaning. The series also provided him with another opportunity to work out the organic nature of Christianity and the church, with Christ incarnate being the life source of the church and the creed functioning as the embodiment of that vitality. The Apostles' Creed, Nevin wrote, "represents not a system of thought, but a system of life. . . . It is the free spontaneous externalization of the christian [*sic*] consciousness, the substance of living christianity [*sic*] as a whole, in its primary form of faith." As such, the early church was not the "artificer that hammered" the creed into shape, "part by part, and one article after another." Instead, the church was "the organ, through whose life as an actual fact it brought itself to pass."[17] One of the practical implications that Nevin drew late in the series from the significance of the creed was that it functioned as the lens through which the Bible needed to be understood, not the other way around. Again, this was an assertion sure to upset the Bible-only wing of American Protestantism. Nevin acknowledged this dimension of his argument. But his point had much to do with the way in which his American Protestant peers were using the Bible and the implicit hermeneutic of private judgment to cut themselves off from the historic pattern of faith, from the ancients through Rome and down to the Reformers.

Nevin concluded the four-part series with an essay entitled "Puritanism and the Creed." In many respects this piece put the others in perspective. His aim all along was to show, as he had in *Mystical Presence*, that modern Protestantism was a novelty, a deformed variety of Christianity that had departed from the ways of historic Protestantism because it was unmindful of standing upon the soldiers of saints who had gone before. Nevin thus implied that the divide between modern and historic Christianity was greater than that between Protestants and Roman Catholics. Nevin articulated that division in a manner reminiscent of the binary categories he used in the conclusion to *Anxious Bench*:

> Here are two *minds*, two theological habits, the old catholic consciousness and the modern Puritan consciousness, "having no kindred spirit," each of which claims to be, not at once the Bible, (neither the Creed nor the New England Primer is *that*,) but still the only true and safe preparation for coming to the right sense of the Bible. . . . *I* build upon the Scriptures, it exclaims; the Creed is a human production, and teaches false doctrine; follow *me*. Truly, a very great and solemn demand! Let it be heard with all becoming seriousness and respect. Still, we tremble at the thought of such a deep rupture with the old Christian consciousness, and venture to ask: By what authority doest *thou* this thing, and who *gave* thee *such* authority?[18]

Nevin stressed that he did not want to be misunderstood. He conceded that Puritanism's Bible-only faith had many merits. But so did Catholicism. And as of 1849 Nevin was prepared to believe that both the one extreme (the Bible plus private judgment) and the other (church and outward authority) could be harmonized. Still, the contemporary descendants of New England Puritanism had a duty to search for that agreement, for without it the Puritan faith was "at war with reason and right."[19]

Two years later, when Nevin returned to the topic of early Christianity, he was much less convinced that harmonization was possible. By 1851 the stakes had been raised from whether America's low-church Protestantism was out of step with the faith of Calvin and Ursinus to whether Protestantism was inherently suspicious of the church as a mediator of grace. A contributing factor was the wave of anti-

Catholicism among American Protestants that associated Rome with everything un-American—papal tyranny versus individual freedom, religious superstition versus enlightened inquiry, ecclesiastical hierarchy versus popular sovereignty—the list of contrasts could go on. This anti-Catholic prejudice was in many respects one of the chief catalysts for Nevin's theological development. It characterized the initial reaction to his and Schaff's mid-1840s arguments in the likes of Joseph Berg. The latter held the view, common to many Protestant apologists, that Roman Catholicism was a perversion of the earliest Christian faith and that the Reformation was a restoration of ancient Christianity after the so-called Dark Ages. Initially, Nevin's response to such Protestant triumphalism had been to show that modern Protestantism differed significantly from its original convictions and impulses. By the 1850s he took up the challenge of defending Rome itself. He did so by looking precisely at the earliest Christian expressions and comparing them with Roman Catholicism. The point of the comparison was to see whether the anti-Catholic prejudice of his Protestant peers was plausible. Was it truly the case that the faith of American Protestantism, which stressed the Bible-only view and the rights of private judgment, was the repristination of the ancient church?

In a three-part series written in 1851 for *Mercersburg Review* on early Christianity, Nevin weighed in against any number of recent expressions of Protestant sanctimony regarding Roman Catholic superstition and bigotry. His chief point in these essays was to challenge precisely the "Puritan" theory of church history, a term with broad application not simply to New England Congregationalists but also Baptists, Presbyterians, German Reformed, and low-church Episcopalians. The basic idea was that Christianity began unadulterated as a religion solely of the Bible and individual interpretation. Worship resembled that of New England or Scotland. No papacy, priesthood, liturgy, or superstitious ceremonies encumbered genuine Christianity. This pure form of the Christian religion lasted until only the third century when "the prelatical system with its whole sea of corruptions and abominations" began to prevail.[20] This system turned the church into a synagogue of Satan, thus requiring the Reformation of the sixteenth century to recover the early church's pure and simple devotion and unencumbered church.

In one of his most compelling critiques of this form of Protestant myopia, Nevin raised the question of whether the Puritan theory actually made any sense of the wonder of the incarnation, the earthly ministry of Christ, and the witness of his apostles. "The whole course" of the early church's history, he wrote, "seemed to show clearly, that the powers of a higher world were at work in the glorious movement, and that it embodied in itself the will and counsel of heaven itself for the full accomplishment of the end towards which it reached." In fact, many Christian apologists cited the success of the early church as "one of the external proofs of its divine origin, a real supernatural seal of its truth."[21] But after such an amazing and divinely blessed beginning, the work of Christ and the apostles virtually came to naught "hardly [before] the last of the apostles [had] gone to heaven, before signs of apostasy began to show themselves in the bosom of the infant church." So far did the church depart from the truth of the gospel in Puritan accounts that its fall was not only partial and transient but universal "in its collective and corporate character, with an apostasy that was to reach through twelve hundred years." Thus, Nevin concluded, "Satan in the end fairly prevailed over Christ."[22] Nevin believed that this implication of the Puritan theory was enough to show that it was wrong.

Aside from the intellectual difficulties attending this understanding of Christian history, Nevin made explicit that Puritanism differed from the early church in six significant ways. The first concerned the church, whether it was a human institution designed basically to teach or whether it was a divine institution that actually mediated grace by virtue of membership in it. The rest of the differences stemmed directly from this one: the ministry (pastors as "religious counsellors and teachers" versus being part of a "divinely established hierarchy"); the sacraments (gestures of the faithful versus disclosures of divine grace); the rule of faith (the Bible interpreted privately versus Scripture interpreted corporately by the church); the order of doctrine (theological novelty versus the Apostles' Creed); and faith in miracles (supernaturalism versus rationalism).[23] This last point was the newest in Nevin's litany of charges against Puritanism, and by it he was referring to the early church's belief in signs and wonders that accompanied the spread of Christianity as opposed to the charge of superstition that many American Protestants hurled against Roman Catholics. This series of contrasts led inevitably to the conclusion that "no scheme of Protestantism . . . can be vindicated, on the ground of its being a repristination simply of what Christianity was immediately after the age of the Apostles." Furthermore, Nevin added, "to take away from the church its divine historical existence," to place a large set of brackets around the period from the fifth to the sixteenth centuries, "is to turn it into a wretched Gnostic abstraction. To conceive of it as the mere foot-ball of Satan from the beginning, is to suppose that Christ was either totally unmindful of his own word that the gates of hell should not prevail against it, or else unable to make his word good."[24]

In Nevin's second historical series on the ancient church, church father Cyprian, the third-century bishop of Carthage, was the focus of study. This four-part series mainly added depth to the point already made, namely, that modern Protestantism was far removed from the earliest Christian forms of faith. In the first article Nevin sketched Cyprian's life. In the second he looked at the persecution that the church suffered and the controversies that ensued over how to address believers who had forsaken their faith in the face of such opposition. Nevin could not help observing that in the context of persecution membership in the church became an issue of life and death and its ministry a source of hope for Christians under siege. "Cyprian lays so much stress on the solemnity of penance and absolution in the case of the lapsed, as the necessary condition of their being restored to her communion and peace," Nevin wrote, because of the bishop's understanding of the church as "the real organ and medium of salvation."[25] Still, the historical circumstances that prompted Cyprian to require penance from the lapsed and to make absolution a formal rite of public restitution was not Nevin's main point. Cyprian's larger significance was to represent a high view of the church pervading the entire span of early Christianity. In this regard, Cyprian's faith was not significantly different from Augustine. According to Nevin, "no one had ever a deeper sense of [the church's] glorious significance. It lay at the foundation of his spiritual life. It formed the very hinge of his conversion."[26]

Yet, even as Nevin wrote these two series of articles, he could read in the religious press of the United States ongoing attacks upon Roman Catholicism for holding a view of the church like that of the church fathers. He singled out an article in the *New York Observer*, which opined that the "introduction of *a sacramental religion*" into Christianity was "a complete perversion of the gospel" because it removed the necessity of "an intelligent reception of the truth" and rested the "whole affair" in the hands of a priest. The writer for the *Observer* even ridiculed "some learned men in the Protestant churches [who] are seeking to exhume from the catacombs of a past age, and impose upon the wonder-loving credulity of the nineteenth century."[27] Nevin appeared less to take offense from the *Observer* than to interpret the editorial as a sign of his own vindication. Here was an understanding of Protestantism "which boldly repudiates as an apostasy and mystery of iniquity the whole sense of what Christianity was taken to be in the beginning, back at least to the very age next following that of the Apostles." Nevin elaborated his gripe with his American Protestant contemporaries:

> For it is not with this or that questionable point only, that the issue of the N.Y. Observer is concerned. It goes at once to the very foundations of the ancient faith. The idea of a sacramental religion, we are told, overturns the Gospel. A ministry exercising in any true sense Divine powers, is taken to be such a conception as opens the way at once for the full reign of the Antichrist. Why? Only of course because the *Church*, the proper home of such a ministry and sacraments of such supernatural force, is not believed to be the grand and awfully solemn mystery which it was held to be in the beginning. All comes to this at last.[28]

By the end of the series in the fall of 1852 Nevin was clearly growing weary of the tension between modern Protestantism and historic Christianity. In his previous historical inquiries, say in *Mystical Presence* or his articles on the Apostles' Creed, he had usually held out hope in the Protestantism of the sixteenth and seventeenth centuries. Puritanism may have been a departure from the early church, Nevin seemed to console himself, but it was also a break from historic Protestantism. Such lines of historical development allowed him a way to remain a Protestant. But by the end of the series on Cyprian, Nevin's tone had changed markedly. He concluded that not even sixteenth-century and seventeenth-century Protestantism could measure up to the ancient church. "Early Christianity," he concluded, "was in its constitutional elements, not Protestantism, but Catholicism."[29] He followed with a line reminiscent of the Princeton Theology's common-sense apologetics and theological method. "Our concern has been simply to give a true picture of the facts," he wrote, not to offer a justification for Protestantism as a legitimate expression of historic Christianity.[30] Nevin was obviously aware of the larger import of his study, namely, that the only place to find the sacramental and churchly conception of the church that he advocated was in the Roman Catholic Church. Nevertheless he concluded the series on a dour note for Protestants, hoping to find some vindication for their faith. It is no wonder that many of the people closest to Nevin believed he was going to convert to Rome.

Still, Nevin had significant reservations about Roman Catholicism. If forced to choose between Puritanism and Rome, he could clearly sound like a convert in the making. But during these same critical years between 1849, when *Mercersburg Review* started, and 1853, when he retired from all things Mercersburg, Nevin published a steady stream of reflections on Roman Catholicism. These pieces revealed that his Protestant faith went even deeper than his anguish over the state of American Protestantism.

Some of his objections to Catholicism were cultural and social. For instance, in a review of J. Balmes's *Protestantism and Catholicity Compared in Their Effects on the Civilization of Europe* (1851), Nevin demonstrated a charity to Rome that was distinct from the prevailing Whig view in the United States, which associated Protestantism with the advance of civilization and Catholicism as a form of cultural barbarity. He conceded many of Balmes's points about the various cultural, educational, and political achievements that Europe enjoyed, thanks to Roman Catholicism's herculean efforts in attempting to preserve the glories of Roman antiquity. Still, Nevin believed that Balmes's contrast of the two versions of Christianity lacked balance, as if assessing the virtues of Catholicism and Protestantism were a zero-sum game with all prizes going to the winner. Instead, Nevin recognized real and substantial accomplishments in the church before the Reformation but at the same time believed that Protestantism stood on the shoulders of Rome's achievements. "Our faith in Protestantism," he wrote, "is conditioned by the assumption, that the succession of the old church life still flows truly and vigorously in its veins."[31] In other words, Protestantism and Catholicism were both contributors to the project of European civilization. Rome's part was substantial and functioned well for a time. Protestantism communicated "a real onward impulse . . . to the life of the modern world." However much modernity was lacking, it nonetheless demonstrated the vitality of the Protestant faith.[32]

Having conceded in his review of Balmes that material prosperity was "no sure sign or proof of social improvement," Nevin also noted Rome's spiritual defects. These observations came to light in an exchange with Orestes Brownson, a former Unitarian and transcendentalist who became one of Rome's prize American converts and stalwart apologists during the middle decades of the nineteenth century. In a review from 1850 of a variety of Brownson's essays on Catholicism, Nevin mixed evaluations of the author's own spiritual constitution with assessments of the relationship between Protestantism and Catholicism. In the former class of comments, Nevin could not help regarding Brownson's conversion to Rome and his concomitant total submission to the church's authority as a form of Puritanism in reverse, the act of a "Puritan Romanist." At the one extreme was the Puritan view of the Bible-only and private judgment, and at the other was the complete authority of the pope in all things. Nevin explained Brownson's defect: "The alternative with him is, law from within or law from without; one *or* the other, and one always so as to exclude the other." Nevin believed that Brownson had convinced himself that Puritanism logically resulted in rationalism and nihilism and that the only alternative to save Christianity was to accept "the opposite rule, as the only form in which it is possible to have part at all in a really supernatural religion." In reaction against his own Puritan past, Nevin argued, Brownson had come to the conviction that "the best Christian" was one who "most resolutely brings both his reason and will into captivity to the authority of this Church, as it is found embodied from age to age in the voice of its hierarchy." Nevin added that Brownson was playing "the very *Yankee* himself in this new game . . . making a king still of his own mind, and wilfully forcing his very will itself, to fall in with the new theory of faith he is thus brought to embrace."[33]

Nevin's observations on the personal contours of Brownson's mind were connected to his more general complaints about Roman Catholicism. The Mercersburg theologian's first objection concerned Rome's subjection of human nature. Catholicism made authority everything and freedom nothing. As such, human nature was completely passive in the reception of religious truth. While Protestantism provided an outlet for private judgment and will, Rome crushed all dissent: "Place the law as an objective force on the outside wholly of the intelligence and will of those who are its subjects, and at once you convert it into an abstract nothing." Protestantism "formed a legitimate and absolutely necessary reaction and protest."[34] Nevin also objected to Catholicism because its assertion of the church's complete authority left no room for organic development. Rome's authority was "mechanical" and "magical." "Humanity," Nevin explained, "accomplishes its destiny by organic co-operation, carried forward in the form of history. Truth is brought to pass for it, through the medium of its own activity, the whole working towards its appointed end by the joint ministry of the parts, in such a way however, as to be something more always than these separately taken."[35] The heavy hand of Rome's rule, however, prohibited such organic cooperation, thus again making Protestantism a necessary corrective.

Here Nevin drew upon the incarnation to explain his criticism of Rome's abstract authority in a way similar, he admitted, to the abstraction of a mechanical notion of biblical authority. In Christ the supernatural entered the natural, and that supernatural life continued to give vigor and sustenance to the church as the body of Christ. "If his incarnation involved a real entrance into [the world's] life," Nevin explained, "it must stand in living inward relation . . . with its entire

159

organization and history under every other view."[36] In other words, Christ's relation to the church was not simply outward, external, or objective, a Gnostic conception that denies his union with human existence. Both Catholicism and Puritanism offered up an abstract religious authority, one in the church hierarchy, the other in a wooden biblicism. Nevin argued that historic Protestantism represented a mediating position, one that incorporated Rome's order, which verged on absolutism, and Puritanism's freedom, which invited anarchy. This placement of the Reformation on the spectrum of Western Christianity was a function of Nevin's quirky idea of historical development, which was an outworking of his understanding of the incarnation. "God moves in history," he asserted.[37] This made it impossible to freeze in time a particular form of Christianity or church life. But because Christ was mystically present in the ongoing ministry of the church, change, correction, and reform were the necessary means of transition for "the Church of God into a higher and better state."[38] In other words, Nevin continued to cling to the belief that Protestantism, purged of its own excesses and reconnected to parts of its Catholic past, offered hope for a better church.

In a subsequent exchange, in which Brownson charged that Nevin's understanding of the incarnation would inevitably result in pantheism, the Mercersburg theologian tried to explain again his objections to Rome's claims to absolute authority. In the same way that Nevin was trying to avoid the extremes of pantheism and deism by articulating theism's proper understanding of God's organic involvement with the world, so he hoped to mediate between Rome and Puritan conceptions of religious authority. "We acknowledge the need of something more here than the Bible," Nevin wrote, "thus made the sport and plaything of private judgment." Christianity, he added, "is a living fact in the world" and so carries "its own evidence and its own authority." This evidence and authority constituted the church: "We own and confess the authority of this body, the one holy catholic Church of the Creed, as both legitimate and necessary for the proper constitution of the Christian faith in all ages and lands."[39] To Protestants who claimed that the Bible was sufficient, as ministered by the ongoing illumination of the Holy Spirit, Nevin again responded that

160

this conception was too abstract and inorganic. He explained that the authority of the Spirit "is to be expected and sought, like all other manifestations of God's will in the world, not under an abstract character, but under the form of concrete life; that is, in the bosom of the Church, by which and through which only it comes to such revelation."[40] But if Puritanism failed on this ground, so too did Roman Catholicism. The pope's authority was as mechanical as the Bible's. To be truly from God, religious authority "must legitimate itself by entering the sphere of the life it seeks to rule; it must take concrete form in the world; it must win for itself a living human activity in the social system, which in the case before us becomes the Church, whereby it may have access to individual thought and will in conformity with the general law of our nature." If the pope's decisions and utterances could be understood to come from the Holy Spirit in this way, Nevin would "listen patiently to the plea that is put in for [the pontiff's] infallibility." But this was not the Catholic view. Instead the pope's infallibility transcended "the process of humanity," ceased to be "concrete and historical," and so lacked "objective mediation in the constitution of the world."[41]

Nevin's ammunition against Romanism was an acquired taste, but it had enough force to keep him from conversion until 1852, when in an exchange of correspondence with Brownson it looked as if he was only shooting blanks. Brownson and other Catholics had been following Nevin's series on early Christianity in *Mercersburg Review*, and to them, like to so many other readers, he sounded as if he was ready to abandon the Protestant fold. Nevin confessed to Brownson in late summer of 1852:

> My Protestantism, you will see thus, is of the poorest sort. I am no longer fit for the defence of its interest in any vigorous style. For this reason, any controversy of a public sort in its behalf, either with yourself or any other champion of Romanism, ought to be in other hands. I find so much of the truth and right on your side, and so much of falsehood and wrong on ours as usually held, that I have no heart for any controversy of the sort, and dread being betrayed by it into the misery of making common cause with principles and tendencies

which all good Protestants no less than Catholics are bound to oppose and hate.[42]

Six months later, as he was relinquishing the last of his duties in the German Reformed Church's college and seminary, Nevin wrote to James Alphonsus McMaster, another Protestant convert to Rome and editor of the *Freeman's Journal*, that he found it more and more difficult to resist the authority of the Catholic Church. But he was still at sea:

> I see well the necessity of something far beyond mere logic or natural evidence to bring the mind to a clear apprehension of the true mystery of the Christian Church and a full and firm acquiescence in it for the purposes of salvation. Meditation and prayer, rather than any dialectic process, must bring to a solution at least the great problem with which I feel myself confronted now every day, and I may almost say every waking hour.[43]

An important difference between 1850 and 1853 was a significant change in Nevin's perception of Rome. In his initial review of Brownson in early 1850 Nevin had asserted that "Romanism, as it now stands, seems to be anything but a facsimile of primitive Christianity, and the evidences of change may be said to meet us from almost every page of Church history." No two centuries of Roman Catholic history "appear to be alike," he complained.[44] But three years later he had come to a markedly different conclusion. After the seven articles on the early church Nevin could not reaffirm his position against Brownson. "Early Christianity," he wrote roughly midway between the letters just quoted to Brownson and McMaster, was "in its constitutional elements, not Protestantism, but Catholicism."[45] In effect, Nevin knew that if apologists for Protestantism were to succeed, they would have to find an argument other than one that regarded Christian history between 500 and 1500 as the Dark Ages. He also knew that an appeal to historical development might help to solve the dilemma. But the problem for him was more than a theoretical one; it was becoming personal.

For some time Nevin had been sensitive to anti-Catholic bigotry since it so often relied upon a caricature of Roman Catholicism and also involved a flawed ecclesiology that denied the church's mediatorial character. He even became the object of some of this prejudice because many Protestants assumed that to go soft on Catholicism, as Nevin appeared to do in trying to recover its high view of the church and sacraments, was akin to giving up the achievements of the Protestant Reformation and the Protestant identity of American society. In a study of nineteenth-century American Protestant converts to Rome, Jennie Franchot observed that the assertion by New England Protestants of a national Protestant culture in reaction to the growing presence of Roman Catholic immigrants during the 1840s and 1850s ironically revealed the "spiritual deficiencies and psychological pressures of Protestant culture."[46] This was certainly true in Nevin's case, where the more his Protestant critics attacked, the more he saw Protestantism's flimsy ecclesiology. After an extended period of strenuous labor, both in trying to achieve institutional stability in the German Reformed Church and in attempting to elaborate a set of doctrines that would restore Protestantism's eviscerated understanding of the church, he was worn out. The only glimmer of hope in early 1853 as he extricated himself from Marshall College and Mercersburg Seminary was the contrast he had drawn in his letter to Brownson between Protestantism "as usually held," that is, the Protestantism of the low-church variety, and some notion of historic succession that could justify Protestantism as part of a providential process of improving the church. The question was whether he had the energy to fan that ember of Protestant faith into a flicker.

The Christian Ministry

After 1852, as Nevin entered into a period of retirement, his literary output dropped significantly. In fact, he would never regain the productivity of the six-year period following the publication of *Mystical Presence*. But for the time being, as Nevin celebrated his fiftieth birthday, his future was uncertain. While onlookers feared his conversion to Rome, Nevin himself grappled with his own mortality. His health was so poor that he believed he was near the end of his life. His reasons for retiring were not simply spiritual, but also physical.

The reading public had little to go on if wanting to chart Nevin's religious status. In 1853 he published only two essays, both in *Mercersburg Review* and both having to do with his last official duties for Marshall College. The first, "Franklin and Marshall College," was an address given at the opening of the newly consolidated institution in Lancaster. The second, "Man's True Destiny," was Nevin's charge to the graduating class at Marshall College, the last to receive a degree from the Mercersburg institution. From the perspective of the history of higher education in the United States, neither speech was remarkable, though in the former Nevin did make some notable points about New England's dominance in American intellectual life and the need for Pennsylvanians and especially the Pennsylvania Germans to pull their own weight. Furthermore, from the perspective of Nevin's own spiritual anxiety, neither address yielded any indication of his plight. To say that Nevin was being reclusive would be an overstatement. But clearly the studies that had stemmed from his own doubts had dried up. The man who had once been a font of theological creativity and keen historical awareness was now mute.

Still, Nevin did not convert to Rome. His reasoning remains a mystery since he had sounded so definite about Rome's superiority at the close of his essays on the early church. His own autobiography stopped at 1840, the year he left Pittsburgh to join the German Reformed Church. Other evidence to illuminate his resolve is hard to find. But 1854 appears to be the turning point. During that year he wrote only two pieces and preached one ordination sermon. Nevertheless, these provide a window into his mind, and they reveal a growing resolve and measure of comfort with his ongoing identity as a Protestant. None of these statements provides the clinching argument to justify Protestantism, nor do they reveal a line of inquiry that helped Nevin come to terms with Protestantism's relation to the rest of Christian history. They simply reveal a man still thinking like a Protestant and still hoping to recover early Protestantism's churchly character.

One of the essays to reveal Nevin's spiritual condition in 1854 was a review of Robert Wilberforce's *Doctrine of the Holy Eucharist* (1853). Nevin and Wilberforce had been traveling down similar theological paths owing to their joint interest in sacramental theology and a common endeavor to root the sacraments in the doctrine of the incarnation. Wilberforce, like Nevin, had also felt the inadequacy of Protestantism, even of high-church Anglicanism, and eventually converted to Rome at roughly the same time that Nevin was wrestling with a similar move. Despite their similarities, Nevin's review of Wilberforce's book drew upon Calvin and the Reformation in ways not seen in the Mercersburg theologian's writing since *Mystical Presence*. After having spent almost three years working through early Christian sources, Nevin's use of Calvin was indeed a surprise. Even more startling was his favorable use of the French Reformer. Nevin still complained of American Protestantism's poor showing. "New England itself must yet come" to see the importance of the church, he asserted, "if Christianity be not doomed to run itself out there into a barren death."[47] Here Nevin's lamentations did not possess the despair that they displayed two years earlier. The reason may have been that he recognized Calvin's doctrine of the Lord's Supper as a way for American Protestants to escape their feebleness. "The theory of Calvin," he explained, "if it can be maintained, would seem to be after all most truly conformed to the wants and conditions of the problem."[48] Then Nevin added in a few lines a revealing glimpse into the way he had handled Protestantism's differences with the early church. He conceded that Calvin "differs from the doctrine of the ancient Church. But must it not so differ, in order to be Protestant?" The question was whether the changes were "essential or simply accidental—the destruction of oneness and sameness absolutely, or such an outward diversity only as may resolve itself fairly into the laws of historical development and growth."[49] Nevin suggested that a link from historic Protestantism's sacramental system and understanding of the church to that of ancient and medieval Christianity was plausible if not actual.

The other statement from Nevin in 1854 that suggested a firmer resolve was a sermon preached in Carlisle at the ordination service of a Baltimore minister, Bernard C. Wolff. Nevin's text was Ephesians 4:8–16, where the epistle takes up the issue of Christ's ascension in relation to the church's ministry. If the sermon had been merely an essay, stripped of ecclesiastical context, it read in a sufficiently generic manner to avoid coming down on either the Protestant or Roman Catholic side of the question. But since Nevin gave such a forceful expression of "The Christian Ministry" only one year after his greatest doubts, and did so in the context of an explicitly German Reformed service, this sermon indicates a newfound resolve. Earlier in his articles on Cyprian he had insisted that any justification for Protestantism had to include awareness and affirmation of the church catholic as articulated by the church fathers and Rome. "However much of rubbish the Reformation found occasion to remove," he had demanded in 1851, "it was still compelled to do homage to the main body of the Roman theology as orthodox and right; and to this day Protestantism has no valid mission in the world, any farther than it is willing to build on this old foundation."[50] In effect, Nevin's ordination sermon in 1854 was his own answer to this previous summons; he was trying to build a Protestant ministry on ancient and medieval Western Christian conceptions of the church.

Nevin's exposition of the Ephesians passage included three points. The first concerned the origin of the Christian ministry, a result of Christ's "glorification at the right hand of God." Because Christ gave the gift of the ministry to the world, the church "by its very nature" possessed "a supernatural constitution, a truly real and abiding fact in the world" that was "destined to outlast and conquer in the end all other institutions, interests, and powers of the earth."[51] His concluding point took up the question of the Christian ministry's design. Here he summarized earlier discussions from *Mystical Presence* about the church's living constitution, its roots in the life of the ascended Christ, and its supernatural and gracious growth through the ministry's sacramental task.

The heart of the sermon came in the second point regarding the nature of the Christian ministry. Here Nevin discussed the principalities and powers of the world and observed that the church's authority and vocation was analogous to that of parents and civil magistrates.

But the church's ministry involved much more than the status accorded these temporal authorities. The "peculiarity" of the church "is that it does not originate in any way out of the order of this world naturally, but proceeds directly and altogether from a new and higher order of things brought to pass by the Spirit of Christ in consequence of his resurrection and ascension."[52] The implications of the church's divine character were indeed broad and breathtaking. On the one hand the church was "higher and greater than the State," and as such government had no right to intervene in the affairs of the church. To do so was to "betray Christ into the hands of Caesar."[53] On the other hand, and here Nevin was going full bore after the democratizing forces that were transforming the church in the United States, "the people" had just as little right to dictate to the church: "The fond notion which some have of a republican or democratic order in Christianity . . . is just as far removed from the proper truth of the gospel as any other that could well be applied to the subject."[54] Nevin's reason for this assertion was that the ministry of Christ and the apostles came before the church, in fact, formed or constituted the church. "The basis of Christianity, as it meets us in the New Testament," he explained, "is not the popular mind and popular will as such in any form or shape." Instead, it started with Christ and reached the world "through the mediation of ministers."[55] The question of the day was church office "in its broad New Testament sense," which involved "a real pastoral jurisdiction over the Church, representing in it immediately the authority of Jesus Christ" and deriving its force from "the sovereignty of heaven and earth to which he has been advanced by his resurrection from the dead."[56]

Of course, this statement of ministerial office did not necessarily resolve the conflict in Nevin's mind and soul. It did not vindicate Protestantism over against the claims of Rome. But it did affirm the only basis upon which Nevin could continue to be a Protestant. If the German Reformed Church could provide a platform upon which he might try to work out such an understanding of the Christian ministry, Nevin was prepared to stay, as this ordination sermon indicated. The sermon did not reveal what had changed to arrest his doubts. Nor did it suggest optimism for a reinvigorated Protestant ministry. In fact, Nevin continued to be profoundly aware of how far what he conceived to be the apostolic notion of church office was from nineteenth-century American practice. But the sermon did indicate a significant turn in Nevin's life. By 1854 he had steadied himself sufficiently to remain within the German Reformed fold. The question that remained was whether he had sufficient physical vigor to continue to mount a defense of historic Protestantism's better self.

6

Relocation and Recovery

n 1852 Nevin's German Reformed nemesis, Philadelphia pastor Joseph F. Berg, resigned from his charge at First German Reformed Church to minister among another ethnic Reformed people, this time the Dutch. On the surface, Berg's choice of the Dutch Reformed appeared to reveal his unswerving commitment to Continental expressions of the Reformed faith. After all, Berg, like one of his German Reformed colleagues, Jacob Helffenstein, could have transferred into one of the American Reformed expressions, such as a Presbyterian denomination. (Helffenstein in fact switched from the German Reformed Church to the New School Presbyterians.) But like most descendants of the magisterial Reformation (i.e., Reformed, Lutheran, Episcopalian), the Dutch were faring no better in preserving Old World faith and practice from the solvents of democratic and populist Christianity of the early American republic than were the Germans, whether Lutheran or Reformed. Indeed, the denomination into which Berg transferred was the Reformed Church in America, the older of the two main Dutch Calvinist denominations in the United States, the other being the Christian Reformed Church. Longevity in the New World, as it turned out, was a better indication of innovation than of maintaining tradition. Like other communions that had come to North America in the seventeenth and eighteenth centuries, the Dutch Reformed had acclimated to the New World and to Anglo-American culture. Indeed, the ethnic denominations with colonial roots were usually the ones fastest to Americanize. In effect, Berg was moving into a denomination not far removed from the German Reformed prior to Nevin's and Schaff's efforts to give the church a coherent theological outlook. Proof of this conclusion came within a few years of Berg's relocation. The Dutch immigrants who settled in Michigan during the 1850s soon became frustrated with the assimilated identity of the Reformed Church in America and in 1857 formed a separate denomination, the Christian Reformed Church, a communion that would continue into the twentieth century to embody a more European, as opposed to American, Reformed identity.

Berg did not leave the German Reformed Church without fanfare. In a formal exit sermon, based on Exodus 17:15, subsequently published under the title *Farewell Words to the First German Reformed Church, Race Street, Philadelphia*, the Philadelphia pastor took a parting shot at the Mercersburg theologians. The issues that continued to animate Berg were the same that had caused him to be one of the most anti-Catholic German Reformed ministers. The Mercersburg Theology was insufficiently Protestant and accordingly too open to Rome. The Bible versus church tradition, the material principle of the Reformation (i.e., justification by faith alone), and sacramental grace were still matters of consequence to Berg. What is more, these theological problems at the German Reformed Church's sole theological institution were so grave that he could no longer minister in a communion that tolerated such laxity.

Nevertheless, Berg was not leaving the German Reformed Church on his own initiative. Instead, he believed that he was a victim of events in the denomination. Here he picked up on the text of his sermon, the verse where Moses constructed an altar with the inscription "the Lord is my banner" after the Israelites had defeated the Amalekites. Berg explained that during the last seven years, since 1845, the German Reformed Church had succumbed to the teaching of Mercersburg. "You know," he told his loyal congregation, "that I protested against [the Mercersburg professors] in their incipiency. And I remember with gratitude the cordiality with which this congregation sustained me, when I stood in the painful position of recording my vote in solitary opposition."[1] The subsequent vindication of Nevin and Schaff in the courts of the church had turned Berg into a martyr. "You see in me, good people, a great and glorious confessor and martyr; who to save his faith, is forced to tear himself away from a fond and pleasant settlement, and go on hard pilgrimage to Gibraltar." Moreover, the German Reformed Church had forced Berg into "this cruel *sacrifice*, by exacting from me terms of communion to which as an honest man I have found it impossible to submit." "I am," he declared, "a victim for righteousness' sake!" His martyrdom functioned, then, as a sacrifice placed upon the altar named "the Lord is my banner." "Upon that altar, inscribed Jehova-Nissi," Berg explained, "I would lay them; and to that blessed Lord who gave them, I here surrender all I have and all I am, for the maintenance of these principles, until He demands the record of my stewardship."[2] The analogy was a bit confusing since what had been a victory for the Israelites was a defeat for the German Reformed Church. But in Berg's mind, he was on the side of the angels, and his former denomination was in the control of infidels.

With the major and at times lone opponent having departed the German Reformed Church, Nevin appeared to be the victor in the war with his critics. In many respects this was exactly the case. The faculty at Mercersburg Seminary and at the denomination's college, first as Marshall and then as Franklin and Marshall, were overwhelmingly cordial to Nevin and carried on his theological program even if the particulars were sometimes shaky. In addition, the denomination at large appeared to be moving into the orbit of the Mercersburg Theology. One indication was the committee charged with revising the denomination's order of worship (to be covered in more detail in chapter 7). With the exception of one or two members, this liturgical committee was supportive of Nevin's and Schaff's understanding of the church, its ministry, and worship. Berg's departure for the Reformed Church of America should have indicated that the prolonged battle between Mercersburg and Philadelphia had concluded with Nevin on top.

But that protracted struggle had also taken its toll on Nevin, both physically and spiritually. Even without his digestive difficulties, Nevin had been working at a feverish pace for almost thirteen years, and that output finally caught up with him. But Nevin's physical condition was intimately connected to his spiritual doubts. Some of Berg's complaints about Nevin had merit. The Mercersburg divine was not simply opposed to anti-Catholic prejudice or to the forced historiography that supposedly vindicated Protestantism. Nevin was drawn to Rome because Roman Catholicism appealed to him, particularly its teaching on the church, its acknowledgment of tradition, and its sacramental theology. Indeed, Nevin's victory over Berg was so decisive that even when the latter's accusations about the former's Roman proclivities appeared to be true, the denomination continued to reject Berg's charges and side with Nevin. Yet, although the Mercersburg theologian won the public struggle in the synods and publications of the German Reformed Church, privately Nevin was hardly triumphant. In fact, he was a spent and for all intents and purposes a defeated man himself.

Ironically, then, as Berg left with the fanfare of his self-ascribed martyrdom, Nevin also retreated from the German Reformed Church but in a much more subdued manner. And while Berg had turned his defeat into vindication, Nevin's decision to retire from affairs at the seminary, college, and other denominational activities colored his victory with the hues of defeat. As a result, the Mercersburg theologian's career went the opposite of most successful educators and churchmen. Just when Nevin was hitting his stride at middle age and should have been collecting on his years of personal and intellectual investment in the institutional life of the German Reformed Church, he withdrew into relative isolation and never regained his earlier vigor or influence. As it turned out, his health was better than he thought, and Nevin would live to the ripe age of eighty-three, surviving for another three-and-one-half decades after his initial resignation at Mercersburg. But during these years he could not muster the same level of energy and intellectual creativity that he had during his initial outburst at Mercersburg during the 1840s and early 1850s. Although Nevin would recover to the point of resuming the presidency of Franklin and Marshall College, he was nonetheless a shadow of the man who had diagnosed the ills of American Protestantism and worked mightily to infuse the German Reformed Church with an alternate Protestant identity.

Gentleman Farmer

Nineteenth-century America abounded with various cures for any number of ills. For physical health some reformers prescribed strange diets consisting of graham crackers, the concoction of New England Presbyterian minister Sylvester Graham. Others recommended abstinence from alcohol and coffee. While still additional prophets had theories about the benefits of water, both outside and inside the body. Nevin himself was not immune to different theories about good health since he was constantly looking for comfort from painful indigestion. He not only tried different diets but was also opposed, as most Anglo-American Protestants were, to the consumption of alcohol and tobacco. But if Nevin's experience supported any one particular theory about good health, it would have been the belief in the physical benefits of manual labor. Some American reformers were prescribing this as a cure to those locked up for various crimes and misdemeanors. But after the 1820s Americans also began to attend to the healthful effects of physical training on mental and spiritual development. Nevin had already witnessed the improvement in his own condition during a time of work and rest at his parents' farm after his studies and teaching at Princeton Seminary. A similar pattern prevailed after his retirement from Mercersburg Seminary and Marshall College. From 1853 until 1861 he discarded the intellectual duties of the classroom and took up the responsibilities of domestic life. The change proved to be physically agreeable.

At first Nevin's regimen of convalescence appeared to be more nomadic than residential, with relocating his family and effects providing the main outlet for his physical labors. In 1854 the Nevin family moved from Mercersburg to Carlisle, the home of Dickinson College, where Nevin's father had studied, and located in Franklin County some twenty miles from the Nevin homestead. Carlisle put some distance between Nevin and the difficulties of Mercersburg Seminary, thus removing temptations to teach or intervene in the school's affairs, while also offering him some intellectual stimulation through Dickinson's faculty and library. One year later, at the urging of one of Franklin and Marshall's faculty, Nevin moved again, this time to the eastern part of Lancaster County, near Churchtown, setting up home at Windsor Place. Here he lived until 1858, still isolated from the city of Lancaster, approximately fifteen miles away, but close enough to enter into some of the town's and college's social life. While living at Windsor Place Nevin led worship services at the nearby Episcopal church with the approval of the local bishop and his friend from Union College, Alonzo Potter. But even these circumstances were too isolated from town and college life. So in 1858 Nevin moved once more, this time to the outskirts of Lancaster City, to a fifteen-acre farm adjacent to President James Buchanan's domestic residence, the Wheatland estate.

Nevin oversaw the design and construction of his new home and entered into a variety of farm chores. His biographer, Theodore Appel, recalled once seeing Nevin on a warm summer day pitching hay, "evidently in a hurry" because of an approaching evening shower. Appel also put into print the story about the extent of Nevin's agricultural labors. Once when Nevin was at home alone, his wife and children being away for several days, the daughter of a neighbor had instructions from Mrs. Nevin to keep an eye on her husband for fear of what he might be up to. At one point, the little girl, who took her charge seriously and peered through the trees to check up on the aging theologian, saw Nevin climb up into a cherry tree to pick its ripe fruit. The girl immediately went to the trunk of the tree and called to Nevin to come down promptly. He put her off, being amused by her concern. But she became all the more urgent and told Nevin that his wife had given her instructions to look after him during her trip. Finally, Nevin complied and returned to footing more fitting a man of his age. According to Appel, this little neighbor girl became "the means of preserving a life which afterwards became fruitful and of extended usefulness."[3] That likely overstates the danger of Nevin's harvesting practices. But the story does indicate the range of his activities as he worked on his home and farm during his first years on the Lancaster estate he called Caernarvon.

Nevin's new home also brought friendship with his neighbor, President Buchanan, especially after the fifteenth occupant of the White House retired from public service to the Pennsylvania Dutch heartland. Buchanan, like Nevin a native of Franklin County, was twelve years the theologian's senior. Born in Mercersburg and a graduate of Dickinson College and reared in the same Scotch-Irish Presbyterian culture in which Nevin had matured, Buchanan was, like Nevin's great-uncle, Hugh Williamson, a Federalist member of Congress, before switching to the Democrats in the mid-1820s with the failure of his old political party and the ascendancy of another Scotch-Irish Presbyterian, Andrew Jackson. Buchanan's ties to Nevin were even closer through the theologian's wife. Martha Nevin was the daughter of Robert Jenkins, a successful businessman and one of Buchanan's cronies in Lancaster's politics. Jenkins, also a Federalist, had served two terms in Congress (1807–11). In 1848, while Buchanan was serving as Secretary of State, Wheatland, whose name owed to its original owner's acknowledgment of the surrounding wheat fields, became Buchanan's permanent home. Although Buchanan remained a bachelor throughout his life, his niece, Harriet Lane, filled the requisite role of hostess at Buchanan's many social functions at Wheatland. Unlike Nevin, Buchanan had a reputation for being a gourmand and having a constitution that held large amounts of alcohol—sherry, Madeira, and rye whiskey being among his favorite beverages. Buchanan not only entertained various public officials and dignitaries, but also regularly invited the local firemen to Wheatland to enjoy his liquid hospitality.

Nevin was likely not a party to Wheatland's libations, but aside from family and political connections he also had professional reasons for befriending his neighbor. The president had served on the board of Marshall College and worked for its merger with Lancaster's Franklin College and the location of the united school in his hometown. After leaving the White House and retiring to Wheatland, Buchanan became concerned about spiritual matters and sought Nevin's counsel. Back in Lancaster permanently after 1861, Buchanan often attended the services at Franklin and Marshall's chapel, where Nevin regularly preached and led worship. The former president had grown up in the Presbyterian Church but had never made public profession of faith. Nevin took an active interest in Buchanan's regular reading of Scripture and study of Christianity's basic tenets. When Buchanan became convinced that he should join a church, he sought

Nevin's advice. The latter recommended Buchanan's ancestral Presbyterian faith, but the doctrine of predestination proved to be a barrier. The Episcopal Church was another option, but Buchanan worried about the public notoriety that would attend his profession of faith, both for his own sake and in the highly charged context of the Civil War, where both sides had fused religion and politics to prosecute their cause. So Buchanan explored membership in the German Reformed Church.

At this point, Nevin began to advocate what had been until then only small talk. For a while the college faculty had discussed the possibility of forming a separate congregation for those connected with the school. One hurdle here was Buchanan's own physical infirmities. He worried about having to kneel for confirmation, a position that his aging frame could no longer assume. Nevin reassured him that he could participate in the rite while remaining standing. A bigger obstacle proved to be the German Reformed in Lancaster. Fears of draining talent and members from the established Lancaster congregation prevented some from supporting the plan for a new church at the college. Buchanan was not in a hurry, but delays in gaining approval for a new German Reformed congregation did eventually prompt him to make further inquiry with the local Presbyterians in Lancaster. Once the congregation's officers assured Buchanan that he would not have to affirm the doctrine of predestination, he decided to become a member of the Presbyterian Church. When Buchanan died in 1868, Nevin delivered the funeral sermon before family and friends at Wheatland.

Interestingly enough, in 1865 the German Reformed congregation that Nevin had encouraged Buchanan to join became a reality. Nevin was active in the college church during retirement, preaching and supervising catechetical instruction. In other words, his life during these years in Lancaster was not characterized by solitude or inactivity. Neither was it the case that his retirement from theological education involved a withdrawal from the life of the German Reformed Church. Despite his limited service for the Episcopal parish in Churchtown, Nevin remained an active churchman. The difference now was that he was not in the public eye of the denomination but carried out his responsibilities at the local level. The fortunes of the German Reformed

Church no longer rose and fell according to his own theological developments or personal crises. The one aspect of the denomination's institutional life that continued to hook Nevin's active participation was Franklin and Marshall College. Here the stakes of denominational politics were not as high, nor was his at times quirky theology as much an issue. Ironically, the college over which he had presided as something of a stopgap measure during his early years in Mercersburg, owing to the unexpected death of Frederick Rauch, turned out to be the one institution that would draw Nevin out of premature retirement and recover part of the vigor that had driven him when he first transferred to the German Reformed Church.

Nevin's Other Instruction

Most of the books and articles on Nevin feature his theological ideas and involvement at Mercersburg Seminary. Indeed, the name *Nevin* and the phrase *Mercersburg Theology* are synonymous. But the close association between the man and a school of theology ignores that Nevin served longer as a college president and professor than he did as a theological educator. He presided over Marshall College from 1841 to 1853, practically the whole time he lived in Mercersburg, a period when the college was in dire straights and when Nevin himself was most productive. Then later in life, Nevin presided over the successor, Franklin and Marshall College, from 1866 to 1876, until his second and final retirement. Of course, his significance as a theologian is greater than that as an educator, hence the propriety of associating Nevin with Mercersburg rather than with Franklin and Marshall. In fact, his views on undergraduate education, though never held up to great scrutiny, were not nearly as creative as his theological scholarship. In other words, simply on the merits of his work at a struggling denominational college Nevin would not have distinguished himself from the rest of the nineteenth century's educational pack. But when added to his theological achievement, his work as a college educator certainly emerges as remarkable, even if not brilliant.

One indication of Nevin's importance to the college in Lancaster was the board's invitation to him to deliver the keynote address at

Franklin and Marshall's 1853 inaugural festivities. He used the occasion to reflect on the significance of the school for the commonwealth of Pennsylvania and for the institution's German-American constituency. On the first score, Nevin believed that the state was on the cusp of greatness, both materially and spiritually, or at least that is how he introduced his remarks. But when he turned to Pennsylvania's intellectual attainments Nevin was not so encouraging. Pennsylvania was not on a par with New England and its "machinery of education."[4] The reason was not the superiority of the Yankees' native intelligence but rather the barrier posed by the German character, the dominant cultural element in Pennsylvania, according to Nevin. He did not attribute any sort of mental inferiority to the Pennsylvania Germans, nor could he if Old World German intellectual life had proved so influential to his own development. The problem with German-Americans lay instead with their cultural isolation, owing partly to their native language. At the same time, by forming separate communities, "devoted almost entirely to agricultural pursuits,"[5] German-Americans shut out the dominant Anglo-American culture and its educational institutions. Eventually, farming produced significant wealth but also an "undue attachment to money for money's sake; and along with this, as a necessary consequence, a low appreciation of all that pertains to the proper care and culture of the mind." Pennsylvania Germans had, in effect, committed treason against "the true, original constitution of the German mind itself" by combining "narrow-minded ignorance and close-fisted avarice."[6]

Nevin's words before the Lancaster dignitaries may not have been the most auspicious, but he had a method to his madness. Ever since his appointment in 1841 as Marshall College's president, which he had agreed to do on a provisional basis and which turned into a twelve-year stint, the school's poor financial health had beleaguered him. During this time, as he taught at Mercersburg Seminary, wrote substantial pieces, and fended off his critics, Nevin served without remuneration as president of the college and president of the school's board of trustees. In 1848 a professor of science resigned because of the college's poor finances, followed by the mathematics professor the following year. By 1850 Nevin had tired of the college's hand-to-mouth budget. He wrote a series for *Weekly Messenger* that advocated relocating Marshall in Lancaster and merging it with Franklin, a plan that offered the combined resources of two institutions, as well as the support of Lancaster City as an important agricultural center. This decision took all of Nevin's persuasive powers to change the minds of local Mercersburg board members and donors, while also requiring administrative muscle to gain the Pennsylvania legislature's approval of both colleges' charters. At one point Nevin admitted that he was "so heartily sick of the whole business of trying to carry forward a College without proper means."[7] That the plan succeeded and that the German Reformed Church became the controlling interest in the united college, combined with an almost complete transfer of the pro–Mercersburg Theology at Marshall faculty to Franklin and Marshall over the protests of Nevin's critics, is an indication of his gifts and foresight as an educator, even if only president *pro tem*. Undoubtedly, this history of struggle, both personal and institutional, informed Nevin's seemingly obtuse remarks at Franklin and Marshall's opening.

Although Nevin was on his way out as president in 1853 and might have felt freer to vent because of his impending independence, he still provided a vision for what the new college could become and how it could best serve Pennsylvania and its German-American citizens. True to his organic conception of spiritual life, Nevin argued that Pennsylvania should not ape New England, however superior the northeastern states' institutions of higher learning might be. Such would be "unnatural" and "unwise." Pennsylvania needed an order of education "in some measure peculiar to herself, and answerable to her own order of life." If the state were to fall back on "the true ground of its own life,"[8] Pennsylvania would need to do justice to "the German mind and the German character." By this Nevin did not mean hostility to English or the repristination of High German language and letters. Instead, he appealed to the German mind, "its distinguishing spirit, its constitutional organization, its historical substance and form."[9] This burden was larger than what a college alone could bear. It would also require reform of the common schools. But the challenge for Franklin and Marshall was to offer a curriculum that followed the reigning American standards and also included the German language and "the German habit of thought." Its task, in other words, was to maintain a "living communication" with the arts and sciences of Germany, "with a proper insight into its merits and wants." The benefits of such an institution would then trickle out to the state at large, "as a college for Pennsylvania and not for some other State, working thus in harmony with the natural spirit of the State itself and finding in it a more congenial element, . . . a source of general education."[10]

Nevin conceded that emphasis on things German could sound sectarian, not simply on ethnic grounds but also on religious ones, since Franklin and Marshall was a German Reformed college. His response involved a simple recognition that the college had an ethnic obligation that was not necessarily culturally divisive. Nevin had no intention of supplanting the English character of America or of setting the German mind against the English. The goal was a common culture to which the German part could make its own and distinctive contribution. Nevin used a similar argument to justify the college's German Reformed patronage. If Franklin and Marshall were to be a religious college, its faith needed to be tied explicitly to "a particular branch of the Protestant Church." At the same time, the German Reformed Church possessed its own liberality and catholicity that would prevent a "narrow spirit of sectarianism" from dominating the school.[11]

Nevin finished where he began, with an appeal that hinted at Marshall's penurious conditions during his tenure as president. Not only Pennsylvania but Lancaster City and County, with the proper encouragement and support, could turn Franklin and Marshall into an "ornament and glory" of the state. Here Nevin, as so many college presidents before him, pulled out the last resort: civic pride and local boosterism. "A mere second or third rate college, a college of no character or force, might answer for other places," he gushed, "but for the Lancaster that now is, and still more for the Lancaster that is to be some ten or twenty years hence, no thought of this kind should be for the moment endured." Better no college at all than "the mere sham or shadow of a college in no right keeping with the central and solid character of the place in other respects." The college needed solid and enduring financial support from the city, Nevin concluded, not a "mere twenty five thousand dollar scheme of public improvement!"[12]

180

From 1853 to 1866 Nevin enjoyed the bliss that came with ignorance of Franklin and Marshall's finances and of the authenticity of the city's support. Once he moved to Lancaster County in 1855 and then to the city proper three years later, he did enter into a closer relationship with the college. But it was several steps removed from Franklin and Marshall's central operations. Nevin continued to enjoy the support of the college faculty and would on occasion participate in Franklin and Marshall's public events. In addition to his ministry at the college chapel and the congregation that emerged there, Nevin also gave the commencement address to the graduating classes of 1853 and the convocation lecture at the opening of the 1858 winter term. In both cases the thought of teenagers listening to Nevin's fairly ethereal reflections on the relationship between nature and the supernatural as it bore on college education inevitably invites images of youthful vigor being slowed down by heavy and somewhat pretentious intellectual bromides. But for those students who listened carefully to Nevin's somewhat distended style, his thoughts usually carried sufficient originality to bring his mystical tendencies down to earth.

In 1861 Nevin's relations with the college became sufficiently official for him to come out of retirement, though not in a full-time capacity. The story goes that his wife, Martha, was shopping at one of Lancaster's markets when one of Franklin and Marshall's faculty greeted her and inquired about her husband. She expressed concern for his general well-being and suggested that if Nevin might be able to engage in some regular intellectual labor at the college his condition might improve. Perhaps the retired professor was becoming something of a nuisance at home now that Martha's mother had died and no longer needed her care. In any event, this happenstance meeting led to an invitation from the faculty for Nevin to give lectures part-time in the department of history, which he accepted. What made this position possible may have been Nevin's own inherent abilities as a polymath. After all, he had during his career taught Hebrew, Greek, Bible, church history, moral philosophy, theology, and even mathematics in the role of a substitute. (Nevin would eventually add to his list aesthetics and ethics during the last ten years of his academic career.) More likely is that in an era before academic specialization nineteenth-century col-

181

lege and seminary faculty could range over any number of disciplines by selecting the appropriate survey texts and examining students in their comprehension of the assigned readings. Even so, this appointment brought Nevin closer into the formal life of the college. It also provided him with ample opportunity to develop a philosophy of world history that drew upon his theological conceptions of the organic relationship between the divine and the human, the spiritual and the physical realms. Again, the image of young students trying to absorb Nevin's highly abstract notions summons up, depending on one's perspective, either feelings of amusement or pity. Nevertheless, his teaching at the college, combined with his ministry at the chapel, kept Nevin intellectually active and afforded a sense of usefulness at a time when his own literary productivity was in decline.

Nevin's philosophy of history was a significant component in the college curriculum and reflected the uniqueness of Franklin and Marshall as a German-American liberal arts college. Since its founding and through the instruction of Frederick A. Rauch, the German Reformed college had employed a philosophical outlook (German idealism) that was different from that of the old elite schools of the northeast: Harvard, Yale, and Princeton (Scottish commonsense realism). Rather than regarding the mind as a passive recipient of fact, Rauch stressed the intellect's active participation in the appropriation of truth. This philosophical perspective dovetailed with Nevin's instruction in history.

Not only did history interest Nevin for understanding the development of Christianity and the organic qualities of the church, but it also proved to be a subject that gave coherence to the college curriculum. Because the study of history involved the "universal relation of the system of nature to the system of living mind in the economy of the world," it offered a means of training the mind to see things whole.[13] This commitment to a unified conception of knowledge in turn gave momentum to the Franklin and Marshall idea of liberal education. Since history included more than facts but also discerned in them their relation to, as Nevin put it, the "economy of the world," it was quintessentially a form of liberal education that required knowledge, faith, and imagination. For Nevin, then, history was crucial to the development of a liberally educated mind. It required, he explained, "a sympathy with the organic movement of human life, in which the old and new are continually joined as one and the same existence."[14] According to historian Sally F. Griffith the history course was the "linchpin of the College's philosophical curriculum."[15]

In 1866 Nevin's more or less informal ties to Franklin and Marshall became decidedly official with his appointment as president. Similar to the situation in 1841 when Nevin took the reins of Marshall College as a measure to strengthen a weakening institution, the board of the college turned again to the Mercersburg theologian to help with a school that was underfunded and experiencing malaise. E. V. Gerhart, the united college's first president, had performed competent service for Franklin and Marshall during the 1850s, and during that time the college grew. But the Civil War exposed the institution's structural weaknesses and hurt fund-raising. During the conflict the student body remained remarkably strong. In 1862 the college graduated twenty-eight students. By 1866 that figure had declined to six. At this time the board also recognized the need for a more substantial endowment, increasing its goal from an originally modest figure of $50,000 to the ambitious one of $200,000. Complicating these deficiencies was ongoing discontent within the church over the composition of the faculty, who were almost to the man in the pro-Mercersburg camp. The anti-Mercersburg German Reformed, though a minority, continued to look for ways to unseat the Mercersburg Theology's grip on the denomination. Accordingly, with the search for a new president to strengthen the college, some also called for a reconstruction of the faculty so that it might represent the entire composition of the church. At first the board debated whether simply to appoint Nevin with the honorary title of president emeritus, thus adding the strength of his name to the school's meager resources. He declined the offer, insisting that he did not want to be merely a figurehead, at which point the board offered to make him president, with Gerhart serving as Nevin's vice president in charge of fund-raising. As Nevin indicated in his letter of acceptance, the board believed that his name would significantly improve the college's chances of raising the necessary endowment, but Nevin was not so sure. "Too much account is made of my name, I am afraid, in this view," he wrote, "but where, in a case like this, so much importance is attached to it by others, a sort of necessity is placed upon me not to withhold it from the service of so worthy an enterprise."[16]

Nevin's acceptance of the arrangement demonstrated again the majority of the church's confidence in him—and once again marked defeat for the anti-Mercersburg contingent. At the same time, Nevin's selection was curious, if only because he was partly responsible for opposition to the school. Why make the target of vigorous criticism the chief executive of the struggling college? The answer may very well have been that Nevin represented exactly what Franklin and Marshall needed if it were ever going to compete with other American colleges. He was the German Reformed Church's lone Anglo-American intellectual who could show that the college was serious in its academic ambitions. At the same time, as he had argued at the 1853 opening of the school, Nevin was devoted not only to high educational standards, but was eager to preserve as much of the German Reformed Church's ethnic heritage as possible. To appoint another German-American was to risk further cultural isolation and consequently fewer contacts with non-German donors and students.

Although the reasons for Nevin's second term as college president may have said more about the market value of his name than it did about the brilliance of his intellect, he still showed himself to be a keen observer of trends in American higher education. In an 1867 commencement address Nevin demonstrated insight into how the recent American war was transforming advanced learning. Some of the address suffered from ideas swollen as large as Nevin's sometimes inflated rhetoric. The war had proved that the United States' progress was of "world-historical" significance. "The greatest questions of life, the last problems of history, are fast crowding upon us for their solution."[17] Furthermore, in Nevin's list of issues to be resolved in America he could not resist putting the church question at the top. On this score Nevin was naïve if he thought that the church question had not been mostly settled in American Protestantism. Even so, Nevin's powers of observation, even about religious matters, were not without real discernment. He noted in a way remarkably prescient for the time that the great temptation of postwar America was to so identify the kingdom of God with American sociocultural progress that Christianity itself was becoming obscure.

Nevin asserted that it was hard "to stand firm and fast in the faith of Christ," exceedingly so in the euphoria of the war's conclusion. The reason was that the relation between grace and nature was closer in the minds of many Christians than it ever had been, so intimate that "the very elect are in continual danger of being deceived by it to the loss of their own steadfastness." As such, Nevin felt compelled to go on record that "Nature is not Grace." "That which is born of the flesh," he added, "is at last, in its highest sublimation, flesh only, and not Spirit." Whatever the merits of the earth or its assistance to the church, "it is not in the power of the earth to create the Church, or to take into its own hands the office and work of the Church." In a statement that surely steered Nevin's organicism away from the religiously based progressivism that would in the decades ahead characterize liberal Protestantism, he insisted: "The race can never be brought right, and made to be what it ought to be by machinery, or mere outward social economy of any sort; and just as little can it be redeemed by politics, education, or science."[18] The world's "true regeneration," then, had to come from above. "Humanitarianism is not Christianity; and the Gospel of such men as Emerson, Theodore Parker, Garrison, Wendell Phillips, and others . . . is not the Gospel of Jesus Christ." No matter how beneficent the signs of the times were for political and cultural progress, "we have no assurance in [them], that the change will move on victoriously in the line of universal righteousness and truth." In fact, Nevin feared that the very elements and forces that were the firstfruits of a new era were also "volcanic" in character: "The very effort that is made to scale the heavens, in the way of material aggrandizement and politico-social self-exaltation, seems to invite upon itself the thunderbolts of Divine wrath, and to foreshadow a confusion worse than that of old on the plains of Shinar."[19]

The effects of humanitarian utopianism were especially evident, according to Nevin, in the sphere of knowledge and education. Here he complained about the significance of the Smithsonian Institution in Washington, D.C. Its aim of increasing the "diffusion of knowledge" had become reductionistic in simply promoting the natural sciences. "Physical Geography, Coast Surveys, Aboriginal Monuments, Palaeontology, Geology"—the list went on—had entirely eclipsed "Morality, Humane Literature, Metaphysics, and Philosophy." It was a sign both "curious" and "significant" and a proclamation to the world "of what Science, Education and Progress are coming more and more to mean for the spirit of the Nineteenth Century, as it is now sweeping all things before it in the new-born life of these United States."[20] Such a message required institutions like Franklin and Marshall "to maintain in vigorous force" a devotion to liberal education, "in the old and proper sense of the term." A liberal education, accordingly, involved a freedom "from all bondage to merely outside references and ends," and had to do chiefly with "the enlargement of the mind in its own sphere." Nevin did not use the word *humanities*, but his vision of liberal education was clearly one that exalted those spheres of study having to do with the improvement and capacity of the human mind and spirit. Such an education was not opposed to forms of "utilitarian, practical, and professional" training. But these spheres were insufficient to "complete the organization of a true human culture." Material progress, if it were to stand, required a foundation of "solid spiritual thought."[21]

As president of the college between 1866 and 1876, Nevin followed through on his idealistic vision of liberal education. Part of the arrangement that led to his installation as president in 1866 was a call from board members to make the college's curriculum more practical. This would have involved the addition of classes in politics and constitutional theory and a three-year course of instruction in natural science. But Nevin refused to comply with the board's demands. He had the advantage of arguing that the extra courses would be impractical—the college could not afford to hire the new professors needed to teach the new subjects. Still, Nevin's more basic argument stemmed from his view that liberal education should not be practical in the sense of providing utilitarian or vocational knowledge or experience. As he explained to the graduating class of 1867:

> Let it be our ambition then, and our care, to maintain in vigorous force here, an institution that shall be devoted supremely to liberal

education, in the old and proper sense of the term; *liberal*, as being free from all bondage to merely outside references and ends, as having to do, first of all, with the enlargement of the mind in its own sphere. This, after all, must remain the true conception of education forever.[22]

In the larger scheme of American higher education, Nevin's outlook was soon to be outflanked by the research university and the academic specialization, especially in the social and natural sciences, that it nurtured. But through the Mercersburg Theology and his cultivation of it, Franklin and Marshall College remained one of the last colleges to hold on to the classical curriculum of the liberal arts colleges. During his own tenure Nevin had little trouble keeping Franklin and Marshall on the path of this traditionalist understanding of liberal education. Part of the reason was financial. And Nevin's primary responsibility for the decade he served as the college's president was to raise sufficient funds for Franklin and Marshall's traditional curriculum. But that vision was insufficient to raise Nevin's visibility in the annals of American colleges and universities. In fact, no matter how noble the vision, it consigned his school, and many denominational colleges like it, to a rank of also-ran. Consequently, although Nevin proved to be a competent administrator in securing Franklin and Marshall's standing among the nineteenth-century liberal arts colleges supported by Protestant churches, educational aims such as his would soon be regarded as retrograde among America's academic reformers. Even so, no matter how conservative his outlook, Nevin knew that he was fighting a losing battle that was still worth fighting. What is more, after America's involvement in twentieth-century wars that were of true world significance, American educators began to consider whether college presidents like Nevin may have had a point.

The Mercersburg Theology Continued

During his first retirement and his second term as college president Nevin did not abandon theological scholarship. His output was, however, significantly diminished. From 1853, when his retirement began, until 1876 when he stepped down from Franklin and Marshall for the last time, he averaged roughly three published articles per year, compared to the nine per year that Nevin was churning out during the seven years after the publication of *Mystical Presence* (1846). Another way of indicating Nevin's decline is to say that he produced almost the same number of published articles between 1846 and 1853 (63) as he did from 1853 to 1876 (62). Even this comparison fails to convey the degree to which Nevin's literary output trailed off after 1853, for most of the articles he published between 1846 and 1853 were usually longish scholarly articles for a theological quarterly. But at least half of the pieces he wrote after 1853 were for the German Reformed Church's weekly newspaper and took up little more than a page of news print. An explanation that used his presidency of Franklin and Marshall as a factor for the latter period's drop off would be wrong-headed since during the earlier period he was president of Marshall College and also professor of theology at Mercersburg Seminary. In other words, after 1853, even though coming out of retirement to preside over the Lancaster college, Nevin was for all intents and purposes still in literary retirement.

Still, his lack of publications does not signify intellectual inactivity. Some of Nevin's most important writing on worship occurred during these years (to be treated in chapter 7). In addition, he continued his interests in the incarnation, historical development, the church's ministry, and the contours of church life in the early Christian fathers. Arguably the most revealing of his theological insights came at the expense of other prominent American theologians. Indeed, the originality of Nevin's doctrinal outlook becomes clear in essays he wrote about the Old School Presbyterian and his former professor, Charles Hodge; Hartford Congregationalist minister and forerunner of Protestant liberalism Horace Bushnell; and confessional American Lutheran theologian Charles Porterfield Krauth.

The occasion for Nevin's resumption of disputing with Hodge was the publication in 1856 of the Princeton theologian's commentary on Ephesians. Whether Nevin felt he had a score to settle with the man who could interpret his Christocentric theology only as Schleiermacher in American guise, the Mercersburg theologian did not hold back his judgment regarding the inadequacies of the Princeton Theology. In his review of Hodge, Nevin vented most clearly his objection to the Calvinist doctrine of predestination and the eternal decree. He was not interested in the Arminian resolution to the apparent difficulties of Calvinism's high doctrine of election. Nevin recognized that the classic fault lines between the Synod of Dort and the Remonstrants was a question of human participation in salvation, with Calvinists stressing rightly in his view divine sovereignty in redemption and the Arminians granting some real power to human agency. The Calvinists had properly, he wrote, defended grace as a "power, distinct from nature and above it."[23] The problem, however, was that Calvinist teaching on election so emphasized divine agency as to obliterate any role for nature or the human. This became a real difficulty, Nevin argued, in Hodge's understanding of the church and the traditional Presbyterian distinction between its invisible (the elect) and visible (church members) forms. In effect, Hodge's rendering of predestination turned Christianity essentially into a "scheme of pure abstract spiritualism" that denied to the church any such "powers of a higher world."[24] For this reason Nevin boldly asserted that Calvin's idea of the elect was at odds with the Apostle Paul's because the Geneva Reformer's ecclesiology also relied upon the visible-invisible distinction. Nevin explained that he did not disagree with the metaphysics informing Calvin's teaching on predestination. Instead, Nevin rejected the way that the eternal decree had been used as a basis for Presbyterian conceptions of the church.

What Nevin had in mind, as he further explained in his review of Hodge, was a notion of salvation grounded in membership in and reliance upon the agency of the church. In Nevin's scheme Christian salvation played out really and concretely in history, in the form of the church, and was not simply an abstract covenant transacted in the Godhead before all time. With Christ and his presence in the church, a "new order of life" had entered human history. As such, those who were baptized into the church stood "in correspondence with the powers of a higher world, the mysterious forces of the new creation in Christ Jesus."[25] Nevin used the image of Noah's ark to explain the way

189

in which he was conceiving of the church. Those outside the patriarch's family had a chance to be saved from destruction by joining Noah and his family, but their unbelief and disobedience condemned them. Those who entered the ark, however, had availed themselves of the means of salvation from the flood. Their fate was not certain since they could through unbelief and disobedience also frustrate divine mercy. But while on the ark, they enjoyed an estate of "glorious miraculous privilege, as compared with the condition of the world at large." "It placed them in a new order of existence, and brought them into living actual communication with the scheme of grace which God had been pleased to provide for the deliverance of His people." In effect, the church of Christ functioned exactly as the ark. It is "the necessary medium of salvation for men."[26] This was the conception of the church that Nevin believed the Apostle Paul clearly taught and that undergirded all his epistles. It was, however, lacking entirely in Hodge's rendering of Ephesians, and Nevin blamed the Princetonian's deafness to the Pauline idea upon the tendency to make predestination the controlling principle of Reformed dogma.

The reaction from Nevin to Bushnell's proposal in *Nature and the Supernatural* (1857) was less extensive and apparently more favorable than his review of Hodge. For some, that might have indicated the Mercersburg Theology's inherently liberal character, since Bushnell would become the inspiration for the liberal wing of the Congregationalist church to break decisively with the confining orthodoxy of Puritanism. What may have accounted better for the seeming discrepancy in Nevin's responses was the old axiom about being hardest on the ones closest to you. Nevin did have more at stake with Hodge, his former professor and cobelligerent in defending Reformed Christianity, except that the Princeton Theology had proved to be a severe disappointment to Nevin in his own quest to recover the sacramental and churchly aspects of the Reformed faith. With Bushnell he had much less to lose. Nevin also had in the Hartford minister another theologian who had found the reigning philosophical paradigms in North America too restraining and was looking to Germany and its various mediators to affirm a more organic and less Scholastic version of Christianity. Bushnell's 1857 book represented precisely that sort of endeavor. While trying to steer clear of pantheism (with which he had been charged after writing *God in Christ* [1849]), he was attempting to bring the divine back closer to the human by expanding the idea of the supernatural. One obvious way of doing this was to explore the relationship between the natural and the supernatural in Christ. Bushnell's goal was not as much to break with theological orthodoxy, as it was to reestablish the importance of Christianity (the supernatural) in human culture (the natural).

Nevin applauded Bushnell's intention to rein in the enlarging influence of naturalism with a defense of supernaturalism. The Mercersburg theologian likewise complimented Bushnell for grounding this effort in Christ. Indeed, Nevin recognized in Bushnell's book a kindred Christocentric spirit. But the devil was in the details, and Nevin was not pleased by the Hartford pastor's execution. One fault was the book's idea of the natural. Although other reviewers took issue with Bushnell for a porous conception of the supernatural, Nevin believed that Bushnell sold nature short by limiting it merely to the physical and material, as if it were in an altogether different sphere than the spiritual and moral. Bushnell also had a faulty doctrine of sin, which turned the fall into a natural transitional stage in the flow of human history. As such, Bushnell had not escaped the grasp of the old Puritanism. "Calvin's supralapsarianism, and the pantheistic world-progress of Hegel," Nevin wrote, "run out here to the same conclusion, a Manichean notion of sin on the one hand, and as the necessary counterpart of this, a Gnostic conception of redemption on the other."[27] The major complaint was Bushnell's "want of ecclesiastical feeling."[28] To Nevin it seemed as if Bushnell's notion of supernatural influence on natural life was like that of heavenly air enveloping all things. Nevin countered that it made much more sense to think of the new creation in Christ as taking shape "as an objective constitution . . . having place in the world under a wholly different form, and carrying in itself relations and powers altogether peculiar, and not to be found anywhere beyond its own limits; an order of supernatural grace, into which men must be introduced" by baptism in order to "come into the full use afterwards of its quickening and saving help."[29] Nevin may have sounded like a Johnny one-note, constantly playing the tune of the church in all of his performances. Yet, his critique of both Hodge and Bushnell on the church question shows how central it was to Nevin's thinking and indicates the creative uses to which he could put the doctrine with which he, like Jacob on the banks of the Jordan, so strenuously wrestled.

The appearance of Krauth's *Conservative Reformation* in 1871 provided Nevin with an opportunity to reflect on the character and history of the Protestant Reformation, as well as the relationship between its two chief branches, the Lutheran and Reformed. A professor of theology at Lutheran Seminary in Philadelphia and of moral philosophy at the University of Pennsylvania, Krauth was an important figure in an attempt, not altogether different from Mercersburg's, of recovering historic Protestant faith and practice from American defections. His book, as the title suggested, likewise attributed greater affinity between Lutheranism and Rome than many American Lutherans, swept up in waves of revival and reform, were willing to grant. In effect, Krauth's project was to portray Lutheranism as the conservative branch of the Reformation, thereby insinuating that modern American Protestantism was a radical break from sixteenth-century impulses. But, as much as Nevin appreciated Krauth's depiction of the original Protestant movement, he was not pleased to read the confessional Lutheran's inference that the Reformed branch of Protestantism was the more radical of the two Reformation churches. Nevin did compliment Krauth for rescuing Lutheranism in the United States from the dangers of Puritanism and Methodism and restoring "sacramental and churchly ideas."[30] At the same time, Nevin used the front page of the *Reformed Church Messenger* from the fall of 1871 to the winter of 1872, in fourteen separate installments, to reconsider the genius of Protestantism on the basis of Krauth's defense of confessional Lutheranism. It was a feat that demonstrated that Nevin had indeed come to terms with his own Protestant identity.

One of the most surprising features of Nevin's review of Krauth was the Mercersburg theologian's defense of Zwingli. Earlier in his life, particularly in *Mystical Presence*, Nevin had shown greater favor for Calvin over Zwingli, particularly since the Zurich Reformer had not seen as Calvin had the importance of affirming Christ's presence in the Lord's Supper. And one of the constant expressions of friction in the German Reformed Church was for Mercersburg's critics to play up the denomination's Zwinglian roots to counterbalance Nevin's use of Calvin for high-church ends. Even so, by 1870 Nevin was sufficiently intent to defend the value of Reformed Christianity that he chided Krauth for portraying Zwingli as a Reformer with radical instincts. He devoted three separate installments to defending Zwingli from the familiar dismissal by high-church Lutherans. On the one hand, Nevin noted that Zwingli's humanism was no more pagan or unbecoming his Christian profession than was Melanchthon's. On the other, the Mercersburg theologian gave Zwingli higher marks than he gave Luther for recognizing a "more originally Christological relation" between Christ and believers.[31] To save Zwingli from the reputation as a radical Reformer, Nevin even asserted that the Lutheran Reformation was equally prone to radicalism. Of course, only in Calvin did Reformed Christianity reach "a more round, full and clear" position. Yet to Zwingli belonged the credit for laying the basis of the Helvetic Reformation upon which Calvin, "the master-builder," would construct the "self-asserting, self-discriminating character of the Reformed Church."[32] Because Krauth had failed to recognize Zwingli's significance, the American Lutheran was guilty, like Hodge at Princeton, of caricaturing the original reforms of Zurich in order to balkanize the Reformed and Lutheran churches—Krauth for high-church ends, Hodge to make room for revival-inspired piety.

Not to be drawn into a divisive reading of Reformed and Lutheran developments, Nevin used his review of Krauth to reiterate his own conviction that the Protestant Reformation was indeed a conservative reform of Roman Catholicism. If he had to identify a difference between Lutherans and Reformed, Nevin put it in terms expressed by Ferdinand C. Baur: "'The Reformed system begins above, and comes down; the Lutheran begins below, and ascends,'" which Nevin paraphrased as "the Reformed begins with God, and reasons down to manhood; the Lutheran begins with man, and reasons up to Godward." Yet, despite these different tendencics, and despite Nevin's own identification with Reformed Christianity, he could not follow Krauth in asserting that his own branch of the Reformation was "the express image and sum total of all Christian truth." Nevin still believed that Rome had too much truth on its side for Protestants to become too confident of their own invincibility. "There is more a great deal in Christianity," Nevin wrote, "I firmly believe, more in the idea of the Holy Catholic Church, than has yet been attained, either in the way of knowledge or the way of life, by the Protestant Reformation."[33] Lutherans and Reformed needed each other in order to explore further the nature of Protestant reform and to recover the older conception of the church. In fact, Nevin used almost half of the series on Krauth's book to reiterate his own evolutionary and organic conception of Christianity in which the incarnation and Christ's glorified body supplied the source of life for the history of the church. Unlike two decades earlier when he unraveled the complex relationship between Roman Catholicism and Protestantism, Nevin was not a man on the verge of losing his tie to the Reformation. Instead, he appeared to be content with the notion that just as Lutherans and Reformed needed each other, so too did Roman Catholics and Protestants. For a true understanding of Christianity, Rome's stress upon the outward and external authority of the church was as crucial as Protestantism's legitimate insistence upon the need to appropriate the faith inwardly and subjectively.

Nevin's responses to these three important American Protestant theologians reveal both the character of his theological reflections while in retirement from theological education and his own resolution of the questions that bedeviled him during the years of his greatest productivity. He continued to reflect on the importance of the church as a means of salvation and critiqued various theological expressions from his own churchly perspective. Nevin also displayed a keen insight into historical development, espousing compelling interpretations of some of the most obscure bits of Protestant history. In addition, he demonstrated an ongoing knowledge of significant theological scholarship from Europe. In sum, as his reviews of Hodge, Bushnell, and Krauth reveal, Nevin remained intellectually sharp even at a time when he appeared to have abandoned academic theology. At the same time, during this period of theological isolation he became an even more pronounced theological maverick with little to hold his idiosyncratic views in check beyond the courage of German Reformed editors who might dare take him on. Without the discipline of teaching and independent of the rhythms and fraternity of a seminary setting, Nevin's solitary observations of American Protestant theology proved to be as peculiar as they were original.

Nevertheless, for all of Nevin's isolation and the idiosyncrasy that it may have fostered, he could still affirm the general doctrines that gave life to Reformed Christianity. Here his introduction to the tercentennial edition of the Heidelberg Catechism is instructive for discerning the content of Nevin's seemingly odd methods. The 1863 edition of the Heidelberg Catechism was an effort by the German Reformed Church to celebrate their confessional standard and produce a critical edition of the Palatinate catechism in English, German, and Latin. Despite his retired status, Nevin served on the committee responsible for the commemorative edition and drew the assignment of writing its introduction. His essay is a testimony to his abiding allegiance to the Reformed tradition even after the difficulties of the previous decade, when he contemplated leaving the Protestant fold for Rome. Nevin's Reformed faith, to be sure, was not that of Princeton, southern Presbyterians, New England Old Lights, or even the strict Calvinists recently removed from the Netherlands and settling in western Michigan. His was a Calvinism with some of its edges worn down. Consequently, Nevin stressed the Heidelberg Catechism's catholicity, its educational (read: churchly) system of religion (as opposed to revivalist, Puritanism, and Baptistic Christianity), its sacramental teaching, its reliance upon and harmony with the Apostles' Creed, and its avoidance of the speculative predestinarianism that in his estimation bedeviled the Westminster divines.

Still, for all the energy that Nevin expended trying to demonstrate the Heidelberg Catechism's comprehensive and nonsectarian spirit, his interpretation of the catechism differed little from the one he had rendered twenty years before when to celebrate the centennial of the German Reformed Church's first coetus, he wrote a series of articles, published in 1847 as a short book, on the German Reformed Church's lone creedal statement. Then, just as in 1863, Nevin emphasized Heidelberg's catholicity, high view of the church, and avoidance of Calvinist extremes. In fact, some of the material for the 1863 introduction comes directly from the earlier essays and book. All of which suggests that despite the depths of Nevin's despair over American Protestantism and no matter how much his theological reflection moved him away from the sixteenth century back to the first three centuries of Christian faith and practice, his own Calvinist faith remained constant. In the 1863 introduction, he wrote:

> Representing, as we have seen it to do, the general confessional life of the Reformed Church in the age of the Reformation, the Heidelberg Catechism carries with it a special historical force for all times. We may say indeed, that its existence is interwoven with the very being of Protestantism itself; inasmuch as we have it in the genial, living expression of what was a necessary constituent of this vast religious movement in the beginning. It belongs to the creative period of the two great Protestant Confessions; and comes before us here as the spontaneous utterance of the Reformed type of faith. . . . It is a mirror of the mind and spirit of the Reformed Confession, as this was comprehended organically in the entire movement of Christianity and the Church, when the distinction first arose; a particular symbol, reflecting throughout the lights and shadows of what may be denominated the comparative symbolism of the age. In this view, history shows it to be of vital account for the whole course of the Reformation.[34]

Again, this was not the Calvinism of Hodge's federal theology or of Thornwell's *jure divino* Presbyterianism. And for that reason, Nevin's Reformed convictions left other Presbyterians and Reformed cold. But Nevin's voice was thoroughly within the bounds of Reformed and Presbyterian expression because the Heidelberg Catechism itself, the gist of which Nevin clearly comprehended, was in the mainstream of Reformed Christianity. He was clearly not always enthusiastic about his Reformed identity, and he needed times dedicated to rest and convalescence in order to remain within the fold. But try as he might, Nevin could not sever himself from lengthy and strong ties to Reformed Christianity, thanks to the comfort provided in the catechetical system of religion taught by the Heidelberg Catechism.

196

7

Mercersburg Theology Embodied and Embattled

With the exception of giving marching orders to a seminary and college and the controversy that absorbed the Eastern Synod of the German Reformed Church between 1846 and 1852, the Mercersburg Theology was generally an abstraction. That is to say it had little direct impact on the lives of German Reformed parishioners unless their pastor happened to have been trained at Mercersburg Seminary or had definite opinions about the school's program. Nevin and Schaff would eventually gain significance in the narrative of American church history, but their theology was a relatively isolated phenomenon in, by nineteenth-century standards, a fairly obscure denomination. This was ironic if only because of Nevin's own understanding of the church. In its organic nature the church was not simply the embodiment of the resurrected Christ but also an ongoing expression of the belief and practices of a particular people. The real test of any school of theology, then, was its effect upon the church's worship. Did the liturgy of a particular communion display and undergird its creed, or was it either a random collection of worshipful acts or an imposition of an element foreign to a specific church? The real issue for the Mercersburg Theology, accordingly, was the German Reformed Church's worship. Here was the measure of whether the seminary's teaching would connect with the church's membership. Even more important, however, was the denomination's liturgy as a barometer of the Mercersburg Theology's teaching on the liturgical and sacramental character of the church's ministry. If Nevin's incarnational views remained simply a matter for the classroom or theological quarterly, then his teaching was as guilty of the charge of abstraction as was the Puritan low-church view against which he so frequently railed.

From roughly 1850 until 1880 the German Reformed Church embarked upon an assessment of Mercersburg's understanding of the Christian ministry through plans to revise the denomination's worship. In many respects the liturgical controversy of the church became an effort to see if the catechetical system that Nevin had held up against the program of revival in *Anxious Bench* could play in Peoria. In fact, the small Illinois town of cliché fame, located in the German Reformed's Western Synod, was too remote from the Mercersburg Theology's limited range of influence. Indeed, as much as the liturgy that Nevin defended was the culmination of his deepest theological convictions, its implementation would turn out to be limited mainly to the Eastern Synod of the German Reformed Church. The Western, or Ohio, Synod proved to be a much more difficult region to influence, since it became the site of the most vigorous dissent to the Eastern Synod's apparent theological and liturgical oddities.

Even in the Eastern Synod Nevin received less support than his stature as president of Franklin and Marshall College might have suggested. His ideas about worship faced two main obstacles. The first was his increasing interest in the early church. Because of the Protestant Reformation's tendency in Nevin's view to result in a Gnostic understanding of the church and its ministry, he felt compelled to press back beyond the liturgies of historic Protestantism to the worship of Christian antiquity. For many in the German Reformed Church, even those sympathetic to the Mercersburg Theology, the liturgical leap to the ancient church was too difficult to execute. The second problem was the ongoing legacy of the denomination's incoherence throughout its first century in the New World. If the German Reformed Church was susceptible to pietism and revivalism, and if that tendency had been both the catalyst for Nevin's critique of American Protestantism and the basis for opposition to Mercersburg, then performing a high-church liturgical make-over on the German communion would be as difficult to accept as the proposition that historic Protestantism had more in common with Rome than with Finney's Oberlin.

Accordingly, the German Reformed liturgical controversy demonstrated that Nevin's influence would be limited mainly to educational institutions rather than the church's corporate life as a worshiping community. It also suggested that Nevin's theological agenda was largely out of step with the communion to which he had tried to give a measure of doctrinal and liturgical coherence. To persuade boards of trustees, secure faculty appointments, and enamor impressionable students was one thing, but to change the attitudes that believers brought into the pews of their local church was quite another. Thus, an irony attended the worship war in the German Reformed Church. It showed the inorganic character of Nevin's theology. As much as he advocated a conception of the church in which its theological developments would be the natural outworking of history, the embodiment of Christ's mystical presence as it were, the effort to revise the German Reformed Church's liturgy revealed how cut off the Mercersburg Theology was from the denomination's own historical development. Even so, the liturgy that the denomination's revisers tried to implement put flesh on Nevin's Christocentric theology. It may have had the unfortunate effect of showing Mercersburg's occasional excesses. Nevertheless, Nevin's ideas about worship reinforced the larger significance of his career: American Protestantism was fast losing touch with the historic currents of Christianity. As believers and pastors in the United States abandoned liturgical forms and the order and stability they provided, America's Protestant churches were moving fast and farther from the churchly faith that had shaped the early church, Rome, and even the original Protestant communions.

The Search for Liturgical Order

The prevailing pattern of worship among American Protestants in the nineteenth century was nonliturgical or "free." *Free* could refer to the practice of praying extemporaneously without recourse to a prayer book or simply not having a set order of worship within all the churches of a particular denomination. This was the legacy of both Puritanism and revivalism. Hostility to set worship and fixed prayers came naturally to Anglo-American Protestants, who in the Old World had been dissenters from the Church of England and its *Book of Common Prayer*. Puritans gave such dissent ammunition with their defense of liberty of conscience against the tyranny of church authorities who tried to force ministers to adopt certain liturgical forms and practices. Revivalism reinforced the Puritan suspicion of liturgical uniformity by demonstrating how much more active the Holy Spirit apparently was when set orders of worship were not rigidly prescribed or followed. In fact, many defenders of revivals conceived of an inverse relationship between formal liturgy and the movement of the Spirit, with the former invariably functioning as a barrier to Spirit-filled worship. A further wrinkle in American Protestant reflection on corporate worship was the objection that prayer books not only lacked spontaneity but failed, in the words of Charles Hodge, "to meet the desires and exigencies of the people."[1] What the Princeton theologian had in mind was more the need for petitions for the particular circumstances of a congregation than simply the liturgical preference of those assembled. If famine or storm or death struck a local church, would a prayer book have the adequate resources to address the church members' legitimate cares?

Continental Reformed churches, that is, the Dutch, German, Hungarian, and French, did not have the same objections to read prayers and set orders of worship that seventeenth-century British politics had taught Puritans and dissenting English Protestants. At the same time, these communions did not have the elaborate prayer book of the Church of England. Nor did these Reformed churches from the Continent have liturgical resources available to them in English, which became a significant concern once these Old World communions settled in the New World and adopted America's mother tongue. In the case of the German Reformed, the Palatinate liturgy was supposed to inform the order and forms used in worship. It was a product of Zacharias Ursinus and Caspar Olevianus, the same men who had composed the Heidelberg Catechism for the Reformed churches of the Palatinate. With its publication in 1563, its order for Sunday services made preaching central, and it included prayers of confession, a prayer for illumination before the sermon, and a general pastoral prayer of thanksgiving and intercession after the preaching of the word. The liturgy also included an order for a Sunday afternoon catechetical service, along with prayers for fast days, prayers for the high holy days (Christmas, etc.), and forms for the administration of the sacraments, church discipline, marriage, and burial. Although the Palatinate liturgy became the order of the day in the Dutch Reformed churches and made its way to North America with some of the earliest European settlers in the New World, its use by the Dutch Reformed added little incentive to their German peers. The German Reformed congregations in America followed a hodgepodge of worship orders. And as these churches lost their native language and increasingly used English, the Palatinate liturgy became even more remote. The free pattern of worship had come to prevail by the 1830s among most congregations, with only some German Reformed ministers using the Dutch Reformed forms for the sacraments and special occasions.

Despite the prevailing practice of Anglo-American Protestants, a liturgical awareness blossomed during the middle decades of the nineteenth century, of which the German Reformed Church's struggles over worship were one example. From Europe to the United States came a variety of liturgical resources. In 1840 John Knox's liturgy became available in Scotland. A year later Scottish ministers produced a resource for the home, *Family Worship* (1841), which gave the implicit approval to the use of written prayers in certain circumstances. Also Scottish Presbyterians in 1849 published an English translation of Calvin's *Form of Prayers*. For German-speaking Protestants, J. H. A. Ebrard, a professor of church history at Zurich, oversaw the publication of *Reformiertes Kirchenbuch* (1846), an anthology of prayers and liturgical forms from various Continental Reformed sources. These European resources for worship were partly responsible for home-grown efforts by Americans during the 1850s. Presbyterian Charles Baird, who had traveled to Europe and experienced liturgical worship, in 1855 collected a compendium of various Reformed liturgical orders in *Eutaxia; or, The Presbyterian Liturgies.* The American relied on Ebrard for information on the Continental churches and supplemented it with his own investigation into English and Scottish materials. Baird's hope was that American Presbyterian ministers and congregations would voluntarily adopt a book such as his to bring worship in the New World into closer conformity with Protestantism's historic practice. He followed this effort with an anthology of prayer, *A Book of Public Prayer* (1857), which included the forms for prayer of Calvin, Knox, Bucer, and others. Adding to the American interest in historic Protestant worship was the Reformed Church in America's effort during the 1850s to produce a liturgy for the Dutch Reformed congregations in the United States. In many respects the Dutch Reformed were working in a parallel capacity with their German Reformed peers since the Palatinate liturgy provided the starting point for both communions' reflection on an appropriate pattern of public worship.

As early as the 1820s the German Reformed began to exhibit the first rumblings of a liturgical awakening. The chief catalyst however was not so much a desire for liturgical order but instead the need of congregations fast losing their German tongue. This demand finally resulted in 1837 in the production of the so-called Mayer liturgy, a rough translation of the Palatinate order by Lewis Mayer, who taught briefly at Mercersburg Seminary before transferring to the Dutch Reformed seminary at New Brunswick, New Jersey. The synod of 1840 adopted Mayer's effort as the form for the churches to use, but it received little use. Mayer's liturgy never went into a second printing, and by 1847 synod was forming another committee to produce resources for the denomination's worship. Not that it was responsible for the neglect of Mayer's liturgy, but the Palatinate liturgy of 1563 was so scarce that when the 1847 liturgical committee began to study the first patterns for the German Reformed order of service they had to go to a pastor in Easton, Pennsylvania, whose father had brought a 1763 printing of a 1684 edition of the original Ursinus-Olevianus service book. Reformed liturgy was about as unknown in the German Reformed church that Nevin joined in 1840 as the Torah was to Israel during the reign of King Josiah.

The committee appointed in 1847 presented its work to synod two years later and thus launched the ingredients of a three-decade-long liturgical controversy. Part of the problem was that the committee had not met, and the proposals it allegedly brought forward were really the work of John H. A. Bomberger, an 1838 graduate of Mercersburg Seminary and pastor of the German Reformed Congregation at Easton and the eventual founding president of Ursinus College (1869). Despite this glitch, Bomberger's recommendations won the support of the 1849 synod meeting at Norristown, Pennsylvania, thus accounting for their designation as the "Norristown Proposals." Part of the reason for the positive outcome were speeches on behalf of the recommendations by Nevin and Schaff. What pleased both Mercersburg professors was the Norristown Proposals' advocacy of liturgical forms, especially in the first two recommendations:

1. That the use of Liturgical forms of church worship, as recognized by our forefathers, has the clear sanction of the practice and peculiar genius of the original protestant churches.
2. That there is nothing in the present circumstances of our Church in this country to call for or justify a total departure from this ancient and long-established practice.[2]

Bomberger's inherent opposition to a free style did generate some opposition from members of synod but not sufficient to prevent a committee from being formed, with Nevin as chairman and the assignment of preparing a revised liturgy for the German Reformed Church.

The timing of Nevin's service on the committee for a revised liturgy was poor since it coincided with his own personal struggle over Roman Catholicism. But even before he reached his nadir of religious depression, Nevin was decidedly ambivalent about the prospects of liturgical renewal in the German Reformed Church. At the Norristown synod of 1849, which appointed him as chairman of the committee, Nevin expressed the view that the church needed to address two questions: the first was one of expedience and concerned what liturgical forms the congregations might actually adopt; the second was the prescriptive issue of what was "theoretically correct." He believed the church should put principle above practice and shoot for a liturgy informed by sound theology. At the same time he admitted on the floor of synod, "I have no personal interest in this matter. Unless the Church, as such, feels the need of it, we had better do without it."[3] Nevin's apparent skepticism stemmed from his own observations of the denomination, a church that he believed was more interested in a few forms for special occasions and services than in a full-blown liturgical system to guide and inform worship each Sunday. Despite this negative estimate, synod voted to appoint Nevin, a further indication of the sway he had in the denomination, as well as a sign that ministers regarded seminary professors as having duties to lead the church in theological formulation. The selection was not a happy one. Nevin never convened the committee, and at synod the following year he reported a recommendation to close the effort to revise the German Reformed Church's liturgy. The best outcome, Nevin advised, was to translate the Palatinate liturgy, though even here he doubted whether it would have wide use. At least it would provide some of the forms that some of the ministers desired. In 1851 Nevin resigned from the committee, the first of his acts to extricate himself from the institutional life of the denomination should he decide to align with Rome.

Synod replaced Nevin with Schaff as committee chairman, again a sign of Mercersburg's influence in the church and of the services that theological faculty were obliged to render. Neither man had particularly strong views about the need for a liturgy in the German Reformed Church. Nevin had his own spiritual anxiety to absorb his time, while his perceptions of the low-church impulses among the German Reformed implied a slim chance of a liturgy ever being adopted or embraced. Schaff also seemed to perform his duties on the committee with a measure of obligatory feeling. His son later observed that Schaff "favored free use of devotional forms" and in family worship would regularly use prayers and forms from the ancient church. Schaff also recognized the immense influence of ecclesiastical forms, whether creeds, hymns, or prayer books, upon the health and identity of a church.[4] "The best state of things," he wrote in 1858, "would perhaps require the equal excellency and harmonious cooperation of the doctrinal and liturgical standards." But, he confessed, he knew of "no denomination which may claim to have at once the best catechism, the best hymn-book and the best liturgy."[5]

Despite misgivings, the work to revise the denomination's liturgy enabled Nevin and Schaff to pool and give coherence to aspects of each other's sometimes esoteric views. In effect, the work of revision played out like a form of tag-team endeavor where Schaff oversaw the production and then, when the liturgy needed defense, Nevin entered the ring to perform the polemics.

With Schaff as chairman, the committee finally began to meet and delegate assignments for different segments of the liturgy. They sought to provide the denomination with forms for all parts of congregational life, from the Sunday service, baptism, Lord's Supper, and marriage to family worship and a lectionary. This was in effect a plan for a prayer book, which amounted to a huge task for a church that had functioned so long with only a vague sense of liturgical order. At Schaff's disposal were fourteen committee members, ten ministers, and four elders. Nevin continued to serve on the committee despite his theological doubts during the years 1851 to 1853 and despite his misgivings about the German Reformed Church's receptivity to a liturgy. The committee was decidedly supportive of the Mercersburg Theology, with only two of its members showing resistance and even then only after the fact.

The Mercersburg character of the group was clear from its statement of liturgical principles. The first, and the one that would later become the chief point of disagreement, was an assertion of intention to look not solely to the sixteenth century for guidance but also, and with greater rigor, to the early church. It read: "The liturgical worship of the Primitive Church, as far as it can be ascertained from the Holy Scriptures, the oldest ecclesiastical writings, and the liturgies of the Greek and Latin Churches of the third and fourth centuries, ought to be made, as much as possible, the general *basis* for the proposed Liturgy."[6] This did not mean that the Reformation was necessarily defective because, as the committee also explained, the "merit of the Reformation" was not to produce new liturgies but to hand down older ones translated into the vernacular, "purifying them from certain additions," "reducing them to greater simplicity," and "subordinating them to the preaching of the Gospel." These forms should not be followed slavishly, and the committee hoped to provide a variety of resources so that congregations might adapt the liturgy to their own needs. Neither did the adoption of forms prohibit extemporaneous or free prayer. The desire was simply to "regulate" and "promote" such manner of prayer in the appropriate setting.[7] One last important principle was the committee's intention to use the liturgy as a prayer book of the laity and not simply a manual for conduct in the pulpit. Schaff believed that if the people could follow the liturgy by reading along during worship rather than simply observing it they would be more inclined to make it their own.

Despite the clarity of its vision and Schaff's leadership, the committee did not begin to meet for four years—not until 1856. The delay owed in part to Schaff's own travels to Europe during the academic year 1853–54. It also stemmed from the actual labor of study and production. In 1854 Schaff had asked Nevin to draft the forms for communion. At the time Nevin was preparing to move from Carlisle to Lancaster County and declined. When Schaff requested the less demanding work of writing family prayers, Nevin was no more encouraging, explaining that he had "no heart, no faith, no proper courage for any such work."[8] But other members of the committee were not so disaffected and complied with their chairman's requests. Traces of their efforts began to show up in *Mercersburg Review* as part of the committee's efforts to let the denomination see what they were doing. By the time the committee met in person to assemble their individual efforts, they had plenty of material. They still required five formal meetings of approximately a week in length between 1856 and 1857. Jack M. Maxwell estimates that they spent the equivalent of seventy-two 24-hour days in committee, usually convening in Lancaster but sometimes in Philadelphia. In turn the committee presented its labors to synod of 1857, and by 1858 copies had been printed and were available for inspection and use. Synod determined to allow the provisional liturgy to be employed voluntarily in congregations and families for a decade before deciding whether to make it the official worship form for the church. Nevin, who by 1857 had recovered from his spiritual despondency, presented the committee's report to synod and concluded with the assertion that "it is not too much to say, that if the present Liturgy should prove inadequate . . . , no other is ever likely to be formed that will be attended with any better effect."[9] Nevin did not prove to be much of a prophet since the liturgy ended up having effects considerably worse than he could have imagined.

The Mercersburg Theology Vindicated

Nevin came to writing about worship relatively late in his theological development, though the subject was implicitly there as early as *Anxious Bench*. To highlight the novelty of Finney's new measures he had contrasted the rival devotional systems of the bench and the catechism, with the latter signifying a churchly piety of which corporate worship was the center. This led Nevin to work out a sacramental understanding of the church, which in turn prompted his explorations of Christ's mystical presence in the Lord's Supper. From there Nevin's move to a christological conception of the church as the body of Christ further bolstered his case for the church as a dispenser of grace, a means of salvation. Worship and the order and forms of a service then were not far from the main themes of his scholarship and reflections. Even so, he did not address liturgy per se or the execution of worship until his service on the committee for the revised liturgy.

One of Nevin's first published comments on worship came in his short 1847 book on the Heidelberg Catechism. There he demonstrated how little liturgical knowledge existed among the heirs of the Heidelberg Catechism—the Dutch and German Reformed—when he wrote that the extant version of the catechism's authors' liturgy, the Palatinate book, included only a bare skeleton of the original.[10] Two years later, once the German Reformed Church's liturgical committee's wheels had started to turn, Nevin felt compelled to editorialize on the recent efforts of the denomination to put its worship in order. He believed that a liturgy's value depended on the end it was designed to serve:

> If it is taken to be a mere outward help and convenience for the purposes of public worship, a sort of crutch to assist the decent conduct

of our sanctuary devotions, it is not to be expected that we shall be able to bring it to anything better than such poor mechanical character. . . . A Liturgy so adopted, is like the notion of civil government, as taken by a certain school to be a prudential compact, in which men part with some of their rights to be more sure of the rest.

For that reason, if the German Reformed were to have a liturgy, it needed an entirely different basis. It needed to be embraced "not as a burden but as a relief, not as a yoke but as a crown, not as a minimum of evil simply, but as a maximum of privilege and good." The true conception of liturgy, in contrast to unliturgical or "*free* worship," was one of a "real emancipation into the liberty of the children of God."[11]

Nevin would not write again until 1856, when he resumed a more active role on the liturgy committee. One of his articles was a historical survey of Christian hymnody, another indication of Nevin's remarkable grasp of church history, and related to the committee's recently added burdens of supplying the German Reformed Church with a hymnal. His only other explicit discussion of worship prior to his writings in defense of the revised liturgy, again from 1856, was an article on the church year. Here, Nevin waxed more philosophical than historical by arguing that the observance of sacred time was as natural to men and women as air and water. "The idea of a sacred or ecclesiastical year," he observed at the start, "is not something peculiar to any particular people or time" but grows naturally "from the religious constitution of man."[12] Nevin's reason for being so certain stemmed from his own understanding of the relationship between the supernatural and the natural. Humans were part of both orders, with spiritual and physical aspects, and since human existence occurred in time, and ways of marking time followed the rhythms of nature, Nevin believed it completely natural to give religious significance to the change of years, seasons, and days: "Time is made to be the mirror thus of eternity."[13] Adding to the natural occurrence of sacred time was Christianity's grounding in historical events that lent themselves effortlessly to rites or observances of commemoration. Nevin turned to the historical origins of the church year in only a brief contrast of pagan, Jewish, and Christian calendars. Here he observed a natural progression from the inferior forms of pagan worship to the superior pattern of the Christian year, with Judaism preparing the way for the church calendar. Notably lacking was any effort to square this conception of the church year with the older Puritan and Reformed hostility to the observance of any holy days lacking scriptural warrant. This was likely an indication that Nevin had clearly come to terms with and rejected his earlier affinities with Puritanism. Even so, it was also a thoughtful set of reflections on the significance of sacred time and gave plausibility to the liturgical committee's decision to incorporate the Christian year in its forms for worship.

One reason for Nevin's silence on liturgical matters even after becoming more involved on the liturgical committee, aside from setting up a new home in Lancaster and being retired, was the absence of controversy in the church over efforts at liturgical revision. This is not to say that Nevin thrived on polemics, though without controversy his literary output would likely have been smaller. Instead, his silence during the decade after 1852 reflected the unity and good will among members of the committee and between committee and the church. Liturgical harmony continued after the publication and release of the revised liturgy in 1857. Even though efforts to introduce the new forms were in some cases slow and in others difficult owing to the denominations unfamiliarity with a book-of-common-prayer manner of worship, the committee's proposed liturgy did not initially ignite a fire of opposition or stir up controversy. Consequently, Nevin could keep his pen in his inkwell.

But the liturgical calm before the worship storm was brief, and soon Nevin would be required to be the spokesman for theological coherence in the German Reformed Church. The chief catalyst in the liturgical controversy that soon engulfed both the Eastern and Western Synods of the denomination was John H. A. Bomberger, a member of the committee, pastor of the congregation in Easton, and a longtime sympathizer of Schaff and Nevin. Although Bomberger would emerge in the history of the denomination as little more than a low-church pastor comparable to Joseph Berg, the Easton minister was in fact one of Nevin's chief defenders. At roughly the same time that Berg left the German Reformed Church to minister among the Dutch

Reformed, Bomberger wrote two articles defending Nevin's teaching on the Lord's Supper, the incarnation, and church history from those who accused him of harboring Roman Catholic sentiments. Bomberger had admitted that he was not in complete agreement with all of Nevin's views. But he also believed that Nevin's accusers had not proven their case and that they carelessly threw around the charge of "papist." Bomberger was also not an advocate of free worship. Since 1849 he had been working for the recovery of the Palatinate liturgy because he believed the church's custom of worshiping without forms was creating liturgical chaos. These affinities between Bomberger and Nevin were largely responsible for the committee's harmonious labors from 1852 to 1858. After 1860 those affinities were hardly discernible, and these two became the chief antagonists in the German Reformed Church's version of civil war.

Part of what contributed to the intensity of the hostility was Bomberger's clear about-face. In 1857, upon the publication of the provisional liturgy, the Easton pastor published a vigorous endorsement of the efforts of the committee on which he had served. He declared that the "Plan and Principles" adopted by synod in 1852 had been "faithfully adhered to in the execution of the work." He also described the provisional liturgy as a combination of the historic resources of Christian worship and the spirit and structure of "our old standard Palatinate Liturgy." In effect, the new and improved German Reformed liturgy was "in essential agreement with the old." Bomberger even went so far as to aver that "it may be said to be what the original framers of the Palatinate Liturgy would have made it, had they lived and labored in such a period as ours." He also recommended it for use in family worship as a book "that parents may safely put into the hands of their children." The liturgical committee could not have asked for a warmer approval.[14]

By 1860, however, Bomberger had begun to change his mind. Maxwell perceptively notices an article that the Easton pastor wrote for *Mercersburg Review* on the church's responsibility to humanitarian causes. He specifically had in mind the German Reformed Church's lack of involvement in the network of voluntary societies that emanated out of the northeast to constitute the Benevolent Empire. Too much theological and liturgical introspection could lead to a form of quietism that was synonymous with irresponsibility. Given the agitation in the nation's sociopolitical life on the eve of the Civil War, Bomberger could very well have hoped that his ethnic communion would play a more vigorous role in moral and constitutional disputes that were dividing Anglo-American Protestants. A year later in 1861 Bomberger wrote a piece in *Weekly Messenger* in which he questioned specific matters related to the provisional liturgy. In effect, he wondered about the wisdom of letting the new book take root and generate responses in an unofficial manner without direct reference to a formal ruling by a classis or synod. Bomberger also suggested that the new forms needed to be revised. To other members of the committee, this was the equivalent of trying to change the rules of the game in the middle of the contest. Synod of 1857 had specified that the provisional liturgy would have a decade for trial before further action or revision. Bomberger was six years ahead of schedule.

Efforts to explain Bomberger's change of heart are largely unsuccessful. Some regard the standoff between him and Nevin as a classic fight between the German Reformed Church's earlier low-church or free worship and Mercersburg's high, sacramental conception of the church. But to place Bomberger in the camp of nonliturgical worship is a mistake. He clearly desired liturgical reform and was serious about recovering the Palatinate liturgy. That 1563 order of worship may not have had the perceived grandeur and mystical character of nineteenth-century high-church liturgies, but it was decidedly on the liturgical side of the spectrum when compared to the average Baptist, Congregational, or Presbyterian service. As Maxwell puts it, Bomberger was not antiliturgical. Rather he was a "medium" liturgical, and the provisional liturgy had offered enough variety of forms and latitude of implementation that he could in good conscience support its production even if not going all the way with the Mercersburg Theology's (read: Nevin's) sacramental worship.[15] Whatever the explanation, by 1860 the reasons for Bomberger's disapproval of the provisional liturgy were obscure. They would become apparent only as the liturgical controversy played out in the politics of the German Reformed Church.

One thing that is clear from the record is that personal dynamics contributed mightily to Bomberger's actions. Once he had begun to raise questions of procedure and suggested the need for revision, his fellow committee members accused him of betrayal. And as the accusations piled up, Bomberger dug in his heels to the point where he became an outright opponent of the revised liturgy. What could have been chalked up to a minor disagreement to be worked out in conversation or correspondence turned into a heated personal dispute between Bomberger and Nevin that ended up involving the entire denomination. Bomberger had clearly changed his mind and should have seen the reaction from others on the committee coming. Nevin did not help matters, however, by plying his polemical gifts and raising the stakes of Bomberger's dissent.

The hint of discord functioned as a wedge to divide the committee further. Soon after Bomberger's reservations went public, two other members of the liturgical committee also voiced dissent. This prompted the synod of 1860 to call for responses from the classes. The verdict that resulted from this solicitation was mixed. All responses favored a liturgy. Half of the classes desired the period of testing to go its full course until 1867. But all of them wanted the provisional liturgy to be revised further. Consequently, synod of 1861 sent the provisional liturgy back to the committee from which it came. Nevin tried to avoid another stint in a work for which he continued to assert that he had "no heart."[16] But synod refused his resignation.

At this point the work of the committee fell mainly on Nevin's shoulders. Inexplicably, Schaff did not attend the meetings, though his inaction suggests that his heart was close to Nevin's. During the ensuing meetings the members rehashed the basic principles informing the provisional liturgy. Here Bomberger's opposition emerged. He chiefly opposed the congregational responses in the forms that he believed departed from the pattern of the Reformation orders of service. Bomberger also desired that the provisional liturgy more closely resemble sixteenth-century Protestant worship than that of the ancient church. In addition, he thought that the book of 1857 harbored baptismal regeneration and veered in a non-Protestant direction with its forms for ministerial absolution. As such, the committee had reached an impasse, at which point its members called for a statement of the two different theories at work behind Bomberger's concerns and those of the Mercersburg adherents. Nevin complied and in 1862 wrote the German Reformed Church's report on worship, *Liturgical Question*, in which he outlined the two sides. Nevin described Bomberger's notions in an unflattering light, calling his conception of a liturgy "a mechanical directory of the manner in which the services of the sanctuary are to be conducted, with written forms of prayer and other public address, more or less full, thrown together in an outward and prevailingly independent way."[17] Nevin believed that Bomberger's position was inherently pro–free worship. This explains why Bomberger submitted a minority report to synod. This was a surprise to the committee, but it did allow the Easton pastor to restate his chief concerns about following more closely the sixteenth-century orders and his belief that revision of the provisional liturgy would not destroy its coherence. With his report Bomberger also submitted a revision that incorporated the first major section of the provisional liturgy but without the congregational responses and that changed the absolution from "I declare" to "the Gospel declares."

When Nevin turned to the majority view, he wrote that its idea of liturgy was that of a "whole order or scheme . . . in which all the parts are inwardly bound together by their having a common relation to the idea of the Christian altar." In sum, the center of Christian worship for Nevin and the majority was "the mystical presence of Christ in the Holy Eucharist."[18] As such, the stress in worship was on the altar—a word chosen intentionally, as opposed to the traditional Reformed idea of table—not the pulpit. If this departed from the sixteenth century, Nevin reasoned, so be it. With the multitude of changes at the time of the Reformation, it was not an age congenial to the "production of good liturgies." The committee had not been bound by the past but instead had attempted to improve upon it. Nevin's organicism again surfaced when he addressed the question of whether the provisional liturgy could be revised. It was, he wrote, "like a work of art," with its "own plan, and is governed through by its own reigning idea."[19] He believed that the work should be left as is or else the church would not have any liturgy at all. The result of synod of 1862's deliberations

213

was a recognition of deep division in the church about the provisional liturgy and a commitment to let the period of optional use go forward until 1867 at least to honor the denomination's contract with the book's publisher.

In 1863 the first General Synod of the German Reformed Church met. This was a combined meeting of the Eastern and Western Synods, and while the regional synods would continue to meet annually, the General Synod was scheduled to convene every third year. To try to bring both synods into closer relationship, the General Synod instructed the Eastern Synod to revise the provisional liturgy and the Western Synod to continue its own preparation of a book of worship. Nevin carried on in his capacity with the Eastern Synod's committee, though not enthusiastically. One advantage of the new work, however, was the absence of Bomberger. And with the minority view removed, the liturgical committee changed the provisional liturgy to follow even more explicitly the Mercersburg Theology. What this involved was the omission of alternative forms and all services explicitly centering in the Eucharist. In effect, Nevin and company damned the torpedoes and went full throttle toward a uniform liturgy that was sacramental and embodied his notion of the church as a medium of salvation. Rather than trying to reflect the diversity of the denomination, Nevin and the committee ironically violated his organic conception of the church and put theory ahead of reality. Some may have wondered if the committee also acted vindictively by showing little tolerance for Bomberger's views. In any case, the Mercersburg program of returning to ancient forms and patterns of worship revealed arguably the chief weakness in Nevin's theology. In an effort to recover the church catholic as a means of grace, he had ignored a central feature of the Reformation, which was to make the word and preaching central in worship. The word could have easily supported Nevin's understanding of the church as a mediator of salvation. But his interest in sacramental teaching and practice bordered on obsession and so obscured the prominence of pulpit over table (not altar) in historic Reformed worship.

The committee's lack of restraint in composing a pro-Mercersburg liturgy may help to explain the events of the General Synod in 1866.

The revised liturgy had received a provisional endorsement from the Eastern Synod. But the General Synod was still waiting for a liturgical submission from the Western Synod. This became the means by which Bomberger and like-minded officers in the Eastern Synod tried to sink the revised liturgy. The majority of the eastern delegation proposed to the General Synod that the revised liturgy be adopted in a provisional manner and that congregations be free to use it until the Western Synod had completed its liturgical report. But a minority report from the Eastern Synod, proposed by Bomberger, received support from the western delegation. It outlined Bomberger's previous opposition to the revised liturgy—that it was out of character with Reformed worship, that it would divide the congregations, and that it would require an episcopal form of government. The minority also called for the creation of a denomination-wide liturgical committee to produce a book of worship that was consistent with the Heidelberg Catechism and the Palatinate liturgy, offered a variety of forms for different services, and made room for extemporaneous prayer. This proposal was clearly the work of a concerted effort by Bomberger to conspire with members of the Western Synod to defeat Mercersburg. Even though the General Synod of 1866 met in Dayton, Ohio, on the Western Synod's home turf, Bomberger's proposal failed, and the revised liturgy of the Eastern Synod prevailed by a slim majority of seven votes. It could be used for three years by congregations until the meeting of the next General Synod in 1869.

This was the setting for Nevin's last major theological effort, his *Vindication of the Revised Liturgy* (1867). Designed specifically to answer the arguments that Bomberger had been making since 1862, this short pamphlet was divided into two sections: the first half covered the history of the liturgical committee's work, the second laid out the theology that had informed the revised liturgy. The historical section indicated Nevin's disgust with the ordeal of liturgical revision and may have been his most sardonic writing to date. Even more biting were such barbs directed at Bomberger as "sublimity of nonsense," "disordered vision," "outrageously preposterous," and "caricature of history." Nevin also wrote of Bomberger that "he abounds in special pleading, and wastes page after page on points, that are, when all is

215

said and done, of no account for the main issue at hand."[20] The historical section also reflected Nevin's irritation at having been drawn into the controversy. He portrayed himself as a bystander at times, which was clearly the case during the years prior to 1857. "My heart was not in it with any special zeal," Nevin wrote, "I was concerned with it only in obedience to the appointment of Synod."[21] This personal dimension of *Vindication of the Revised Liturgy* had less to do with Nevin's attempt to wash his hands of the matter than it did to counter Bomberger's accusations, which implied a Mercersburg conspiracy to foist a high-church liturgy on the lowly German Reformed. Where a real difference existed, such as on the point of whether the original committee was to work mainly from the Palatinate liturgy or to use that as a window on the liturgical heritage of Christianity throughout the ages, Nevin had little trouble using Bomberger's 1857 endorsement of the provisional liturgy against the Easton pastor. Nevin also admitted that the committee had shifted after 1862 by producing a liturgy less flexible and more compliant with the Mercersburg Theology. But he also argued that this was not done surreptitiously since Nevin himself had informed the church in his report, *Liturgical Question*, exactly what the committee was trying to do. He concluded the historical section by asserting that what had happened in 1866 was that one part of the church (the Western Synod) had in complete ignorance rejected years of work on worship by another part of the church (the Eastern Synod) as part of a larger power play. "A beautiful spectacle truly, was it not," he wrote, "this attempt to turn the General Synod . . . into an organ, through which the Synod of the West might be able to rule, as with a rod of iron, the mother Synod of the East!"[22]

In the second half of *Vindication of the Revised Liturgy* Nevin turned from the politics of the 1866 General Synod to the theology of the revised liturgy. It was the culmination of his career. All of the major themes of his earlier writings were evident. Nevin outlined his defense around three themes: the Christocentric character of the liturgy's theology (read: Mercersburg's), its dependence upon the Apostles' Creed, and its objective and historical nature. But these sections were secondary to the topics of Christ's mystical presence, the spirit of the antichrist, and the church as a medium of salvation, each of which followed from Nevin's conception of the incarnation. In effect, all of the topics of Nevin's major writings informed his own justification of the liturgy by appeal to Christ, the Apostles' Creed, and the embodied or historical nature of the gospel.

For instance, Nevin wrote that the gospel of the Apostles' Creed was entirely christological, that is, it "concentrates itself in Christ, throws itself, in full, upon the Incarnation, and sees in the objective movement of this Mystery of Godliness . . . the whole process of grace and salvation." In contrast, the gospel of Puritanism was subjective, "causing metaphysical abstractions to stand for the proper objects of faith."[23] Here was Nevin's criticism of Puritanism from *Anxious Bench*. Bound up with this understanding of the incarnation was his notion that sectarianism bred the spirit of the antichrist by denying that "Jesus Christ is come in the flesh," not just in first-century Palestine but in the ongoing ministry of the church, a theme he had developed in *Anti-Christ*. The theology that opposed the revised liturgy was not of God but "is the very spirit of the Anti-Christ, just because it sets up a Christ which is the creature of its own subjective thinking, over against and in place of the only true objective and historical Christ of the gospel, 'who is over all, God blessed forever.'"[24] Because Bomberger's theology was subjective and denied the ongoing mystical yet objective presence of Christ in the church, it was inherently unchurchly. As such, it failed to affirm the nature of the Christian ministry that Nevin had laid out in his 1854 ordination sermon that lifted him from midlife spiritual depression. The unchurchly opposition to the revised liturgy denied that the office of Christian ministry flowed from Christ's ascension, that ordination was an "investiture with a supernatural commission," and that sacraments were actually "seals of grace present."[25] In sum, the theological rationale for the liturgy brought all of Nevin's previous theological writings together and as such revealed that the liturgical controversy was in effect a referendum on Mercersburg teaching.

Still, Nevin did not stop with his own theological reflection on the incarnation and its significance for the church's ministry. He also appealed, as he had done effectively in *Anxious Bench* and *Mystical Presence*, to sixteenth-century views to justify his own churchly orientation. So when it came to Bomberger's objections to the liturgy's teaching that in the service of ordination with the laying-on of hands comes "the gift and grace of the Holy Ghost," Nevin countered that the Reformers had insisted that ordination was the "sacramental seal of their heavenly commission" and a "symbolical assurance . . . that their consecration to the service of Christ is accepted, and that the Holy Ghost will most certainly be with them."[26] To Bomberger's objection to the declaration of pardon after corporate confession of sin as a form of sacerdotalism, Nevin replied that the forms clearly stated that the minister's authority to absolve sin came strictly from that delegated by Christ. And because of that delegated authority, the minister's official declaration had in its own sphere "a real force."[27] To Bomberger's criticism that the revised liturgy taught baptismal regeneration, Nevin responded that the forms did not state that baptism saved the unbaptized child but instead put him or her in the "way of salvation," thus making the sacrament a means that God designed to "carry with it the benefit it represents." Finally, to Bomberger's criticism that the liturgy implied transubstantiation in its forms for the Lord's Supper, Nevin contended that only a Puritan outlook could read it that way, but that the old Calvinist understanding of the Lord's Supper did actually conceive of the sacrament as a "medium of a real mystical communion with [Christ's] glorified life."[28]

Although Nevin's *Vindication of the Revised Liturgy* constituted a summary of his theology, it also had the weakness of revealing two minds at work that never quite synchronized. The first was the creative one in which he sought to ground a high view of the church and its ministry in the incarnation and Christ's ongoing presence in his body. The second was a mind indebted to the sixteenth-century sense of the church and its ordinances. These two conceptions functioned relatively well when teaching at the denomination's seminary and when formulating one's own distinctive insights into different theological questions. But when these views informed the work of a denominational committee, one with a specific task and beholden to a certain confessional standard, in this case the Heidelberg Catechism, Nevin's two minds ended up antagonizing each other. After all, to engage in creative theological reflection without requiring the church's approval and without contradicting the church's accepted views, as Nevin had done between 1844 and 1852, was a fairly standard practice among theologians. But to use one's own peculiar doctrinal constructions to underwrite practices and forms to be used by the whole church, no matter how voluntarily, was to contravene the very strictures against private judgment and ideals of organic development that Nevin himself had so ably advocated. In other words, Nevin's *Vindication of the Revised Liturgy* was an apology for a high-church liturgy that may have resonated deeply with the Christian church catholic, but that in the particular circumstances of German-American Reformed church life fell flat. Earlier in his career Nevin could range between his creative and traditional modes and capably defend his own views. But in this case, with his originality providing the primary basis for the new liturgy, Nevin's shifting from historical to creative argument was unsuccessful because he was appealing to a range of opinion that was not the public or official standard for the German Reformed Church. Ironically, then, Nevin's own ecumenical liturgy, with its deep roots in the ancient church, was a sectarian effort because it was only mechanically connected to the German Reformed Church's Old World roots and New World ethos. The original provisional liturgy with its variety of forms and room for free prayer was much more organically connected to the denomination's history than was the revised liturgy of 1866. That Nevin did not see that his own efforts to tap the church catholic had resulted in an abstract liturgy disconnected from his communion is a sign of his abiding frustration with American Protestantism and the German Reformed Church's complicity in its low-church devotion.

The Mercersburg Theology Refuted

If Nevin thought his would be the last word, he was mistaken. Bomberger himself wrote two pamphlets in response to Nevin: *Reformed, Not Ritualistic* (1867) and *The Revised Liturgy: A History and Criticism of the Ritualistic Movement in the German Reformed Church* (1867), the former of which constituted a minority report at the General Synod of 1866. Despite these warring pamphlets from the most vocal members of the liturgical committee, the German Reformed

Church would not find liturgical peace and order for another fifteen years.

Initially, prospects for the revised liturgy of 1866 looked hopeful. Having gained no matter how narrowly the approval of synod for congregations to adopt it voluntarily, the new liturgy at least had the advantage of being the only liturgical option aside from the default position of free worship. Still, its implementation was selective and confined mainly to pockets in the Eastern Synod where the Mercersburg proponents ministered or had an influence. Nevin wrote in September 1869 that "it is now perfectly plain, if it has not been before, that no Liturgy can be introduced among us, and made to be of general binding force, by Church authority." He blamed "the hue and cry" of 1866 and concluded that "the general introduction of the book is now out of the question."[29] Another factor was concerted opposition to the liturgy led by Bomberger. He was active in promoting the Myerstown Convention, an informal gathering of officers whose concern was to protest the innovations of the revised liturgy. Although the Myerstown group received a reprimand from the Synod of the East as an unconstitutional body, it continued to meet and plot. The Myerstown Convention established a rival newspaper, *Reformed Church Monthly*, and in 1869 also took the lead in starting a new college, Ursinus, located in Collegeville, Pennsylvania, approximately thirty miles northwest of Philadelphia, over which Bomberger presided. The college also included the aim of training German Reformed pastors untainted by Mercersburg's views.

By 1869, the next General Synod, the Western Synod had finished its own effort at a revision, and it became a rival to the Mercersburg-inspired revised liturgy. Bomberger had assisted the Western Synod, and its order of worship was much closer to what he first wanted. It was a directory, not a prayer book, and it excluded a confession of sin, absolution, and congregational responses and downplayed the centrality of the Lord's Supper. Consequently, almost two decades after the denomination had first called for a liturgical committee with the Norristown Proposals, the German Reformed Church contained two distinct positions on worship that continued to divide and antagonize. The General Synods of 1872 and 1875 managed to avoid disputes over worship, but the issue continued to generate suspicion and spite. As a result, the General Synod of 1878 formed a Peace Commission to promote good will and unity in the church. This body also became in effect another liturgical committee whose task was to find a compromise that would accommodate advocates of both Mercersburg's and the Western Synod's books for worship. Its work would last until 1887, when the General Synod of that year adopted a *Directory of Worship* for the denomination. It restored the variety of forms and options for free prayer that the provisional liturgy of 1857 had allowed, but it also followed the outline and included as options most of the forms from the revised liturgy of 1866 that showed Nevin's handiwork. For Jack Maxwell, who has studied most closely the German Reformed debates over worship, the *Directory of Worship* did not compromise any of Mercersburg's essential positions. At the same time, the document was a political, rather than a liturgical, effort. And by allowing congregations the option of not using the *Directory of Worship*, many sections of the denomination slipped back into (if they had ever changed) the freedom they enjoyed and the low-church worship they had practiced prior to 1850. Nevin may have succeeded in forcing the church to be more self-conscious about worship, mainly through his own theology and only partially through his service on the liturgical committee. But the outcome of the liturgical controversy was hardly a victory for the Mercersburg position. His school of thought was legitimate but by no means dominant.

In his booklet *Reformed, Not Ritualistic*, Bomberger offered one clue to the failure of Nevin's views. The Easton pastor wrote that the debate over worship had forced a decision upon the denomination between the faith of the Apostles' Creed "delivered to us by our fathers, in that incomparable standard of the Heidelberg Catechism" or one "fanciful, speculative construction and interpretation . . . somewhat in accordance with its fifth or sixth century sense."[30] Of course, Bomberger's reading of the issue was partial to his own personal constructions of the Heidelberg Catechism and the German Reformed Church. Still, his comment suggests that Nevin was unsuccessful in convincing the church of his theology because he had not connected the dots between the Apostles' Creed and the Heidelberg Catechism.

If he had, then he could have insisted that his views were bound up with the theological standard that provided unity and borders for his communion. As it was, Nevin could successfully refute critics who said his notions were outside the bounds; he could appeal to the Heidelberg Catechism to show his affirmation of German Reformed norms. But what he failed to do more generally with his most creative theology, and this became particularly evident in the debates over liturgy, was to take the next step and demonstrate that his system was the logical or spiritual or doctrinal culmination of the Heidelberg Catechism, the inevitable point from which the church should not depart. Without that argument, the liturgical controversy exposed Nevin's views as rather "fanciful" and "speculative," in Bomberger's words. To be sure, academic theologians regularly engage in fancy constructions and speculate on doctrinal implications. But in this case the German Reformed Church was unprepared to follow Nevin in his constructive theology. The denomination had a need for less-fanciful speculation, no matter how creative and smart, and for more-basic theological instruction.

Bomberger was successful in diverting the denomination from Nevin's lead by raising the question of Reformed identity. Again, in his booklet he asserted that with Nevin's theology many in the German Reformed Church had left Reformed circles for the Episcopal or Roman Catholic churches. Indeed, one test of Nevin's proposals was to see how his own theological development affected his children. Here Bomberger's generalization gained credible evidence. Nevin's youngest daughter, Martha, became an Episcopalian at least in later life when she married Bethlehem industrialist Robert Sayre. Their two sons both remained in the Episcopal church, and John Nevin Sayre, the older of them, studied at Union Seminary in New York on his way toward becoming an Episcopal priest. The younger of the two, Francis, who married one of Woodrow Wilson's daughters, reared his son, Frank Jr., to become, like his uncle, a priest in the Episcopal church. Of Nevin's three sons, Robert and Richard also affiliated with the Episcopal church, the former serving with distinction at St. Paul's Church in Rome, a church built by J. P. Morgan for Americans in residence in the ancient city. Of course, the status of Nevin's children became a sign of Mercersburg's damaging influence, a case that Bomberger did not make explicitly. Although parents have little control over the faith of their children, that so many of Nevin's offspring settled in the Episcopal rather than the German Reformed communion is striking if not indicative of his own higher regard for a liturgical as opposed to a Reformed theology.

To be fair, Nevin did come the closest of nineteenth-century Reformed theologians to making a case that liturgical worship was a consequence of Reformed Christianity. Even so, the doctrinal creativity he used to justify his own interests failed to take deep root in the German Reformed Church. According to Bomberger, the cause of Nevin's failure was the Mercersburg theologian's "High Church ritualistic new measures."[31] Whether Nevin's measures were ritualistic or any higher than those of Ursinus or Calvin is open to question. But Bomberger did have a point in calling Nevin's methods *new*. Ironically, then, the very charge that Nevin had registered against Finney, that the revivalist's measures were a departure from historic Protestantism, turned out to be a plausible critique of Nevin's own efforts to provide liturgical worship for the German Reformed. Unlike Finney, Nevin's efforts fell clearly within the bounds of historic Christian worship. But like Finney, Nevin could not show how the worship and theology he advocated conformed to historic patterns of the sixteenth century or the German Reformed. Unable to demonstrate continuity, the Mercersburg Theology, to which Nevin had given most of his life, became a religious transplant that would not take root in German Reformed soil and that looked like strange fire to his former Presbyterian contemporaries.

223

Conclusion:
The Critical Period for
American Protestantism

By the time the Peace Commission had undertaken its work to restore a measure of harmony in the German Reformed Church, Nevin was well advanced in years and no longer capable of the polemics in which he engaged off and on between 1843 and 1867. In 1876 Nevin stepped down once again from his teaching and administrative duties as president of Franklin and Marshall, and this retirement proved to be his last.

He remained relatively active as a septuagenarian, producing a dozen or so articles on diverse theological topics and yielding to his spiritual inclinations in ways that prompted him to read the works of Emanuel Swedenborg, the eighteenth-century Swedish engineer and philosophizing mystic. Nevin's critics used some of his positive statements about Swedenborgianism to discredit further Mercersburg's innovative teaching. Theodore Appel, Nevin's biographer, attributes his subject's mystical interests in part to a desire to flee the suffering of the present life and find meaning and purpose completely in the realm of the spirit. Within a five-year span Nevin and his wife Martha suffered the loss of two adult sons: Richard Cecil in 1867 and John Williamson in 1872. These deaths, Appel believed, coincided with Nevin's reading of Swedenborg, an activity that carried over into retirement. Even so, Nevin remained active in the local German Reformed Church in Lancaster, preaching, administering baptisms, even teaching Sunday school to children. After 1883, he began to slow down considerably, owing to his failing eyesight. Walking the mile or so to church was no longer possible, and even negotiating the church steps became sufficiently difficult to prevent regular attendance.

A year before the Peace Commission produced its *Directory for Worship* (1887), on June 6, 1886, Nevin died at his home after a ten-day illness. The funeral service that took place three days later was undoubtedly a moving tribute to one of the most creative American theologians of the nineteenth century. At the same time, it also indicated the relative obscurity in which Nevin had labored for practically all of his career. Seven men either spoke or officiated the ceremonies, and six of them came from the provinces of Lancaster or the German Reformed Church. Archibald Alexander Hodge, son of Charles, was the only speaker with a reputation outside the local network of German Reformed institutions. To be sure, Nevin's theological fits and starts, not to mention his acerbic pen, had not nurtured lots of good will. Still, his polemics were no greater than other nineteenth-century intellectuals whose memorial services drew larger crowds and a roster of more prominent names. Here was a theologian who had attracted the notice and engaged the minds of some of Europe's leading theological scholars, never mind the interest that Nevin had generated in North America. When Hodge spoke in the Lancaster church he mentioned that Nevin was one of the Presbyterian Church's few great theologians and one of the greatest three or four citizens of the Commonwealth of Pennsylvania. Yet, despite his stature Nevin died in relative obscurity within the small ethnic denomination that he had served for over four decades.

At the time of Nevin's death Anglo-American Protestantism continued to dominate Christianity in the United States. Consequently, Congregationalists, Episcopalians, Presbyterians, Baptists, and Methodists were for all intents and purposes the mainstream of American religion. One sign of such English-speaking Protestant religious dominance was the series on American church history that in the 1890s Philip Schaff would oversee and edit. All of the denominations just mentioned received coverage in separate volumes. But the German Reformed had to settle for treatment in a volume that included the Dutch Reformed and Moravians, a combination that eluded either ethnic or theological consistency. Furthermore, within the German Reformed tradition the theological outlook that Nevin had so mightily worked to construct, the Mercersburg Theology, was a minority position. This was evident in the way that the worship wars had functioned to check Nevin's influence beyond a small network of institutions and pastors. As James Hastings Nichols concludes, "By the early twentieth century the Mercersburg theology had ceased to exist as an aggressive theological force, although the Mercersburg liturgy was still a living tradition in many congregations."[1]

The point here is not to pay disrespect to Nevin or his efforts. Instead it is to be sober in estimating the man's influence. Nevin continues to be a source of fascination to a handful of historians and academic theologians—and rightly so. His intellectual creativity and insight, along with his mediation of German scholarship to the United States, was as impressive as it was singular. His answers to questions being posed in mid-nineteenth-century America were indeed so unusual and combined such diverse elements in intriguing ways that Nevin's contribution remains worthy of study. Perhaps even more impressive were the questions regarding revivalism, the church, and worship that he introduced to American theological conversations. Few pastors or seminary professors were raising such queries. And that Nevin was able to pull off these thoughtful reflections in the context of a denomination ill suited to entertain them—and while establishing himself as an administrator of the first educational institutions of his church— is a testimony to an indefatigable spirit that constantly warred with physical and spiritual distress. (For the sake of perspective, Nevin's work as administrator would be the equivalent of Charles Hodge teaching and writing all that he did while also presiding over the College of New Jersey for two decades and functioning as the chief liaison between Princeton Seminary and the General Assembly of the Presbyterian Church.) In other words, Nevin's attainments as a scholar, editor, and president were truly remarkable. But within the confines of his own denomination Nevin's contributions were less impressive. And if his own communion ended up neglecting his scholarship and convictions, how much more the average American Protestant pastor or church member beyond a lecture in a seminary or college class on American church history? Had Nevin remained in the Presbyterian Church and finished his career at Princeton (an unlikely possibility because of the stiffer and better organized opposition that his views would have faced), he could have attained greater visibility in the chain of American theological letters and learning running from the Puritans and Jonathan Edwards, through Charles Hodge and Horace Bushnell, down to Reinhold Niebuhr and Carl Henry.

The history of the German Reformed Church in the twentieth century further indicates the limits of Nevin's legacy. During the first decades, the denomination, like the rest of the Protestant communions in the United States, engaged in ecumenical dialogues with other churches. While the German Reformed participated in broader cooperative ventures like the Federal Council of Churches (1908) and the Plan for Organic Union (1919), its leaders were particularly interested in merging with the Evangelical Synod of North America, a predominantly German denomination of nineteenth-century origin that reflected the 1817 Prussian union of Lutherans and Reformed. By the early 1930s these ecumenical conversations, begun in 1925, took shape in formal plans for a merger of the German Reformed and Evangelical Synod. In 1934 the united church took as its name the Evangelical and Reformed Church. As one historian of the union characterizes it, the new denomination combined the Evangelical Synod's "interconfessional, unionistic, and liberal evangelical stance" and the German Reformed's "witness of its Calvinist heritage."[2] How these two aspects combined, in the same historian's words, to form an "essential character" of "liberty of conscience inherent in the Gospel" is not altogether obvious.[3] But aside from Nevin's effort to recover the catholicity of the Reformed tradition, a conception of catholicity that was distant from the twentieth-century ecumenical movement despite its leaders' efforts to appropriate Nevin, the Evangelical and Reformed Church had largely forgotten the points that Nevin made about the ongoing presence of Christ and the church as a medium of salvation.

The extent of this neglect became evident when, only twenty-three years after its formation, the Evangelical and Reformed Church became absorbed in the United Church of Christ. At this point these formerly German-American Protestants had finally entered the mainstream of Anglo-American Protestantism just prior to the mainline denominations' loss of their hegemonic status during the last three decades of the twentieth century, the so-called second disestablishment of the Protestant mainline. This is not to say that cultural status or influence was the sole reason for merging with the United Church of Christ. The cooperative impulse that had emerged after the Civil War among American Protestants actually turned out to be the fuel propelling the most significant aspects of twentieth-century Protestantism in the United States. To resist it was difficult, doubly so for German-Americans who, thanks to two world wars, desired to show their assimilation of the American way. But the eventual situation of the German Reformed tradition in and among the New England Congregationalists who dominated the United Church of Christ has to rank as one of the great ironies of American church history. After all, the German Reformed provided a safe haven for John Williamson Nevin, whose theological scholarship not only helped to give his communion a measure of self-consciousness but also took dead aim on Puritanism (read: New England Congregationalism) as the chief agent responsible for dissolving older Protestant conceptions of the church and worship. If Nevin's theology had an influence on the United Church of Christ, which some propose, his attacks on Puritanism clearly lacked any. In fact, to extract Nevin's high-church views from his critique of Puritanism is a feat hardly accomplished—and this difficulty may explain why one student of Mercersburg reasons that the United Church of Christ possesses "marks of the church catholic, apostolic, reformed and evangelical" and that wherever those elements are visible the influence of Mercersburg is felt.[4] That is an intriguing argument, but a long way to go in order to find traces of Nevin's continuing sway.

The trouble with the Mercersburg theologian's proposal was its originality. Nevin's scholarship was creative and at times obscure and so requires sustained reading, the sort of activity in which academics engage. It was also occasional in the sense that his theology failed to amount to a system that could easily be handed down to another generation. This aspect also made it difficult for Nevin to convince the German Reformed that his unique views were embedded within the denomination's own confessional heritage of the Heidelberg Catechism. He was effective at showing that his own notions were permissible within the church and that they were plausible implications of the sixteenth-century and seventeenth-century Reformed standards. But since he also argued at several points that the theology of Calvin and Ursinus was inadequate in certain respects, he had a real problem then in persuading his peers that his own Mercersburg outlook was normative for the German Reformed Church, which is partly what the liturgical controversy turned out to illustrate. And without some appeal to a binding corporate doctrinal standard, the Mercersburg Theology was bound inevitably to become the view of a select group, based more on affection for a former professor, than on the demands of faithful ministry or theological integrity. Once those ties of affection faded, so too did most traces of Nevin's outlook, thus leaving his fate to the fickle minds of academic historians and seminary professors.

The Critical Period for American Protestantism

If Nevin's significance is difficult to find among his own German Reformed and United Church of Christ successors, it is only because they have failed to address his most basic insight. The same can be said for his academic admirers, who usually miss Nevin's abiding discernment about the nature of American Protestantism on the way to explorations of his theological method, hermeneutics, employment of German philosophy, or ecumenical teaching. One way to recover Nevin's wise perceptions about the churches in the United States is to contrast them with an interpretation of American Christianity that continues to obscure a profound aspect of nineteenth-century Protestantism seldom accounted for in the history of the American churches.

Arthur Schlesinger Sr. established the predominant narrative of nineteenth-century Protestantism in a short essay written in the 1930s. The Harvard historian categorized the last three decades of the century as the "critical period" for the Protestant churches and used the

intellectual challenges of Darwinism, higher criticism, and compara-
tive religion, along with the social difficulties caused by urbanization,
industrialization, and immigration, to highlight a new environment in
which the churches fared poorly. "Perhaps at no time in its American
development," Schlesinger wrote, "has the path of Christianity been
so sorely beset with pitfalls and perils as in the last quarter of the nineteenth century."[5] Although he wrote at a time when fundamentalists
were losing to the modernists, Schlesinger was generally evenhanded
in his essay by observing that the former actually ministered better to
those undergoing significant social dislocation while exploring the successful ways in which the latter responded to the challenges of new
knowledge. Whatever Schlesinger's own sympathies in the polariza-
tion that developed between conservatives and liberals thanks to these
new ideas and social dynamics in the United States, his periodization
has become a mainstay in the literature on American Protestantism.
Until 1865 Protestant churches generally flourished, if not prevailed,
in a friendly environment. But after 1865 hostile intellectual and social
forces compelled Protestants to go on the defensive. Interestingly
enough, this interpretation also characterizes Nichols's sensitive and
important study of Nevin and the Mercersburg Theology. He writes
that even though this doctrinal outlook continued to inform prominent German Reformed theologians and educational institutions, "the
post–Civil War generation had new interests": "Darwinism, biblical
criticism, the social problems of urbanization and industrialism, psychology of religion, and the religious education movement crowded
aside Christology, the church, and sacraments."[6] In other words, in
the critical period of American Protestant history Nevin's arguments
became antiquated and irrelevant.

Any number of books could be marshaled to demonstrate the influence of Schlesinger's periodization. James Turner's *Without God, without Creed* (1985) is a fascinating study of the rise of unbelief in the
United States after the Civil War. To his credit, Turner locates the seeds
of such disbelief in the decades prior to the war, when Protestants
argued for the truth of Christianity in ways that made their teaching
easy targets for the new knowledge to emerge in the late nineteenth
century. Even so, this book conforms to the general pattern of Chris-

tian theologians thriving (even if naïvely) before 1870 and going into decline after Darwin became a household name.[7] Another book, Bruce Kuklick's *Churchmen and Philosophers* (1985), adds to the pivotal nature of the nineteenth century's last three decades. Kuklick supplements the narrative with a compelling institutional wrinkle. He observes that after 1870, roughly the time when the research university replaced the denominational college as the standard-bearer for American higher education, the discipline of theology could not attract the same caliber of individuals as philosophy attracted. The reason stemmed in part from theology's irrelevance to the new social arrangements of the United States in which questions of free will and divine sovereignty looked hopelessly out of touch. At a time when the urban masses and the so-called social question suggested that important sectors of the American populace were victims of large impersonal bureaucratic forces beyond their control, theologians needed to shift to a different set of questions. Again, the period after 1870 is critical in Kuklick's account.[8] One last book to show the ongoing vitality of Schlesinger's argument is George Marsden's *Soul of the American University* (1994). Here the narrative explores the decisive turn that American higher education took after 1870 away from its Christian orientation in the form of church-run colleges to science-dominated universities. The secularization of the academy in the United States, accordingly, coincided with Schlesinger's critical period, when the new knowledge that the Harvard historian pinpointed took root in America's centers of research and learning.[9]

To suggest that this way of understanding changes in American Protestantism is inaccurate is to border on perversity. Who would possibly quarrel with the notion that the United States, the Western world, in fact, changed dramatically after 1870 and that the churches faced a remarkably different, if not new, set of circumstances in which to minister? One answer is that the person who reads Nevin sympathetically might challenge the prevailing periodization of Christianity in modern America. This is not to deny Nichols's point that Nevin and the Mercersburg Theology, with their emphasis on the church as the body of Christ and the sacramental character of Christian ministry, were out of step with post–Civil War developments in the mainstream

Protestant churches. Nevin's concerns were indeed distant from the realities that pastors and theologians believed they needed to address if Christianity were to remain influential. At best the constellation of sacramental and liturgical sensibilities that Mercersburg nurtured might qualify as a form of antimodern protest that some historians attribute to the Victorian fascination with medievalism and Gothic art and architecture.[10] But even that sort of charitable reading involves the implicit critique that such a studied embrace of the premodern West was simply an escape from the pressing realities unleashed during this critical period of social and intellectual history.

Notwithstanding the reasons for minimizing the relevance of the Mercersburg Theology, adding Nevin to the picture of nineteenth-century developments introduces an arresting twist to the standard narrative. His articulation of the church question stands the periodization of American Protestantism on its head because Nevin's understanding of the church poses a different set of criteria than that of Schlesinger and the company of historians who followed his lead. If, as historians assume, the measure of the church is its healthy relationship to matters external to it, such as the economy, the world of learning, or domestic or international affairs, then the period after 1870 was indeed a critical one for American Protestants. But if, as Nevin argued, the well-being of the church is determined by its own internal affairs, its worship, its sacramental life, its creed, then the critical period for American Protestants came well before the late nineteenth century. Of course, evaluations of nineteenth-century Protestantism need not be so one sided, as if the right view is either the historians' or Nevin's. But the Mercersburg Theology does pose a different conception of the church that reveals the hidden assumptions of those evaluating the health of American Protestantism. Generally speaking, academics study the church to see how strong its standing is in society, whether it speaks with a respectably authoritative voice to the major questions of a particular time and place. Nevin's point, in contrast, is that the church has a different standard for performance, one that stems from its status as a medium of salvation. As such, the work of establishing the kingdom of God, not through political muscle or classroom intelligence, but by engrafting people onto the vine

233

of Christ, establishes a different criteria for evaluating Christianity. This is a yardstick, to be sure, that scholars might understandably resist because it appears to require a degree of religious commitment. Still, the point stands. Nevin's posing of the church question raises further queries about the critical period in American Protestantism.

If, as Nevin contended, the church's mission is a redemptive one, unique among all institutions because of the church's singular sacramental ministry, then well before American Protestants had to reckon with Darwin or monopolies they had settled the church question. That was surely Nevin's own realization as early as 1843, with the publication of *Anxious Bench*, a discovery that would only deepen over the course of the next decade. Only three years after joining the German Reformed Church, almost two decades before Darwin's bombshell and almost three decades before the transformation of intellectual life that research universities heralded, he recognized not simply the historical discontinuity between Calvin, Ursinus, and the Westminster divines on the one side and Edwards and Finney on the other. Nevin also articulated the fundamental incompatibility between revivalism (the system of the bench) and the historic branches of the Protestant Reformation (the system of the catechism). The former was subjective, individualistic, and didactic, while the latter was objective, corporate, and sacramental. In a word, the bench located religious authenticity inside the believing individual, the catechism in the corporate practices of the church.

In 1846 Nevin continued his historical and theological diagnosis of modern American Protestantism most perceptively with *Mystical Presence*. Here again he hammered away at the historical breach between early modern and American Protestantism. And the basis for this critique was the sacrament of the Lord's Supper. The American Protestant disregard for this rite, he argued, highlighted the unchurchly or nonliturgical character of Calvin's, Luther's, and Cranmer's ecclesiastical descendants. Nevin may have been carried away in suggesting that these different forms of Protestantism constituted two different religions. And this implication clearly accounts for his own doubts about the Protestant enterprise during the 1850s when he contemplated joining the Roman Catholic Church. Did the faith of the Reformers, he wondered, inherently lead to a devaluation of the sacraments, both the Lord's Supper and baptism, or was this mainly a tendency among New England Puritans, the whipping boys for so much of his invective? The opposition to Nevin's speculation often took issue with his own theological creativity in formulating a Christology that would justify and give added meaning to the significance of the Lord's Supper in the corporate life of the church and believers. Even so, Nevin's larger point remained. American Protestants had dropped a practice that had been central not only for the Eastern church or Roman Catholics but also for the Protestant Reformers. As such, the churches in the United States had launched a new era in Christian history, one that was more like a revolution than a reformation.

In 1854 Nevin finally recovered from his introspection about Protestantism's poor observance of Christian sacramental life with a vindication of the Christian ministry. At a time when ministers themselves had lost significant status and when lay-run forms of evangelism, small groups, and voluntary associations were increasingly providing alternatives to the denominations or dissolving denominational identity altogether, Nevin articulated one of the most vigorous defenses of the pastor or priest as a mediator of divine grace to be produced by a Protestant in the United States. Again, his polemical style clearly upset the timid, while his theological support sometimes so echoed German statements that those who heard Nevin's argument could too easily dismiss his point as a novelty. But, as was the case with his theology of the catechetical system or his teaching on the Lord's Supper, Nevin's understanding of the ministry was far closer to the early modern Protestant conception than were those of his American peers. As such, he continually raised the specter of American Protestant faithlessness, showing the irony of American Protestant novelty and error among those believers who considered themselves to be the preservers of Protestant orthodoxy.

To be sure, Nevin was not infallible in his assessment of Protestant history or the significance of the church among Reformed Christians. But because of his work on the Lord's Supper, Nevin was able to see much more continuity between Rome and the Protestant Reformers than did the average American Protestant minister or church member, who regarded Roman Catholicism as a threat to the American way of life. With that insight, he perceived the extent of American Protestantism's divergence from its sixteenth-century roots. Of course, to read Calvin or Ursinus and see the anomalies of an Edwards or Finney did not require the intelligence of a genius. Nor, for that matter, did such recognition settle the debate of whether modern or historic Protestantism was right on the church question. But Nevin was one of only a few Reformed Christians in the nineteenth century to see the tension and develop its implications. And the reason stemmed from his own sensitivity to the claims of the institutional church through its officers and rites upon the lives of believers.

Consequently, from his first critique of the Second Great Awakening's new measures to the 1854 ordination sermon he delivered on the nature of the Christian ministry, Nevin relentlessly demonstrated the breach between historic and modern Protestantism. The central issue, unlike most American Reformed or Presbyterians of his day, was not the five points of Calvinism or the imputation of Adam's sin. Instead, it was the church and it ministry. Old School Presbyterians may have excelled in defending the uniqueness of the church in contrast to the social-reform efforts of voluntary associations. But those Presbyterians were reluctant to employ the language of mediation in their arguments for the Christian ministry. This was not the case for Nevin. He understood that the only possible way of saving the church for Protestants was by recovering the older Reformation sense that church membership was necessary for salvation. This proposition alone could transform the apparently ineffective instruments of baptism and the Lord's Supper into genuinely redemptive transactions between God and humanity. Had he not neglected preaching in his conception of the Christian ministry, he might have actually gained more support from skeptical Old Schoolers. Yet, despite this defect, thanks to his historical diagnosis of contemporary American Protestantism combined with his prescription of the church as a real site of mediation, Nevin's emerged as nineteenth-century America's most original and deeply Christian insight into the plight and promise of Protestantism.

Nevin's Singular Contribution

If Nevin was right about the discontinuity between the Protestant Reformation and American Protestantism, then the standard accounts of American church history may very well need to be revised. The critical period for American Protestantism, accordingly, is not the time that the churches adapted to or resisted the new knowledge and social conditions of modern society that emerged after the Civil War. Instead, it occurred earlier, as Nevin argued, sometime when Protestants no longer regarded the church as a medium of grace but more or less as a voluntary society of Christian disciples. He did not supply the specifics for pinpointing exactly when the change took place, though Nevin's critique of revivalism, which is as applicable to the First Great Awakening as it to the Second, suggests that the revivals of the 1730s were a significant factor in the transformation. Whenever the date of the transition, Nevin's diagnosis of American Protestantism's health circa 1850 does suggest a plausible revision of the major turning points in the history of American Protestantism.

But Nevin's significance lies beyond the somewhat abstract enterprise of accounting for change over time. History books may arguably benefit from the perspective that Nevin adds to the narrative of American Christianity. Yet, the writing of history pertains only to the surface of his arguments. Nevin's ongoing relevance is not merely one of determining important transitions in the history of Christianity. Instead it concerns the claim that buttressed his own historical scholarship, namely, whether the institutional church has a unique work to perform with instruments unlike those of any other human organization or institution. At the same time, this question significantly informs whether the period after Darwin or the one after Edwards is of more significance in the history of Christianity. So the issue of periodization is intimately bound up with the church question. If the church is mainly a transformer of culture, then when the culture changes in ways hostile to the church, a period of critical importance has indeed emerged. But if the church is primarily an agency of grace through word and sacrament, then when those means of salvation become marginal, Christianity has entered an era fraught with abiding significance.

For this reason, Nevin continues to offer instruction to historians and believers alike. But the more important lessons he still teaches are the ones that American Protestants failed to learn from him in the nineteenth century. Had Protestants heeded his counsel during his life, Schlesinger and subsequent historians might well have written different accounts of the so-called critical period in American Protestant history. Indeed, for a new kind of history to be written, Protestants themselves will have to learn to think about the church more like Nevin did. What that history will look like is, of course, difficult to predict. But if Protestants could actually follow Nevin in conceiving of the church and its liturgical life as the only site of eternal significance, not the halls of Congress or the university seminar room, they might inaugurate a new era in American church history, one that scholars may or may not notice. What would characterize that new period of American Protestantism would be the prevalence of Nevin's abiding insight: Christianity's primary influence needs to be evaluated not by the church's ability to influence society, but by its performance of sacred rites and recitation of holy words through which the body of Christ grows. Nevin's recognition that the church has something to offer that no other institution can is still as pertinent at the beginning of a new millennium as it was in 1843 when he first articulated it. That he saw it so early and so clearly is a reason why Nevin should continue to be read and studied by believers and academics alike.

Notes

Introduction: Romantic or Reformed?

1. David F. Wells, ed., *Reformed Theology in America: A History of Its Modern Development* (Grand Rapids: Eerdmans, 1985). In fairness it should be noted that this book does include sections on H. Richard Niebuhr and Reinhold Niebuhr, who grew up in the Evangelical Synod of North America, a denomination with German Lutheran, Reformed, and pietist roots that would eventually unite with the German Reformed Church in 1934 to become the Evangelical and Reformed Church. One of the classes to abstain from this merger was the Eureka Classis of Illinois, which as the Reformed Church in the U.S. today is the lone independent remnant of the German Reformed tradition.

2. Sydney E. Mead, *The Lively Experiment: The Shaping of Christianity in America* (New York: Harper & Row, 1963), 62.

3. Daniel Walker Howe, "Religion and Politics in the Antebellum North," in *Religion and American Politics: From the Colonial Period to the 1980s* (ed. Mark A. Noll; New York: Oxford University Press, 1990), 130–36.

4. Nathan O. Hatch, *The Democratization of American Christianity* (New Haven: Yale University Press, 1989), 6–7.

5. Mark A. Noll, *America's God: From Jonathan Edwards to Abraham Lincoln* (New York: Oxford University Press, 2003), 3.

6. Ibid., 11.

7. As becomes clear, Nevin used the word *Puritan* in a sense distinctly different from Noll. For Nevin it was synonymous with revivalist-friendly, low-church Protestantism of the Second Great Awakening. Although the nineteenth-century revivals tapped older Puritan ideals and flourished in regions where the Congregationalist churches were influential, the Puritanism described in the quotation from Noll was

239

in its earlier forms more churchly and sacramental. But throughout this book the word usually has the significance that Nevin gave to it.

8. Noll, *America's God*, 173–74.

9. Robert Bruce Mullin, *Episcopal Vision/American Reality: High Church Theology and Social Thought in Evangelical America* (New Haven: Yale University Press, 1986), xiv.

10. Ibid., xv.

11. Bruce Kuklick, "The Place of Charles Hodge in the History of Ideas in America," in *Charles Hodge Revisited: A Critical Appraisal of His Life and Work* (ed. John W. Stewart and James H. Moorhead; Grand Rapids: Eerdmans, 2002), 76.

12. Bruce Kuklick, *Churchmen and Philosophers: From Jonathan Edwards to John Dewey* (New Haven: Yale University Press, 1985), 182.

13. Sydney E. Ahlstrom, "John Williamson Nevin: Romantic Church Reformer," in *Theology in America: The Major Protestant Voices from Puritanism to Neo-Orthodoxy* (ed. Sydney E. Ahlstrom; Indianapolis: Bobbs-Merrill, 1967), 371.

14. James Hastings Nichols, *Romanticism in American Theology: Nevin and Schaff at Mercersburg* (Chicago: University of Chicago Press, 1961), 1, 4.

15. B. A. Gerrish, *Tradition and the Modern World: Reformed Theology in the Nineteenth Century* (Chicago: University of Chicago Press, 1978), 52.

Chapter 1: Presbyterian Provincialism

1. Glenn T. Miller, *Piety and Intellect: The Aims and Purposes of Ante-Bellum Theological Education* (Atlanta: Scholars Press, 1990), 5.

2. Sydney E. Ahlstrom, "John Williamson Nevin: Romantic Church Reformer," in *Theology in America: The Major Protestant Voices from Puritanism to Neo-Orthodoxy* (ed. Sydney E. Ahlstrom; Indianapolis: Bobbs-Merrill, 1967), 371.

3. Theodore Appel, *The Life and Work of John Williamson Nevin* (Philadelphia: Reformed Church Publishing House, 1889), 26.

4. John Williamson Nevin, *My Own Life: The Earlier Years* (Lancaster, Pa.: Historical Society of the Evangelical and Reformed Church, 1964), 4.

5. Some discretion is necessary when using Nevin's memoirs, *My Own Life*. On the one hand, when Nevin wrote these recollections in 1870 he was at the end of a stormy career in the German Reformed Church, and he could well have used this occasion to justify some of the bad weather he had brought to his denomination. On the other hand, Nevin had a theological agenda that included a high view of the church and its ministry, and so he could well have written his autobiographical reflections to further his aims. While one must be discerning when reading *My Own Life*, at the same time, memoirs filled with detailed descriptions about everyday life in times past are sources that make historians glad. And Nevin's own autobiographical reflections, covering his life only before joining the German Reformed Church, are the best source on his early life. For that reason, Nevin's memoirs should not be doubted any more

than the average reflections found in diaries, letters, and personal narratives so often welcomed and cited by historians. In sum, Nevin's memory may not be infallible, but it is sufficiently reliable to be of help.

6. Ibid., 2.

7. Ibid., 4–5.

8. James Hastings Nichols, *Romanticism in American Theology: Nevin and Schaff at Mercersburg* (Chicago: University of Chicago Press, 1961), 7.

9. Nevin, *My Own Life*, 5.

10. Guy S. Klett, *Presbyterians in Colonial Pennsylvania* (Philadelphia: University of Pennsylvania Press, 1937), 157.

11. Nevin, *My Own Life*, 4.

12. Ibid., 6.

13. Codman Hislop, *Eliphalet Nott* (Middletown, Ct.: Wesleyan University Press, 1971), 167–68.

14. Ibid., 230.

15. Nevin, *My Own Life*, 7.

16. Ibid., 8.

17. Ibid.

18. *Letters of the Rev. Dr. Beecher and Rev. Mr. Nettleton on the "New Measures" in Conducting Revivals of Religion* (New York: Carvill, 1828), 13, quoted from William G. McLoughlin Jr., *Modern Revivalism: Charles Grandison Finney to Billy Graham* (New York: Ronald, 1959), 33.

19. Nevin, *My Own Life*, 9–10.

20. Ibid., 11.

21. Ibid., 12–13 (emphasis original).

22. Ibid., 13–14.

23. Ibid., 16.

24. Ibid., 18–20.

25. Elisha Swift, *Requisites to the Successful Cultivation of Christian Theology: Address at the Inauguration of Rev. Wm. S. Plumer* (Pittsburgh: Haven, 1854), 11–12, quoted from David B. Calhoun, *Princeton Seminary*, vol. 1: *Faith and Learning, 1812–1868* (Edinburgh: Banner of Truth, 1994), 91.

26. Archibald Alexander Hodge, *The Life of Charles Hodge: Professor in the Theological Seminary* (New York: Scribner, 1880), 554, quoted from Calhoun, *Princeton Seminary*, 91.

27. Nevin, *My Own Life*, 21.

28. Ibid.

29. Ibid., 24, 27.

30. Ibid., 27–28.

31. Ibid., 29.

32. John Williamson Nevin, *A Summary of Biblical Antiquities* (1829–30; repr. Philadelphia: American Sunday-school Union, 1849), 7–8.

33. Nevin, *My Own Life*, 30.

34. Ibid., 31.

35. Nichols, *Romanticism in American Theology*, 18.

36. Nevin, *My Own Life*, 36.

37. Ibid., 76.

38. Ibid., 78.

39. John Williamson Nevin, "The Grand Heresy," *The Friend* 24 (Feb. 5, 1835), quoted from Nichols, *Romanticism in American Theology*, 28.

40. Nevin, *My Own Life*, 84.

41. Ibid., 88.

42. Ibid.

43. Ibid., 77.

44. Ibid., 150.

45. Ibid., 8.

46. Ibid., 11.

Chapter 2: Becoming German Reformed

1. Archibald Alexander quotation from James Hastings Nichols, *Romanticism in American Theology: Nevin and Schaff at Mercersburg* (Chicago: University of Chicago Press, 1961), 36.

2. Theodore Appel, *The Life and Work of John Williamson Nevin* (Philadelphia: Reformed Church Publishing House, 1889), 132.

3. David F. Wells, ed., *Reformed Theology in America: A History of Its Modern Development* (Grand Rapids: Eerdmans, 1985).

4. Joseph Henry Dubbs et al., *A History of the Reformed Church, Dutch; the Reformed Church, German; and the Moravian Church in the United States* (New York: Christian Literature, 1894), 271.

5. Ibid., 323.

6. Ibid., 330.

7. John B. Frantz, "Revivalism in the German Reformed Church in America to 1850, with Emphasis on the Eastern Synod" (Ph.D. dissertation, University of Pennsylvania, 1961), 92–93.

8. Ibid., 93.

9. Dubbs, *History of the Reformed Church*, 346.

10. Letter quoted from Appel, *Life and Work*, 98.

11. Ibid., 97.

12. Ibid., 98.

13. John Williamson Nevin, *My Own Life: The Earlier Years* (Lancaster, Pa.: Historical Society of the Evangelical and Reformed Church, 1964), 121.

14. John Williamson Nevin, "The Active Christian," *The Friend* 22 (Aug. 1833), quoted from William DiPuccio, "Nevin's Idealistic Philosophy," in *Reformed Con-*

fessionalism in Nineteenth-Century America: Essays on the Thought of John Williamson Nevin (ed. Sam Hamstra Jr. and Arie J. Griffoen; Lanham, Md.: American Theological Library Association/Scarecrow, 1995), 49.

15. Nevin, *My Own Life*, 139.

16. Ibid., 145–46.

17. DiPuccio, "Nevin's Idealistic Philosophy," 55.

18. John Williamson Nevin, "Inaugural Address," in *Addresses Delivered at the Inauguration of Rev. J. W. Nevin, D.D., as Professor of Theology in the Theological Seminary of the German Reformed Church, May 20, 1840* (Chambersburg, Pa.: Publication Office of the German Reformed Church, 1840), quoted from Appel, *Life and Work*, 112.

19. Ibid., 113.

20. Ibid., 113–14.

21. John Williamson Nevin, "The Heidelberg Catechism," *Weekly Messenger* (Aug. 10, 1842), quoted from Richard Kern, *John Winebrenner: Nineteenth Century Reformer* (Harrisburg, Pa.: Central Publishing House, 1974), 57.

22. Ibid.

23. John Winebrenner, "Letter 4," *Gospel Publisher* (Nov. 1, 1843), quoted from Kern, *John Winebrenner*, 63.

24. Ibid., 59.

25. John Williamson Nevin, "Letter 9," *Gospel Publisher* (Nov. 29, 1843), quoted from Kern, *John Winebrenner*, 70.

26. John Williamson Nevin, "The Sect System," *Mercersburg Review* 1 (1849): 487.

27. John Winebrenner, "Nevin on the Sect Spirit," *Church Advocate* (Oct. 15, 1849), quoted from Kern, *John Winebrenner*, 79.

Chapter 3: The Comforting Church

1. Charles Grandison Finney, *Finney's Systematic Theology: Lectures on Classes of Truths* (1878; repr. Minneapolis: Bethany, 1994), 234.

2. Ibid., 235.

3. Charles Hodge, "Finney's Lecture on Theology" (1847), in *Essays and Reviews: Selected from the Princeton Review* (New York: Carter, 1879), 249.

4. Ibid., 284.

5. Ibid., 253.

6. Finney, *Finney's Systematic Theology*, 245.

7. Ibid., 247, 249.

8. James Hastings Nichols, *Romanticism in American Theology: Nevin and Schaff at Mercersburg* (Chicago: University of Chicago Press, 1961), 8.

9. Theodore Appel, *The Life and Work of John Williamson Nevin* (Philadelphia: Reformed Church Publishing House, 1889), 158.

10. Ibid., 159.

11. John Williamson Nevin, *The Anxious Bench* (Chambersburg, Pa.: Publication Office of the German Reformed Church, 1843), 4.

12. Ibid., 5.

13. Ibid., 7.

14. Ibid., 13 (emphasis original).

15. Ibid., 14–17.

16. Ibid., 15–16 (emphasis original).

17. Ibid., 29–30.

18. Ibid., 32–33.

19. Ibid.

20. Ibid., 34–35.

21. Ibid., 49.

22. Ibid., 52.

23. Ibid., 53.

24. Ibid., 54.

25. Ibid., 53.

26. Ibid., 56.

27. John Williamson Nevin, *The Anxious Bench* (2nd ed.; Chambersburg, Pa.: Publication Office of the German Reformed Church, 1844), reprinted in *Catholic and Reformed: Selected Theological Writings of John Williamson Nevin* (ed. Charles Yrigoyen and George H. Bricker; Pittsburgh Original Texts and Translation Series 3; Pittsburgh: Pickwick, 1978), 105–6.

28. Ibid., 106.

29. Ibid., 107.

30. Ibid., 110–11 (emphasis original).

31. Ibid.

32. Ibid., 113.

33. Ibid., 114.

34. Ibid., 115–16.

35. Ibid., 118–19 (emphasis original).

36. Ibid., 121.

37. Ibid., 123.

38. Ibid., 124–25.

39. Horace Bushnell, *Christian Nurture* (1861; repr. New Haven: Yale University Press, 1947), 4.

40. John Williamson Nevin, "Educational Religion," *Weekly Messenger* (July 7, 1847): 2458. This article responded to essays by Bushnell that would go into his book *Christian Nurture*.

41. Nichols, *Romanticism in American Theology*, 59.

42. Nevin, *Anxious Bench* (2nd ed.), 107.

43. Ibid., 68, 86.

44. Ibid., 52n.

45. Ibid., 49.

46. Philip Schaff, *The Principle of Protestantism* (1845; repr. New York: Garland, 1987), 49 (emphasis original).

47. Ibid., 112.

48. Ibid., 114.

49. Ibid., 161.

50. Ibid., 163.

51. Ibid., 190.

52. Nichols, *Romanticism in American Theology*, 9.

53. David S. Schaff, *The Life of Philip Schaff, In Part Autobiographical* (New York: Scribner, 1897), 104.

54. John Williamson Nevin, "Catholic Unity," in Schaff's *Principle of Protestantism*, 201–2.

55. John Williamson Nevin, "Introduction," in Schaff's *Principle of Protestantism*, 26.

Chapter 4: Reformed Catholicism

1. Quoted from Lawrence Rast, "The Influence of John Williamson Nevin on American Lutheranism to 1849" (M.Div. thesis, Concordia Theological Seminary, 1990), 27.

2. Berg's criticisms are enumerated in James Isaac Good, *History of the Reformed Church in the U.S. in the Nineteenth Century* (New York: Board of Publication of the Reformed Church in America, 1911), 212–13.

3. Philadelphia Classis Resolutions, Sept. 16, 1845, quoted from James Hastings Nichols, *Romanticism in American Theology: Nevin and Schaff at Mercersburg* (Chicago: University of Chicago Press, 1961), 312.

4. Ibid.

5. *Acts and Proceedings of the Synod of the German Reformed Church in the United States (Eastern Synod) 1845*, 80, quoted from George H. Shriver, "Philip Schaff: Heresy at Mercersburg," in *American Religious Heretics: Formal and Informal Trials* (ed. George H. Shriver; Nashville: Abingdon, 1966), 39.

6. Ibid.

7. John Williamson Nevin, "Pseudo-Protestantism," *Weekly Messenger* (Aug. 13, 1845), quoted from Theodore Appel, *The Life and Work of John Williamson Nevin* (Philadelphia: Reformed Church Publishing House, 1889), 231.

8. John Williamson Nevin, *The Mystical Presence: A Vindication of the Reformed or Calvinistic Doctrine of the Holy Eucharist* (Philadelphia: Lippincott, 1846), 54.

9. Ibid.

10. Ibid., 58 (in this and the following quotations from *Mystical Presence* the emphasis is original).

11. Ibid., 56.

12. Ibid., 56–57.

13. Ibid., 59.

14. Ibid., 60.

15. Ibid.

16. Ibid., 61.

17. Ibid.

18. Ibid., 62.

19. Ibid., 66.

20. Ibid., 80.

21. Ibid., 101–2.

22. Ibid., 126.

23. Ibid., 127.

24. Ibid., 137.

25. Ibid., 4.

26. Ibid., 5.

27. Ibid., 158.

28. Ibid., 166–68.

29. Ibid., 173.

30. Ibid., 175.

31. Ibid., 176.

32. Ibid., 177.

33. Ibid., 247.

34. Ibid., 256.

35. Charles Hodge, "Doctrine of the Reformed Church on the Lord's Supper," *Biblical Repertory and Princeton Review* 20 (1848): 269–70.

36. Ibid., 266–67.

37. Ibid., 271–72, 264.

38. Ibid., 234, 241, 251.

39. Ibid., 253–54.

40. John Williamson Nevin, *The Anti-Christ; or, The Spirit of Sect and Schism* (New York: Taylor, 1848), 27.

41. Ibid., 54.

42. Ibid., 9.

43. Ibid., 12–13.

44. Ibid., 17n.

45. Ibid., 16–17.

46. John Williamson Nevin, "Doctrine of the Reformed Church on the Lord's Supper," *Mercersburg Review* 2 (1850), reprinted in John Williamson Nevin, *The Mystical Presence and Other Writings on the Eucharist* (Philadelphia: United Church Press, 1966), 287–88.

47. Ibid., 287.

48. Ibid., 282.

49. Ibid., 289.

50. Ibid., 294.

51. Ibid., 400.

52. Ibid., 354.

53. Ibid., 401.

Chapter 5: Between Lancaster and Rome

1. Theodore Appel, *The Life and Work of John Williamson Nevin* (Philadelphia: Reformed Church Publishing House, 1889), 439.

2. Jacob Heyser Diaries (Lancaster Seminary Archives), January 13, 1853, quoted in James Hastings Nichols, *Romanticism in American Theology: Nevin and Schaff at Mercersburg* (Chicago: University of Chicago Press, 1961), 215.

3. Appel, *Life and Work*, 299.

4. Nichols, *Romanticism in American Theology*, 140.

5. John Williamson Nevin, "Wilberforce on the Incarnation," *Mercersburg Review* 2 (1850): 169.

6. John Williamson Nevin, "Trench's Lectures," *Mercersburg Review* 2 (1850): 618.

7. Nichols, *Romanticism in American Theology*, 147–48.

8. John Williamson Nevin, "Cur deus homo," *Mercersburg Review* 2 (1850): 238.

9. Nichols, *Romanticism in American Theology*, 150.

10. John Williamson Nevin, "The Anglican Crisis," *Mercersburg Review* 3 (1851): 369.

11. Ibid., 371.

12. Ibid., 372.

13. Ibid., 374–75.

14. Ibid., 377.

15. Ibid., 379.

16. Ibid., 378.

17. John Williamson Nevin, "The Apostles' Creed," *Mercersburg Review* 1 (1849): 219.

18. John Williamson Nevin, "Puritanism and the Creed," *Mercersburg Review* 1 (1849): 601.

19. Ibid., 603.

20. John Williamson Nevin, "Modern Civilization," *Mercersburg Review* 3 (1851): 208.

21. John Williamson Nevin, "Early Christianity," *Mercersburg Review* 3 (1851); 4 (1852), reprinted in *Catholic and Reformed: Selected Theological Writings of John Williamson Nevin* (ed. Charles Yrigoyen and George H. Bricker; Pittsburgh Original Texts and Translation Series 3; Pittsburgh: Pickwick, 1978), 211.

22. Ibid., 212.

23. Ibid., 232–54.

24. Ibid., 309.

25. John Williamson Nevin, "Cyprian [Part 2]," *Mercersburg Review* 4 (1852): 382.

26. John Williamson Nevin, "Cyprian [Part 3]," *Mercersburg Review* 4 (1852): 443.

27. Ibid., 447–48.

28. Ibid., 449.

29. John Williamson Nevin, "Cyprian [Part 4]," *Mercersburg Review* 4 (1852): 561.

30. Ibid., 563.

31. Nevin, "Modern Civilization," 173.

32. Ibid., 203.

33. John Williamson Nevin, "Brownson's Quarterly Review," *Mercersburg Review* 2 (1850): 39.

34. Ibid., 59.

35. Ibid., 61–62.

36. Ibid., 65.

37. Ibid., 79.

38. Ibid., 80.

39. John Williamson Nevin, "Brownson's Quarterly Review Again," *Mercersburg Review* 2 (1850): 320.

40. Ibid., 321.

41. Ibid., 321–22.

42. John Williamson Nevin to Orestes Brownson, Aug. 18, 1852; Brownson Papers, Hesburgh Library, University of Notre Dame.

43. John William Nevin to James Alphonsus McMaster, Feb. 26, 1853; McMaster Papers, Hesburgh Library, University of Notre Dame.

44. Nevin, "Brownson's Quarterly Review," 47.

45. Nevin, "Cyprian [Part 4]," 551.

46. Jennie Franchot, *Roads to Rome: The Antebellum Protestant Encounter with Catholicism* (Berkeley: University of California Press, 1994), xx.

47. John Williamson Nevin, "Wilberforce on the Eucharist," *Mercersburg Review* 6 (1854): 183.

48. Ibid., 186.

49. Ibid., 187.

50. Nevin, "Early Christianity," 226–27.

51. John Williamson Nevin, *The Christian Ministry* (Chambersburg, Pa.: Kiefer, 1855), reprinted in *The Mercersburg Theology* (ed. James Hastings Nichols; New York: Oxford University Press, 1966), 353.

52. Ibid., 356.

53. Ibid., 357.

54. Ibid., 358.

55. Ibid., 359.

56. Ibid., 360.

Chapter 6: Relocation and Recovery

1. Joseph F. Berg, *Farewell Words* (Philadelphia: Lippincott, Grambo, 1852), quoted from John Williamson Nevin, "Dr. Berg's Last Words," *Mercersburg Review* 4 (1852): 298.

2. Ibid.

3. Theodore Appel, *The Life and Work of John Williamson Nevin* (Philadelphia: Reformed Church Publishing House, 1889), 444–45.

4. John Williamson Nevin, "Franklin and Marshall College," *Mercersburg Review* 5 (1853): 396.

5. Ibid., 398.

6. Ibid., 399.

7. John Williamson Nevin, "The Removal of Marshall College," *Weekly Messenger* (May 1, 1850), quoted from James Hastings Nichols, *Romanticism in American Theology: Nevin and Schaff at Mercersburg* (Chicago: University of Chicago Press, 1961), 193.

8. Nevin, "Franklin and Marshall College," 404–5.

9. Ibid., 407–8.

10. Ibid., 409–10.

11. Ibid., 414.

12. Ibid., 417–18.

13. John Williamson Nevin, "Philosophy of History," Lecture 1, January 1873, quoted in Sally F. Griffith, "Mercersburg Theology and the Liberal Arts at Franklin and Marshall College," unpublished paper, 14.

14. John Williamson Nevin, "College Days," quoted in Griffith, "Mercersburg Theology and the Liberal Arts," 15.

15. Griffith, "Mercersburg Theology and the Liberal Arts," 15.

16. John Williamson Nevin to Board of Trustees, Franklin and Marshall College, quoted from Appel, *Life and Work*, 643.

17. John Williamson Nevin, "Commencement Address," *Mercersburg Review* 14 (1867), quoted from Appel, *Life and Work*, 643.

18. Ibid., 647–48.

19. Ibid., 648.

20. Ibid., 651.

21. Ibid., 652.

22. John Williamson Nevin, *Address to the Graduating Class of 1867, and the Alumni of Franklin and Marshall College, Lancaster, Pa., July 25th, 1867* (Philadelphia: Fisher, 1867), 24, quoted in Griffith, "Mercersburg Theology and the Liberal Arts," 19–20.

23. John Williamson Nevin, "Hodge on Ephesians," *Mercersburg Review* 9 (1857), quoted from Appel, *Life and Work*, 575.

24. Ibid., 573.

25. Ibid., 579.

26. Ibid., 580–81.

27. John Williamson Nevin, "Natural and Supernatural," *Mercersburg Review* 11 (1859), quoted from Appel, *Life and Work*, 542.

28. Ibid., 547.

29. Ibid., 546.

30. John Williamson Nevin, "Krauth's Conservative Reformation," *Reformed Church Messenger* (Oct. 4, 1871).

31. Nevin, "Krauth's Conservative Reformation" (Dec. 13, 1871).

32. Nevin, "Krauth's Conservative Reformation" (Dec. 20, 1871).

33. Nevin, "Krauth's Conservative Reformation" (Jan. 3, 1872).

34. John Williamson Nevin, "Introduction," in *The Heidelberg Catechism in German, Latin, and English: Tercentenary Edition* (New York: Scribner, 1863), 124–25.

Chapter 7: Mercersburg Theology Embodied and Embattled

1. Charles Hodge, "Presbyterian Liturgies," *Biblical Repertory and Princeton Review* 27 (1855): 461, quoted from James Hastings Nichols, *Romanticism in American Theology: Nevin and Schaff at Mercersburg* (Chicago: University of Chicago Press, 1961), 282.

2. *Acts and Proceedings of the Eastern Synod* (1849), quoted from Jack Martin Maxwell, "The Liturgical Lessons of Mercersburg: An Examination of the Issues Which Emerged during the Mercersburg Liturgical Controversy with a View toward Establishing Procedural and Theoretical Principles for Liturgical Committees in the Reformed Tradition" (Ph.D. dissertation, Princeton Theological Seminary, 1969), 61–62.

3. Quoted from ibid., 66.

4. David S. Schaff, *The Life of Philip Schaff, In Part Autobiographical* (New York: Scribner, 1897), 204.

5. Philip Schaff, in *Mercersburg Review* 10 (1858): 199, quoted in ibid., 205.

6. Report of the Liturgical Committee, *Weekly Messenger* (Nov. 3, 1852), quoted from Maxwell, "Liturgical Lessons of Mercersburg," 126.

7. Ibid.

8. John Williamson Nevin to Philip Schaff, Dec. 3, 1855, quoted from Nichols, *Romanticism in American Theology*, 300.

9. *Acts and Proceedings of the Eastern Synod* (Oct. 1857), quoted from Maxwell, "Liturgical Lessons of Mercersburg," 168.

10. John Williamson Nevin, *The History and Genius of the Heidelberg Catechism* (Chambersburg, Pa.: Publication Office of the German Reformed Church, 1847), 155–56.

11. John Williamson Nevin, "The Liturgical Movement," *Mercersburg Review* 1 (1849): 611–12.

12. John Williamson Nevin, "The Church Year," *Mercersburg Review* 8 (1856): 456.

13. Ibid., 463.

14. J. H. A. Bomberger, "The Provisional Liturgy," *Weekly Messenger* (Nov. 11, 1857), quoted from Maxwell, "Liturgical Lessons of Mercersburg," 252.

15. Maxwell, "Liturgical Lessons of Mercersburg," 254.

16. John Williamson Nevin, *Vindication of the Revised Liturgy* (Philadelphia: Rodgers, 1867): 29, quoted from *Catholic and Reformed: Selected Theological Writings of John Williamson Nevin* (ed. Charles Yrigoyen and George H. Bricker; Pittsburgh Original Texts and Translation Series 3; Pittsburgh: Pickwick, 1978), 339.

17. John Williamson Nevin, *The Liturgical Question with Reference to the Provisional Liturgy of the German Reformed Church* (Philadelphia: Lindsey & Blakiston, 1862), 1, quoted from Maxwell, "Liturgical Lessons of Mercersburg," 263.

18. Nevin, *Liturgical Question*, 15, quoted from Maxwell, "Liturgical Lessons of Mercersburg," 263.

19. Nevin, *Liturgical Question*, 62, quoted from Maxwell, "Liturgical Lessons of Mercersburg," 265.

20. John Williamson Nevin, *Vindication of the Revised Liturgy* (Philadelphia: Rodgers, 1867), 15, 16, 13, 10, reprinted in *Catholic and Reformed: Selected Theological Writings of John Williamson Nevin* (ed. Charles Yrigoyen and George H. Bricker; Pittsburgh Original Texts and Translation Series 3; Pittsburgh: Pickwick, 1978), 325, 326, 323, 320.

21. Ibid., 15 (325).

22. Ibid., 44 (355).

23. John Williamson Nevin, "Theology of the New Liturgy," *Mercersburg Review* 14 (1867): 49.

24. Ibid., 50.

25. Ibid., 52.

26. Ibid., 54.

27. Ibid., 57.

28. Ibid., 63.

29. John Williamson Nevin, "Provisional Liturgy," *Weekly Messenger* (Sept. 15, 1869), quoted from Maxwell, "Liturgical Lessons of Mercersburg," 297.

30. John H. A. Bomberger, *Reformed, Not Ritualistic: Apostolic, Not Patristic: A Reply to Dr. Nevin's Vindication* (Philadelphia: Rodgers, 1867), 140, 141.

31. Ibid., 145.

Conclusion: The Critical Period for American Protestantism

1. James Hastings Nichols, *Romanticism in American Theology: Nevin and Schaff at Mercersburg* (Chicago: University of Chicago Press, 1961), 309.

2. Louis H. Gunnemann, *The Shaping of the United Church of Christ: An Essay in the History of American Christianity* (New York: United Church Press, 1977), 195.

3. Ibid.

4. John C. Shetler, "The Influence of Mercersburg on the United Church of Christ," *New Mercersburg Review* 3 (1987): 3.

5. Arthur M. Schlesinger Sr., "A Critical Period in American Religion, 1875–1900," *Massachusetts Historical Society Proceedings* 64 (1930–32), reprinted in *Religion in American History: Interpretive Essays* (ed. John M. Mulder and John F. Wilson; Englewood Cliffs, N.J.: Prentice-Hall, 1978), 302.

6. Nichols, *Romanticism in American Theology*, 309.

7. James Turner, *Without God, without Creed: The Origins of Unbelief in America* (Baltimore: Johns Hopkins University Press, 1985).

8. Bruce Kuklick, *Churchmen and Philosophers: From Jonathan Edwards to John Dewey* (New Haven: Yale University Press, 1985), 227–29; see also chaps. 13–15.

9. George M. Marsden, *The Soul of the American University: From Protestant Establishment to Established Nonbelief* (New York: Oxford University Press, 1994), especially part 2.

10. See, for instance, T. J. Jackson Lears, *No Place of Grace: Antimodernism and the Transformation of American Culture, 1880–1920* (New York: Pantheon, 1981).

Bibliographic Essay

Nevin's Obscurity

For all of John Williamson Nevin's literary productivity, his writings are relatively hard to access. The reasons for this state of affairs are twofold. First, the nature of Nevin's most important writings was occasional; that is, he was often responding to particular matters of concern either to his own theological development or to his church. If he had written a textbook or works more systematic and comprehensive, his writings might have had a better chance of securing a longer shelf life. Even so, many of Charles Hodge's writings were occasional, and they continue to be read in ways not true of Nevin. The second reason for the obscurity of Nevin's writings is instructive. Unlike Hodge, for example, whose teaching and thought continued to be studied by believers who share most of the Princetonian's convictions, Nevin's religious descendents in the German Reformed Church were not as large as Hodge's in the Presbyterian Church and lacked the institutional outlets that conservative Presbyterians had in seminaries and splinter denominations. (It should be noted that a small group of ministers, academics, and laypeople, largely from the German Reformed wing of the United Church of Christ, have recently formed the New Mercersburg Society in part to keep alive Nevin's thought.)

These considerations help to explain why so much of what Nevin wrote is out of print. Even so, the search for his thought is well worth the effort. Five long essays or tracts from the 1840s represent some of the most compelling and significant pieces of American Reformed theology: *The Anxious Bench* (2nd ed.; Chambersburg, Pa.: Publication Office of the German Reformed Church, 1844); *The Mystical Presence* (Philadelphia: Lippincott, 1846); *History and Genius of the Heidelberg Catechism* (Chambersburg, Pa.: Publication Office of the German Reformed Church, 1847); *The Church* (Chambersburg, Pa.: Publication Office of the German Reformed Church, 1847); and *Anti-Christ; or, The Spirit of Sect and Schism* (New York: Taylor, 1848). Although Nevin never recovered the energy he exuded during the 1840s, later in life during the liturgical debates of the German Reformed Church he did write another important tract: *A Vindication of the Revised Liturgy* (Philadelphia: Rodgers, 1867). One last stand-alone volume, originally written as a series of articles in 1870 for *Weekly Messenger*, was Nevin's autobiographical memoir, published as *My Own Life* (Lancaster, Pa.: Historical Society of the Evangelical and Reformed Church, 1974). Otherwise, aside from some sermons and addresses separately published, readers need to go to theological quarterlies, the most important of which was the *Mercersburg Review*, to find the bulk of Nevin's writings. For a very good and almost complete chronological bibliography of Nevin's published writings, readers should consult the one included in *Reformed Confessionalism in Nineteenth-Century America: Essays on the Thought of John Williamson Nevin* (ed. Sam Hamstra Jr. and Arie J. Griffoen; Lanham, Md.: American Theological Library Association/Scarecrow, 1995). His unpublished papers, with few exceptions, are held in the archives of the Evangelical and Reformed Historical Society in Lancaster, Pennsylvania, and across the street at Franklin and Marshall College. These institutions also have notes from Nevin's lectures as both a seminary and college professor.

Because so much of Nevin's published writing was occasional, the only way for it to be preserved is in the form of an anthology, a genre that seldom remains in print. In fact, the only substantial republications of the Mercersburg theologian's writings came during a brief flurry of interest during the 1960s and 1970s on ecumenical relations and liturgical renewal among mainline Protestants. The first of these collections was James Hastings Nichols, *The Mercersburg Theology* (New York: Oxford University Press, 1966), which includes essays, sermons, and excerpts from larger works by both Nevin and Philip Schaff. Another anthology of Nevin's writings originated in the Pittsburgh Original Texts and Translation Series, a short-lived four-volume effort that also included a collection of Schaff's writings, along with those of an obscure sixteenth-century Anabaptist and a translation of ancient Samaritan texts. This volume, *Catholic and Reformed: Selected Theological Writings of John Williamson Nevin* (ed. Charles Yrigoyen Jr. and George H. Bricker; Pittsburgh Original Texts and Translation Series 3; Pittsburgh: Pickwick, 1978), includes *Anxious Bench*, essays from *Mercersburg Review* on sectarianism, and *Vindication of the Revised Liturgy*. The third anthology came from a projected five-volume series by the United Church of Christ on its German Reformed heritage that produced only two titles, one by Nevin and one by Schaff. *The Mystical Presence and Other Writings on the Eucharist* (ed. Bard Thompson and George H. Bricker; Philadelphia: United Church Press, 1966) reproduces what are arguably Nevin's most insightful writings, those on the history and substance of the Reformed doctrine of the Lord's Supper. The failure of the series on Mercersburg Theology is indicative of the hurdle that Nevin's writings have faced in gaining circulation since 1900. Not even the denomination that incorporated the German Reformed Church showed sufficient interest in Nevin's thought to carry a five-volume paperback series to completion.

If Nevin has languished in obscurity among Protestants who read theology for edification, those who study theological writings for a living have not had the easiest time finding their way to the Mercersburg theologian's corpus either. Bruce Kuklick's valuable editorial effort from the 1980s, American Religious Thought of the Eighteenth and Nineteenth Centuries, includes a reprint of Nevin's writings: *The Anxious Bench* [*and*] *the Mystical Presence* (New York: Garland, 1987). Here Kuklick is primarily following the lead of Yale historian Sydney Ahlstrom, who in the anthology he edited for the American Heritage Series, *Theology in America: The Major Protestant Voices from Puri-*

255

tanism to Neo-Orthodoxy (Indianapolis: Bobbs-Merrill, 1967), included excerpts from Nevin's *Mystical Presence*. Indeed, to judge by the efforts of anthologizers, Nevin's most important titles are *Anxious Bench* and *Mystical Presence*. But to judge by whether those titles are in print, which they are not, Nevin's most important writings remain confined primarily in the pages of *Mercersburg Review* and the German Reformed Church's *Weekly Messenger*. The discussion in the preceding chapters indicates those texts, whether tracts or journal articles, that I found to be most useful for understanding Nevin and assessing the import of what he argued. Readers who have access to a good theological library, complete with holdings in nineteenth-century theological quarterlies and church weeklies will not be disappointed and may even constitute a sufficient audience for a new collection of the Mercersburg theologian's writings. (Hint: editors still reading may want to consider producing another anthology of Nevin's work.)

Nevin's Significance

Even if Nevin's views were quirky and his career was uneven, his theological creativity and observations of American Protestants were sufficiently penetrating to attract the interest of various scholars. This literature may represent more a trickle than a stream, but the appeal, even if limited, has been steady. The most thorough and the only substantial biography of Nevin is Theodore Appel, *The Life and Work of John Williamson Nevin* (Philadelphia: Reformed Church Publishing House, 1889). The most insightful treatment of Nevin comes from James Hastings Nichols, *Romanticism in American Theology: Nevin and Schaff at Mercersburg* (Chicago: University of Chicago Press, 1961). Nichols in fact deserves credit, because of this book and the anthology mentioned above, for making Nevin's writings accessible after years of neglect and for rendering a sympathetically critical portrait of one of the more unusual developments in American Protestant theology. B. A. Gerrish in *Tradition and the Modern World: Reformed Theology in the Nineteenth Century* (Chicago: University of Chicago Press, 1978) includes a perceptive assessment of Nevin. *Reformed Con-*

fessionalism in Nineteenth-Century America: Essays on the Thought of John Williamson Nevin (ed. Sam Hamstra Jr. and Arie J. Griffoen; Lanham, Md.: American Theological Library Association/Scarecrow, 1995) is another book that is extremely valuable for placing Nevin in his context and for interpreting significant features of his teaching.

Most of the other books on Nevin have approached him to advance a particular perspective on the study of religion or theology in the modern academy and so explore a particular aspect of his thought. These include Richard E. Wentz, *John Williamson Nevin: American Theologian* (New York: Oxford University Press, 1997); and William DiPuccio, *The Interior Sense of Scripture: The Sacred Hermeneutics of John Williamson Nevin* (Macon, Ga.: Mercer University Press, 1988). Nevin continues also to be the subject of various doctoral dissertations. Among those consulted for this book were Verlyn L. Barker, "John Williamson Nevin: His Place in American Intellectual Thought" (Ph.D. dissertation, St. Louis University, 1971); Glenn Alden Hewitt, "Regeneration and Morality: A Study of Charles Finney, Charles Hodge, John W. Nevin, and Horace Bushnell" (Ph.D. dissertation, University of Chicago, 1986); Sam Hamstra Jr., "John Williamson Nevin: The Christian Ministry" (Ph.D. dissertation, Marquette University, 1990); and Warren Earl Crews, "Three Men, One Vision: Samuel Schmucker, John Nevin, William Muhlenberg; and A Church Universal and Catholic" (Ph.D. dissertation, St. Louis University, 1995).

Of the several contexts for assessing Nevin's importance and contribution, the denominational one is arguably most important because his work as educator and intellectual were always under the auspices of a church, not to mention his own high regard for the church. Nineteenth-century Presbyterianism has still not received the attention it deserves, but George M. Marsden's *Evangelical Mind and the New School Presbyterian Experience: A Case Study of Thought and Theology in Nineteenth-Century America* (New Haven: Yale University Press, 1970) is a valuable resource and model for future work. Older studies that shed light on Nevin's family background include Guy S. Klett, *Presbyterians in Colonial Pennsylvania* (Philadelphia: University of Pennsylvania Press, 1937); and Alfred Nevin, *Churches of the Valley; or, An Historical Sketch of the Old Presbyterian Congrega-*

tions of Cumberland and Franklin Counties in Pennsylvania (Philadelphia: Wilson, 1852). For consideration of Nevin's Scotch-Irish Presbyterian background, readers should consult Leigh Eric Schmidt, *Holy Fairs: Scottish Communions and American Revivals in the Early Modern Period* (Princeton: Princeton University Press, 1989); and Ned C. Landsman, *Scotland and Its First American Colony, 1683–1765* (Princeton: Princeton University Press, 1985).

The German Reformed Church has been neglected almost universally by historians outside the tradition. Accounts by insiders that are good for covering the main events and people, though often with certain ecclesiastical scores to settle, include James Isaac Good, *The History of the Reformed Church in the United States, 1752–1792* (Reading, Pa.: Miller, 1889); idem, *The History of the Reformed Church in the United States in the Nineteenth-Century* (New York: Reformed Church in America Board of Publications, 1911); Harry M. J. Klein, *The History of the Eastern Synod of the Reformed Church in the United States* (Lancaster, Pa.: Eastern Synod, 1943); and Joseph Henry Dubbs et al., *A History of the Reformed Church, Dutch; the Reformed Church, German; and the Moravian Church in the United States* (New York: Christian Literature, 1894). The predicament that the revivalism of the Second Great Awakening posed to this ethnic communion is the subject of John B. Frantz, "Revivalism in the German Reformed Church in America to 1850, with Emphasis on the Eastern Synod" (Ph.D. dissertation, University of Pennsylvania, 1961). Although a history of Lancaster Theological Seminary, George W. Richards's *History of the Theological Seminary of the Reformed Church in the United States, 1825–1934: Evangelical and Reformed Church, 1934–1952* (Lancaster, Pa.: The Seminary, 1952) is a good account of German Reformed developments, since the history of the seminary was bound up with the centralization and identity of the denomination. Louis H. Gunnemann's *Shaping of the United Church of Christ: An Essay in the History of American Christianity* (New York: United Church Press, 1977) provides an account of the German Reformed from the hindsight of merger with the United Church of Christ. *The Living Theological Heritage of the United Church of Christ*, vol. 3: *Colonial and National Beginnings* (ed. Charles Hambrick-Stowe; Cleveland: Pilgrim, 1995) provides primary sources for the German Reformed part of the United Church of Christ. German-Americans in Pennsylvania have also not received the attention they deserve, but for hopeful signs of remedying this neglect readers should consult Steven M. Nolt, *Foreigners in Their Own Land: Pennsylvania Germans in the Early Republic* (University Park: Pennsylvania State University Press, 2002).

For understanding Nevin's contribution as a theological educator, readers have more contemporary scholarship than is available on nineteenth-century Reformed and Presbyterian denominations. For the influence that Princeton Theological Seminary left on Nevin and his later reaction to his training there, readers should consult David B. Calhoun, *Princeton Seminary*, vol. 1: *Faith and Learning, 1812–1868* (Edinburgh: Banner of Truth, 1994); and idem, *Princeton Seminary*, vol. 2: *The Majestic Testimony, 1869–1929* (Edinburgh: Banner of Truth, 1996); Lefferts A. Loetscher, *Facing the Enlightenment and Pietism: Archibald Alexander and the Founding of Princeton Theological Seminary* (Westport, Ct.: Greenwood, 1983); Mark A. Noll, ed., *The Princeton Theology, 1812–1921: Scripture, Science, and Theological Method from Archibald Alexander to Benjamin Warfield* (Grand Rapids: Baker, 1983); and Andrew W. Hoeffecker, *Piety and the Princeton Theologians: Archibald Alexander, Charles Hodge, and Benjamin Warfield* (Phillipsburg, N.J.: P&R, 1981). Pittsburgh Seminary, where Nevin taught for a decade, is less well known than Princeton, but James A. Walther's *Ever a Frontier: The Bicentennial History of Pittsburgh Theological Seminary* (Grand Rapids: Eerdmans, 1994) provides a useful source of information on the school. Glenn T. Miller's *Piety and Intellect: The Aims and Purposes of Antebellum Theology Education* (Atlanta: Scholars Press, 1990) gives a nuanced account of the variety of institutions that emerged to train pastors for American Protestant denominations.

Mercersburg Seminary and the theology for which it became famous has mainly attracted the interests of those studying Nevin and his colleague, Philip Schaff. George W. Richards's *History of the Theological Seminary of the Reformed Church in the United States, 1825–1934: Evangelical and Reformed Church, 1934–1952* (Lancaster, Pa.: The Seminary, 1952) is the most thorough history of the seminary, though H. M. J. Klein's *A Century of Education at Mercersburg, 1836–1936* (Lancaster, Pa.: Lancaster Press, 1936) provides another perspective. James Hastings Nichols's *Romanticism in American Theology: Nevin and Schaff at Mercersburg* (Chicago: University of Chicago Press, 1961), despite its misleading title, is a remarkable study of the combined genius of Nevin and Schaff. Because of his career after Mercersburg, and because it was in a cosmopolitan city (New York) not a provincial village, Schaff has generated much more scrutiny than Nevin. Of the many books on Schaff, David Schley Schaff's *Life of Philip Schaff* (New York: Scribner, 1897) is the old-fashioned biography, complete with autobiographical portions; while George H. Schriver's *Philip Schaff: Christian Scholar and Ecumenical Prophet* (Macon, Ga.: Mercer University Press, 1987) and Stephen R. Graham's *Cosmos in the Chaos: Philip Schaff's Interpretation of Nineteenth-Century American Religion* (Grand Rapids: Eerdmans, 1995) pursue broader themes to emerge from Schaff's notable career. The Mercersburg Theology attracted both loyal defenders and fierce critics, of which the following are worth examining: Benjamin Schroder Schneck, *Mercersburg Theology Inconsistent with Protestant and Reformed Doctrine* (Philadelphia: Lippincott, 1874); and Samuel Miller, *A Treatise on Mercersburg Theology; or, Mercersburg and Modern Theology Compared* (Philadelphia: Fisher, 1866). The liturgical controversy of the second half of the nineteenth century among the German Reformed also implicated the Mercersburg Theology at the most basic level. The best guide to this piece of history is Jack Martin Maxwell, "The Liturgical Lessons of Mercersburg: An Examination of the Issues Which Emerged during the Mercersburg Liturgical Controversy with a View toward Establishing Procedural and Theoretical Principles for Liturgical Committees in the Reformed Tradition" (Ph.D. dissertation, Princeton Theological Seminary, 1969).

Theology in the United States has not received as much attention as the more contemporary subject, religious thought. Nevertheless, the literature on this topic is substantial and of use for putting Nevin and the Mercersburg Theology in a larger context. The books and dissertations that I found particularly helpful included Nathan O. Hatch,

The Democratization of American Christianity (New Haven: Yale University Press, 1989); Mark A. Noll, *America's God: From Jonathan Edwards to Abraham Lincoln* (New York: Oxford University Press, 2003); idem, *Princeton and the Republic, 1768–1822: The Search for a Christian Enlightenment in the Era of Samuel Stanhope Smith* (Princeton: Princeton University Press, 1989); Bruce Kuklick, *Churchmen and Philosophers: From Jonathan Edwards to John Dewey* (New Haven: Yale University Press, 1985); E. Brooks Holifield, *The Gentlemen Theologians: American Theology in Southern Culture, 1795–1860* (Durham, N.C.: Duke University Press, 1978); idem, *Theology in America: Christian Thought in the Age of the Puritans to the Civil War* (New Haven: Yale University Press, 2003); Walter H. Conser, *Church and Confession: Conservative Theologians in Germany, England, and America, 1815–1866* (Macon, Ga.: Mercer University Press, 1984); Claude Welch, *Protestant Thought in the Nineteenth Century* (2 vols.; New Haven: Yale University Press, 1972–85); Timothy L. Smith, *Revivalism and Social Reform in Mid-Nineteenth-Century America* (2nd ed.; Baltimore: Johns Hopkins University Press, 1980); Robert Bruce Mullin, *Episcopal Vision/American Reality: High Church Theology and Social Thought in Antebellum America* (New Haven: Yale University Press, 1986); Allen C. Guelzo, *For the Union of Evangelical Christendom: The Irony of Reformed Episcopalians* (University Park: Pennsylvania State University Press, 1994); Paul K. Conkin, *The Uneasy Center: Reformed Christianity in Antebellum America* (Chapel Hill: University of North Carolina Press, 1995); David A. Gustafson, *Lutherans in Crisis: The Question of Identity in the American Republic* (Minneapolis: Fortress, 1993); and William Borden Evans, "Imputation and Impartation: The Problem of Union with Christ in Nineteenth-Century American Reformed Theology" (Ph.D. dissertation, Vanderbilt University, 1996).

Another beneficial resource on nineteenth-century American Protestant theology is the genre of biography, particularly of Nevin's contemporaries. Here the following are especially beneficial: Charles Hambrick-Stowe, *Charles G. Finney and the Spirit of American Evangelicalism* (Grand Rapids: Eerdmans, 1996); Robert Bruce Mullin, *The Puritan as Yankee: A Life of Horace Bushnell* (Grand Rapids: Eerdmans, 2002); Douglas A. Sweeney, *Nathaniel Taylor, New Haven Theology, and the Legacy of Jonathan Edwards* (New York: Oxford University Press, 2003); John W. Stewart and James H. Moorhead, eds., *Charles Hodge Revisited: A Critical Appraisal of His Life and Work* (Grand Rapids: Eerdmans, 2002); and Preston D. Graham Jr., *A Kingdom Not of This World: Stuart Robinson's Struggle to Distinguish the Sacred from the Secular during the Civil War* (Macon, Ga.: Mercer University Press, 2002).

Of course, Nevin was more than a theologian and interacted significantly with philosophy, teaching it as well to undergraduates at Marshall College and at Franklin and Marshall College. For perspective on philosophical trends narrowly conceived and on larger themes in American intellectual life, the following should be consulted: Henry F. May, *The Enlightenment in America* (New York: Oxford University Press, 1976); Theodore Dwight Bozeman, *Protestants in an Age of Science: The Baconian Ideal and Antebellum American Religious Thought* (Chapel Hill: University of North Carolina Press, 1976); Allen C. Guelzo, *Abraham Lincoln: Redeemer President* (Grand Rapids: Eerdmans, 1999); Herbert Hovenkamp, *Science and Religion in America, 1800–1860* (Philadelphia: University of Pennsylvania Press, 1978); J. David Hoeveler Jr., *James McCosh and the Scottish Intellectual Tradition: From Glasgow to Princeton* (Princeton: Princeton University Press, 1981); Walter H. Conser, *God and the Natural World: Religion and Science in Antebellum America* (Columbia: University of South Carolina Press, 1993); Donald Harvey Meyer, *The Instructed Conscience: The Shaping of the American National Ethic* (Philadelphia: University of Pennsylvania Press, 1972); William M. Shea and Peter A. Huff, eds., *Knowledge and Belief in America: Enlightenment Traditions and Religious Thought* (New York: Cambridge University Press, 1995); David N. Livingstone, D. G. Hart, and Mark A. Noll, eds., *Evangelicals and Science in Historical Perspective* (New York: Oxford University Press, 1999); James Turner, *Without God, without Creed: The Origins of Unbelief in America* (Baltimore: Johns Hopkins University Press, 1985); and Thomas E. Jenkins, *The Character of God: Recovering the Lost Literary Power of American Protestantism* (New York: Oxford University Press, 1997).

One final context for understanding Nevin is the history of Protestant denominational colleges like the ones over which he presided. Big-picture interpretations of the fate of religious higher education can be found in the following: Walter P. Metzger, *The Development of Academic Freedom in the United States* (New York: Columbia University Press, 1955); Laurence Veysey, *The Emergence of the American University* (Chicago: University of Chicago Press, 1965); George M. Marsden, *The Soul of the American University: From Protestant Establishment to Established Nonbelief* (New York: Oxford University Press, 1994); and William C. Ringenberg, *The Christian College: A History of Protestant Higher Education in America* (Grand Rapids: Eerdmans, 1984). For studies of individual institutions that illuminate many of the strains, both intellectual and organizational, under which administrators like Nevin labored, the following are particularly appropriate: Louise Stevenson, *Scholarly Means to Evangelical Ends: The New Haven Scholars and the Transformation of Higher Learning in America, 1830–1890* (Baltimore: Johns Hopkins University Press, 1986); Marilyn Tobias, *Old Dartmouth on Trial: The Transformation of the Academic Community in Nineteenth-Century America* (New York: New York University Press, 1982); W. Bruce Leslie, *Gentlemen and Scholars: College and Community in the "Age of the University," 1865–1917* (University Park: Pennsylvania State University Press, 1992); David F. Almendinger, *Paupers and Scholars: The Transformation of Student Life in Nineteenth-Century New England* (New York: St. Martin's, 1975); David Potts, *Baptist Colleges in the Development of American Society, 1812–1861* (New York: Garland, 1988); and Howard Miller, *The Revolutionary College: American Presbyterian Higher Education, 1707–1837* (New York: New York University Press, 1976).

Index